Unionism or Hearst
The *Seattle Post-Intelligencer* Strike of 1936

UNIONISM OR HEARST

The Seattle Post-Intelligencer Strike of 1936

William E. Ames
Roger A. Simpson

Pacific Northwest Labor History Association
Seattle, 1978

14

DEDICATION

Slim Lynch always contended there should be a monument erected to the man most responsible for the first major strike victory of the Newspaper Guild. May this volume stand as that monument.

To Bart Guild

TABLE OF CONTENTS

ACKNOWLEDGMENTS

Too few pages of American histories have been devoted to labor history. *Unionism or Hearst* is offered to help remedy that deficiency. This book began in a communications history seminar taught by one of the authors in 1958. He and the seminar students discovered more than just another strike in the Newspaper Guild's 1936 strike against the *Post-Intelligencer*. The professor and one of those students agreed to pursue the strike story beyond that brief examination. Years later, thousands of hours of research, interviewing and writing has resulted in our version of the first major Newspaper Guild strike victory. The story of the birth, development and loss of innocence of the Seattle Guild is told in detail out of our respect and affection for the men and women who fought that first battle.

Our search for records took a thrilling turn when we found the storage trunks in a shed back of the Newspaper Guild headquarters in Washington, D.C. The trunks contained the complete correspondence between the Seattle Guild and the national which has since become part of the manuscript collections of the Archives of Labor History and Urban Affairs at Wayne State University in Detroit. We are especially grateful to Ellis Baker who showed the way to the storage trunks and who has supported our research in Guild history ever since.

The Hearst side of the story is less complete, despite the help of Charles Lindeman and Harvey Kelly and the existence of useful documents in the collections of the Bancroft Library at the University of California. Some records, however, have been destroyed, others could not be located, and still others may not be accessible until the papers of William Randolph Hearst are organized and opened to researchers. We are grateful to Virgil Fassio, publisher of the *P-I*, for permitting us to use photographs from the newspaper's files and to the newspaper's librarian, Florence Frye.

Ross Rieder, president of the Pacific Northwest Labor History Association, was in a great measure responsible for seeing this manuscript into print. The Pacific Northwest Newspaper Guild provided a grant to offset publication costs.

Robert Burke, professor of history, and Rich Berner, archivist, both at the University of Washington, provided information and guidance to manuscript collections which aided greatly. Their encouragement of the project also was appreciated. We are grateful to Don Pember and Vernon Carstensen for their aid and support.

Thanks go also to those who read the complete manuscript and offered their detailed suggestions: Jerry Baldasty, Bob Burke, Mary Joan O'Connell, Terry Pettus, Henry Ladd Smith, and Ken Turay. Hank Smith's enthusiasm for the persons and events of the story returned us to a manuscript which was for many years neglected. Terry and Berta Pettus helped us feel the excitement of the time, and understand the courage of the early Guild members.

Merritt Benson's offer to unleash his own plane to fly us to Coeur d'Alene to interview Harvey Kelly won our unceasing gratitude. Finally, we thank Jan Ames for carrying out numerous unofficial and unheralded editorial duties with patience, care and good humor, and Beverly Simpson, who married into the project but still encouraged and abetted its completion with all the zest of an original conspirator.

If there are errors of fact, we accept responsibility. If we repeat ourselves, please forgive. Both of us sometimes felt the necessity to deal with the same facets of the story. If the book communicates our fascination with these people and events, we will be pleased.

      William E. Ames
      Roger A. Simpson

LIST OF ILLUSTRATIONS

The Guild Striker, August 14, 1936
The Guild Daily, August 15, 1936
The Guild Daily, August 26, 1936
The Guild Daily, September 13, 1936
The Guild Daily, September 25, 1936
The Guild Daily, November 4, 1936
The Guild Daily, November 16, 1936
The Guild Daily, November 26, 1936
"Guildsmen Join in Labor Parade," *The Guild Daily,* September 8, 1936
City Room of the *Seattle Post-Intelligencer,* 1934
    (Courtesy *Post-Intelligencer*)
"Here's a 'Striking' Picture," *The Guild Daily,* August 24, 1936
Dave Beck, about 1936 (Courtesy University of Washington)
Charles B. Lindeman, 1962 (Courtesy *Post-Intelligencer*)
Mayor John F. Dore, *The Guild Daily,* August 19, 1936
Joseph Corbett (Courtesy *Post-Intelligencer*)
Emerson Daggett (Courtesy Mr. Daggett)
John Boettiger and Anna Roosevelt Boettiger, 1935
    (Courtesy *Post-Intelligencer*)
"At Crux of Fight for Guild": Everhardt Armstrong, Richard Seller and
    Frank Lynch, *The Guild Daily,* September 12, 1936
Frank M. (Slim) Lynch, 1937 (Courtesy *Post-Intelligencer*)
Everhardt Armstrong, 1937 (Courtesy *Post-Intelligencer*)
"Governor Martin Greets Guild Supporters," *The Guild Daily,* October
    14, 1936
"He's on Strike But They Wed" (Forrest Williams), *The Guild Daily,*
    November 12, 1936
Morgan Hull, 1936 (Courtesy *Post-Intelligencer*)
Richard Seller, 1936 (Courtesy Seattle Historical Society)
"Hearst Behind Skirts" (Seattle women picketing Teamsters offices),
    The Guild Daily, October 13, 1936

"Three Men in a Quandary" (cartoon: *Star, Post-Intelligencer, Times*),
    The Guild Daily, August 15, 1936

Post-Intelligencer plant (Heffernan Building) at Sixth Avenue and Pine
    Street about 1921 (Courtesy *Post-Intelligencer*)
Raymond D. Holmes, 1940 (Courtesy Seattle Historical Society)

Cover by Allen Auvil

INTRODUCTION

The often-turbulent labor history of the state of Washington has been treated in a very large number of books and articles, as well as many theses and dissertations. These have been made possible by the collection of manuscripts and ephemera, as well as the development of oral history projects, particularly at the University of Washington. A very useful guide to these writings — and to much more as well — is Jonathan Dembo, **An Historical Bibliography of Washington State Labor and Laboring Classes** (Seattle, 1978). Dembo's study was supported by grants from the Washington State Labor Council and the Pacific Northwest Labor History Association.

I think it is fair to say that few of these works are definitive, due at least as much to the uneven quality (and "coverage") of the sources as to any inherent limitations in the authors. But, in history, what is definitive, anyhow? Those who engage in this sort of work are well aware that they are often pioneers, collecting as they go along, and this they find rewarding in itself.

The Pacific Northwest Labor History Association, whose annual spring meetings provide an important forum for papers, panels and reminiscences, now enters the publishing field. It does so with a lively and colorful book on the *Seattle Post-Intelligencer* strike of 1936, *Unionism or Hearst*. The authors are faculty members of the School of Communications of the University of Washington, where they are identified with the continuing scholarship in journalism history. They and their students have done much to enlighten all of us interested in Pacific Northwest history.

You will not read far in this book until you discover that it is labor-oriented. This may or may not bother you, but there is not much that you, or the authors, can do about it. Bill Ames and Roger Simpson are sympathetic with the aspirations of the new American Newspaper Guild and most of their documentation comes from the labor side. They have repeatedly sought, without success, to get access to the employer records. The William Randolph Hearst Collection, still being assembled at the Bancroft Library of the University of California in Berkeley, is not yet arranged, let alone available for research.

So read this book for what it is — a valuable account, from the labor side, of one of the great organizational struggles of the 1930s. You will, incidentally, discover that it is enlightening about a major episode in the career of that most fascinating of Pacific Northwest labor leaders, Dave Beck.

I welcome the publication of *Unionism or Hearst* as the first of what we hope will be a long series of monographs to be published by PNLHA.

Robert E. Burke

PREFACE

Seattle in the mid-1930s was a restless city. It felt sharply the grip of the nationwide depression which many thought might bring the great American experiment in democracy to an end. Chaotic economic conditions left millions unemployed and millions more with tenuous holds on their jobs. Nearly all who were employed had seen their pay checks cut severely, and employees daily faced the possibility of losing their jobs.

Such threats proved a boon to labor organizing. Under the administration of President Franklin Delano Roosevelt there seemed little doubt that the legality of labor unions and the right of collective bargaining would be settled.

Business watched the rise of labor with alarm and stoutly resisted such new legislation as the National Industrial Recovery Act and the National Labor Relations Act, both of which helped secure the position of the unions. The near collapse of the American economy in the early 1930s left both labor and management insecure and fearful of the future. The revolution through which the economy passed helped to widen the breach which separated management and labor, even though it aided greatly in defining the role each would play in the future development of the nation.

The worker revolution in the Soviet Union had provided management with an alarming portent of what could happen in the United States. The instability of the American economy in the 1930s did much to accent the fears. Throughout the country trade unionism was on the rise. Millions signed union cards, hoping for some measure of security in both jobs and wages. Many workers, who in the 1920s had considered unionism radical, now were finding the movement acceptable. Radicals within the labor movement were labeling William Green and his crafts-union alliance, the American Federation of Labor, backward in philosophy and out of step with the modern trends. Some argued that labor, in order to be effective, could not confine itself to narrow crafts and expect to use the strike as an effective weapon. John L. Lewis argued for union organization along industry-wide lines, and in the eyes of the business world this posed the most serious labor threat. To many Americans, Lewis's Committee for Industrial Organization was somehow associated with communism, and many even thought the "C" in the initials stood for the Marxian philosophy.

Advocates of new, philosophies active within the labor movement were widening their membership base. White-collar workers, who only a few years before would have been unwelcome in the labor movement, now were organizing and becoming recognized as having common interests with the blue-collar elements. College-educated workers were finding they shared interests with those who had fought their ways upward in the ranks of labor. To many of the radicals within the labor movement, the eventual triumph of the working man was not far away.

The Seattle labor scene, always a turbulent one, boldly illustrated these conflicts. Still dominant on the Seattle scene was the Central Labor Council. The Council moved from the center of labor radicalism following World War I to a conservative position dominated by the crafts unions. At the hub of the conservative element was the powerful Teamsters Union, presided over by a former laundry truck driver who had strongarmed his way to the most powerful position in Seattle labor. No move was made by the Central Labor Council without the support of Dave Beck and his Teamsters Union.

But Seattle was not without its radical element, centered largely along the waterfront where Harry Bridges's Longshoremen were posed as a threat to the complete dominance of Beck and his Teamsters. These two elements symbolized the rising ferment within the entire labor movement, which in 1935 saw ten industrial unions break with their crafts' counterparts in the AFL to form the Committee for Industrial Organization. Both Teamster and Longshore strikes had been long and turbulent, and in the mid-thirties both continued to wage a battle to dominate the warehouse union and to control the link between water and land transportation.

This intra-labor fight was used effectively by anti-union forces to demonstrate the violence which was fostered by unions and to point up the revolutionary nature of labor's fight for dominance. To many businessmen, the rise of labor posed a threat to the entire business function of the country.

The threat in Seattle seemed more serious to some citizens who had lived through the turbulent days following World War I. Seattle was a center for the militant unionism of the Industrial Workers of the World (Wobblies), the scene of the first city-wide general strike, and had been strongly affected by the two so-called massacres near Seattle involving the Wobblies — at Everett and at Centralia.

All these conditions made large elements of society fearful of the rising power of labor, and many felt that labor unions were un-American and tied to foreign ideologies. The Franklin Roosevelt administration which had helped win labor a firm place within society was damned by much of the business world. Newspaper publishers had balked at such supposed threats of labor, communism, socialism, and the federal government.

None of the publishers had been more active in red-baiting and witch-hunting than William Randolph Hearst, probably the most famous American newspaper figure of the time and owner of the *Seattle Post-Intelligencer*. Hearst's anti-labor, anti-Roosevelt tirades had won him the scorn of much of the labor movement, as well as the vast majority of the nation's voters who favored the Roosevelt New Deal.

Within this Seattle setting, the attempt of fewer than thirty-five newspaper employees to organize and secure recognition for a chapter of the American Newspaper Guild would bring all these forces together in a three-and-one-half month struggle which was to have nationwide importance. Such a foolhardy effort should have won only martyrdom for its organizers, but forces working within the labor scene on both the national and Seattle levels, the personal ambitions of a Seattle labor leader, and the ineptness of business management gave the fledgling American Newspaper Guild its first major victory against Hearst. It was a victory against the most outspoken critic of the Guild. Only two months before the strike, national Guild officers were certain Hearst never would recognize the Guild until he faced a nationwide strike on all his papers. This would take years to organize. Yet the pitifully weak Seattle chapter accomplished the task fewer than seven months after its organization.

That it was a victory that paled by comparison with later Guild battles in the United States and Canada does not detract from its roles at that time in inspiring newspaper employees, spurring growth in the Guild and fostering white-collar militancy. The Guild victory in Seattle was the first agreement with Hearst that directly recognized the union. While the Seattle strike was in progress, a Guild strike against Hearst's *Wisconsin News* in Milwaukee had been settled, but without the essential acknowledgment of the Guild. Seattle and Milwaukee, however, were only the first battles in a long war with Hearst, a bitter fight that erupted in bloody dimensions in a 508-day strike that ended on Hearst's two Chicago newspapers in 1940.

The *Post-Intelligencer* strike also is important for the opportunity it afforded Dave Beck, boss of the Teamsters Union in the West, to assume even greater power within the region and over Seattle's newspapers. While the Guild gained recognition, Beck gained a pinnacle of power which was to go unchallenged for twenty years — a power which made it unhealthy for the newspapers to speak out against his dominance.

It was a strange union of Beck and the Newspaper Guild in 1936. Without Beck's support the strike never would have been called and certainly never would have been a success. Yet for only a few days after the opening of the strike was there a feeling of cooperation between the Guild and Beck. Then each pursued quite different objectives.

This book is a history of the *Seattle Post-Intelligencer* strike of 1936. In that strike, the Guild, born in Washington, D.C., in 1933, came of age in Seattle in 1936. Beck and Hearst each shaped that outcome.

CHAPTER I

THE SWING OF THE IRON BALL

To many employees of the *Seattle Post-Intelligencer,* journalism was frustrating work at the beginning of 1936. The newspaper's writers, unprotected by union contracts, knew what it meant to take unnegotiated pay cuts. More fear was created among the higher paid employees by the Hearst policy of replacing high-salaried "stars" on a newspaper staff with inexperienced youngsters who could be hired for a pittance. 1

The effects of the depression on the *Post-Intelligencer* staff were as diverse as the backgrounds of its members. To many it was the insecurity of the situation which bothered them most. Should they be fired without warning, as many were, there was no severance pay; should they receive a pay cut, there was no way to negotiate the amount; should they have complaints about working hours, assignments, and conditions, there was no guarantee that anyone would heed them. Many of the staff felt trapped at the same time they were grateful for having a job.

There were also the frustrations of working for William Randolph Hearst, one of the nation's most powerful publishers. There were his arbitrary ways of doing things. Telephone calls or sharply worded memos were received by those who failed to measure up to the "Gee Whiz" approach which "The Chief" expected on each front page. There were his increasingly conservative political views. During Franklin Roosevelt's first term, Hearst had broken completely with the New Deal President and by 1936 was leading the forces rallying behind Alfred M. Landon, the conservative governor of Kansas who was eventually to win the Republican nomination. 2 Hearst's attacks on the New Deal coupled with his notorious attacks on communism made many of his staff uneasy. Still, such resentments had to be buried in favor of holding a job.

The situation was complicated further by the fact that the *Post-Intelligencer* was not one of the strong newspapers in the Hearst chain. Three daily newspapers fought for what profits could be realized from depression-ridden Seattle and in the mid-thirties, the *Post-Intelligencer's* share was pitifully small. 3 The largest and most prosperous of the three was the *Seattle Times*, usually looked upon as a home-owned newspaper of the Clarance B. Blethen family, although a sizeable portion was held by the Ridder chain. The *Times* was dominated by the narrow conservatism of General Blethen and its editorial pages were apt to burst forth with wild, exaggerated outbursts against Franklin Roosevelt, labor unions, and communists.

The *Seattle Star* was a member of the Scripps League and the weakest of the Seattle papers. Wages, working conditions, and advancement were probably poorest on the *Star*, but because of its reputation for being sympathetic to labor, its shortcomings were greeted with less hostility than those of the *Post-Intelligencer*.

The *Post-Intelligencer*, founded as the *Intelligencer* in 1867 and combined with the *Post* in 1881, in the early years of the century enjoyed a reputation for somewhat more reliability than did its chief rival, the *Times*. By 1919, though, the paper's financial troubles made it easy prey for a stealthy takeover by Hearst. On December 27, 1921, Hearst's first editorial appeared in the newspaper whose purchase he had never announced.[4] By 1936, the newspaper had a daily circulation of 102,000 copies and more than double that number on Sundays, when delivered to distant points in Oregon, Idaho, Montana, Alaska, and British Columbia. [5]

Hearst management had decided by the mid-thirties that something would have to be done to improve the profitability of the *Post-Intelligencer*. The man picked to improve the financial standing of the paper was Bart P. Guild, business manager of the *Los Angeles Examiner* and the chain's West Coast operations manager.[6] Bart Guild may have had sound knowledge of business practices, but his personal relations were based on fear rather than warmth and understanding. He had been in Seattle on numerous occasions and staff members had come to expect dismissals while he was around or soon thereafter. In the slang of the day, this was known as "the swing of the iron ball." [7] There were those who characterized Bart Guild as a cold, unfeeling, almost demonic person who each day built himself up to a high level of hostility against the inefficiency of the staff. By late afternoon, they said, firings could be expected. Such a view exaggerated the man and his role, but it indicated how thoroughly the executive played on the fears and frustrations which so many of the staff felt. ". . . He has a mania for intrigue and politics, and under the stimulus of even a slight amount of alcohol becomes wild and irresponsible," a Hearst executive wrote in early 1936. [8]

There is no better way to improve the financial situation of a newspaper than to improve its income, and on a newspaper income is improved by raising the advertising revenue. Bart Guild devoted a considerable portion of his time in Seattle to developing special promotions around which advertising sales could be built. Some worked and some did not. It wasn't so much the promotions which annoyed staff members, particularly photographers, but the pride and protectiveness which Bart Guild held for his ideas. Ridicule of these projects behind his back was frequent and, on at least one occasion, led to the firing of one of the paper's top photographers. Art French had been with the *Post-Intelligencer* for years and was generally respected as a man of considerable ability. French was fairly typical of newspaper photographers in the thirties. He had technical ability which he was rarely able to use in routine newspaper assignments; he was satisfied with a reasonable wage and felt lucky to have a job in the middle of the depression; he was a warm, friendly person liked by nearly all the staff, and he was something of a cynic.

French encountered the Hearst efficiency expert when assigned a special "Reach for a Peach" section which was to push Washington State peaches through pictures, articles, and recipes sprinkled among advertisements. Even a peach-colored newsprint was used in the printing. Such newspaper promotions are frequent and French, who thought Bart Guild was exaggerating the originality and impact of the idea, showed his disdain by calling the slogan, "Screech for a Peach." When the word got to the executive, French was promptly dismissed. Calmer minds managed to keep French on the payroll, but he had to sneak in at night and complete his work after Bart Guild left the building. [9]

French's closest friend on the paper was an affable, overweight Irishman named Frank Lynch. Lynch never answered to his given name, however, because early in life his size had earned him the name "Slim." To most of the world he was a friendly and outgoing Irishman always ready with a touch of wit and humor, the cynical, the profane. Although he was a good photographer, he was apt to play down his ability and considered himself lacking in any adminis-

3

trative competence. He was a photographer, resigned to the fact that he would probably be at the *Post-Intelligencer* the rest of his working life. He was a wild mixture of emotions, a warm affectionate man who yearned for more than the *Post-Intelligencer* was offering him. His sense of being trapped by the limitations of his job was heightened by his inability to meet the financial burdens which his family placed on a limited income. His wife had been ill for a number of years with tuberculosis and the Lynchs had heavy debts. They rented a place on Bainbridge Island, further straining a limited budget. Also, his son, early in 1936, suffered a mastoid infection and needed a long period of recuperation.

Much of the time Lynch was annoyed and bored by his job, and at times he was angry with the insignificance of his work. Years later, he recalled one of those annoying assignments:

I remember one time I went out on a story. It was on my mother's birthday and I think the last birthday she had on this earth. Well, they picked up a woman for narcotics. She lived out here in the northend and so some Goddamned rumor went around that she had a trained bear in the basement so if the narcotics agents came down, she'd eat them up or something. Well, I know and anybody with any sense knows these narcotics agents used to pick those hopheads up on a Saturday because then they couldn't get before the commissioner until Monday, and then they'd wait until they got withdrawal pains good, then they'd go in and talk to them. . . . So I know this broad's in jail and I know she isn't going to get out 'til the next day when the commissioner comes and everybody in the city room of the *P-I* must have known the same thing. Goddammit, and they knew there wasn't any bear in that basement. But they made me sit out there all that day until 10 o'clock that night in case that woman came home. Now that might not have made me too mad at the time, but after my mother departed the earth, I — well — I got pretty Goddamned mad about it. What the hell. There wasn't no bear out there, and, if they get a picture of the bear, we'll get hell or something. Hell, they could look in the basement window. Hell, there ain't no bear in there. You wouldn't believe that would you? Oh, hell! [10]

Lynch and his problems contrasted sharply with the secure situation of the chief political writer, Lester Hunt. Hunt's salary was one of the best in the newsroom; he was able to choose the stories he wished to write; and he enjoyed the status of social contact with the area's politicians. His job was secure and he was not particularly bothered about those less fortunate than himself. He found nothing wrong with being a political writer for the *Post-Intelligencer* one week and switching over to handle the press operation for a Republican gubernatorial candidate the next. He was not bothered by becoming a public-relations man for Dave Beck shortly after beginning an investigation of Beck for the *Post-Intelligencer*.[11]

Hunt had the confidence of the Hearst organization and was counted on as a stabilizing force in the newsroom. He could pull together the more conservative newsmen, such as Fred Niendorff and Clayton Fritchett, and balance off the malcontents. At the same time, he could generate a good deal of resentment from many in the newsroom who were not so confident of their jobs.

A good salary didn't always mean a secure position on the *Post-Intelligencer*. Everhardt Armstrong was also among the better paid writers, but he was not so popular with the Hearst management. His $70-a-week salary reflected his ability and his long tenure with the Hearst organization; at the same time he was viewed as a malcontent, a trouble-maker who talked about the cause of labor, the exploitation of the wage earner, and the injustice and failure of the American capitalistic system.

Armstrong was a New Yorker who had somehow found his way to Seattle. He never quite fit into the more casual life of the West Coast city, and even his dress testified to his being something of an outsider.[12] His highly-styled clothes and spats always set him apart from the casually-dressed reporters of the newsroom. His background, education, and interests also made it difficult for him to deal with the more plebeian interests of the sports and police reporters. Yet he made an effort to bridge the gap, particularly to talk to the younger staff members about the injustices which surrounded the employees of the Hearst organization. This won him a few converts and a good deal of animosity from management.

Dick Seller was a young reporter, viewed by both

management and fellow reporters as a "comer." He had a university education, plenty of ability and drive, and he knew his way around the city and the Hearst organization. He was brash, but many of his fellow workers admired the young reporter. As Slim Lynch put it, "Hell, that guy even knew parliamentary procedure."[13] Seller had advanced steadily on the *Post-Intelligencer*, but he had never really been satisfied. He grew bored with the fairly routine assignments and failed to show the enthusiasm for his work which some of the editors desired. He felt that there were serious problems at the *Post-Intelligencer*. In his view, many of the employees were blatantly exploited and were unable to protect themselves. Shortly after hearing about the formation of the American Newspaper Guild, he wrote its national headquarters for information. He was encouraged to organize the Seattle area local, but declined what he considered a certain route to martyrdom.

In 1936, Seller just had been married and appeared ready to settle down to his job on the newspaper. However, management made a decision which put Seller firmly into the camp of the dissident reporters. Shortly after his marriage, he was taken off his daytime news beat and assigned to cover the police department at night. This was a job often given to the single and carefree young men on the staff. Seller complained about the abrupt change in his fortunes, but despite promises that he would be reassigned, nothing happened. As the early months of 1936 wore on, the angry young man became more and more determined to take a hand in his own destiny.[14]

Another long-time employee who lost favor with management, Bernice Reddington, was head of the Prudence Penny department, the home-economics staff of the *Post-Intelligencer*. Reddington had gone to work for the newspaper before she completed a bachelor's degree at the University of Washington and had become head of Prudence Penny. It was an important section of the paper in the 1930s, for Americans were learning to live on a less expensive diet than they had enjoyed in earlier decades. The newspaper sold its advertising to grocers in large part because of the wealth of recipes and advice it offered readers. To the extent that Prudence Penny had a loyal following, the newspaper's advertising income grew. And Bernice Reddington developed a Prudence Penny staff that answered food questions phoned, mailed, and delivered in person by the thousands. The staff tested recipes, developed economical meals and passed the information on through the paper and a popular series of cooking schools.15

By 1936, priorities for the *Post-Intelligencer* had shifted at the expense of the Prudence Penny department. Reddington was told that the newspaper's budget was tight and that some of her better-paid assistants would have to be let go. The word, she was told, had come from Bart Guild. She didn't quite understand the dismissals, but she saw the pattern they were taking. Efficient help appeared to be fired and replaced with younger, lower-paid women who lacked knowledge and experience. Conflicts developed within the department between the experienced and the inexperienced writers and the efficiency of the operation dropped considerably.16 This worried Bernice Reddington. She was no malcontent and was apolitical, yet she was beginning to listen to conversations among some of the more radical staff members. The job which had brought her so much satisfaction for so many years appeared to be turning sour.17

In many cases newcomers to the staff were caught up in the discontent which permeated the *Post-Intelligencer* before they had any opportunity to experience the optimism which usually accompanies a new job. Jack Jarvis, a recent graduate of the University of Washington, had been employed by the *Seattle Star* as a correspondent for the University of Washington campus before going to work full-time on the Scripps League paper. When an opening developed on the *Post-Intelligencer*, Jarvis was hired from the *Star* with a $5-a-week raise. This caused resentment in the Hearst newsroom. Reporters at the *P-I* had nothing against Jarvis, but it was the $20-a-week salary which annoyed many of them.18 Although that is all many of the writers in the women's and home-economics departments received after several years of employment, in 1936 it was assumed that men would be favored with better salaries.

Cliffe Erickson, who worked in the *Post-Intelligencer* library or "morgue," earned only $12 a week, and it was easy to see that the ceiling for his kind of job wasn't much higher. Erickson had little of Jarvis's personal charm or concern for humanity. He would have been a malcontent no matter where he worked but the situation on the *Post-Intelligencer* gave him ample material for airing his frustrations. Erickson had no real professional commitment to the work for which he was hired — it was just a job — a job which paid very little. His frustrations fueled deep dissatisfaction and made him ready to lash out at all he perceived to be responsible for his situation.[19]

There were others who were paid no better than either Jarvis or Erickson but who had not yet begun to feel trapped or unjustly treated. Claude Smith was a novice reporter who for a time was buoyed by the fact that he had a regular job, one with some romance attached to it, and he had enough idealism to think that he could do something about bettering conditions. Also, he was in love with a vivacious young woman named Betty, and for the present, at least, life appeared satisfying to Claude Smith.[20]

Smith's optimism was matched by that of the Swanstrom sisters, Gena and Mary. Daughters of a prominent Seattle family with social position and Junior League ties, the Swanstroms went to work for the *Post-Intelligencer* when the family ran into financial problems early in the depression. The *Post-Intelligencer* hired young women from prominent families to gain entrè to society news and to attract subscribers. The Swanstrom sisters needed the money, yet they were set apart from the other young persons on the newspaper. They were slumming and they had little professional interest. The frustrations they felt concerning salary and the working conditions on the *Post-Intelligencer* were more for others than themselves. And despite all the problems surrounding the newspaper, they were enjoying life and most other employees welcomed the company of two such spirited and attractive girls.[21]

There were about seventy employees on the news staff of the *Post-Intelligencer* in 1936, including the newsroom, library, and home-economics department.[22] Each person met the vexing situations on the newspaper and in the broader world outside in his or her own way. Each carried ambitions, ideals, commitments, and feelings which made it impossible to ignore the tragedies of the depression or their effects on the individuals on the *Post-Intelligencer*. As the tensions, frustrations, and annoyances increased on the newspaper during the early months of 1936, each of these individuals was to react differently. Differences on the newspaper became more clearly defined; emotional issues divided the staff and sent each faction seeking differing solutions; frustrations festered and served to shape the decisions each person made. In many cases, minor annoyances became major issues and helped lay the groundwork for the *Post-Intelligencer* strike of 1936.

FOOTNOTES CHAPTER I

THE SWING OF THE IRON BALL

1. See letters from *P-I* staff members in Terry Pettus Papers (MSS in Manuscript Division, University of Washington Library). Hereafter referred to as Pettus Papers.
2. W. A. Swanberg, *Citizen Hearst* (New York: Charles Scribner's Sons, 1961), pp. 475-479.
3. *Fortune* XII (October, 1935), p. 126.
4. Betty H. Winfield, "Economic Changes in American Newspapers, 1890-1930," unpublished paper, University of Washington, 1975, pp. 14-16.
5. National Labor Relations Board, "Transcripts of Hearings in Case C-136," Board Exhibit 5.
6. Interviews with Lester Hunt, Frank Lynch, Arthur French, Bernice Reddington, Richard Seller, and others, To minimize confusion of names, both given name and surname will be used whenever the Hearst executive is mentioned.
7. Harvey I. Kelly to Roger Simpson, June 13, 1959.
8. John F. Neylan to William Ingram, March 3, 1936, John F. Neylan Papers (MSS in Bancroft Library, University of California, Berkeley).
9. Art French interview, May, 1959.
10. *Ibid.*
11. Lester Hunt interview, April, 1960.
12. Howard Brier interview, October, 1963.
13. Frank Lynch interview, May, 1959.
14. Richard Seller interviews, May, 1959, and June, 1961.
15. Bernice Reddington interview, May, 1959.
16. *Ibid.*
17. *Ibid.*
18. Forrest Williams to Terry Pettus, April 12, 1936, Pettus Papers.
19. Interviews with Terry Pettus, December, 1960, and

Claude Smith, August, 1960.

20. Claude Smith interview, August, 1960.
21. Interviews with Bernice Reddington, April, 1959, and Mrs. Floyd Larkin, May, 1959.
22. Williams to American Newspaper Guild, July 23, 1936, Newspaper Guild Collection, Archives of Labor History and Urban Affairs, Wayne State University, Detroit. The union changed its name to The Newpaper Guild in July, 1971.

CHAPTER II

AN ARMY WITH BANNERS

In the summer of 1935, Terry Pettus, drama editor and general-assignment reporter of the *Tacoma Ledger*, sent off a $2 check for a subscription to the *Guild Reporter*, the publication of the American Newspaper Guild.[1] The Guild issued him a membership card and he became immersed in newspaper union activity. Pettus first organized a Tacoma chapter which was chartered in November, 1935, then turned, at the urging of national Guild officers, to forming a unit in nearby Seattle.[2]

Pettus fit well the role of union organizer. He had come to Puget Sound in 1927 after having worked on newspapers in Minneapolis and Grand Forks, N.D. His father was a minister who felt nearly as strongly about a social gospel for mankind as he did about the Christian gospel. Pettus had been raised in a home where a social conscience and a willingness to act on behalf of man were considered the measure of a person's worth.

Liberal, but not radical, Pettus was alarmed about the weaknesses of American society which the depression had made apparent. Friends of the handsome, personable young writer covered the political spectrum, and for most of them, the home where he and his wife Berta lived at Spanaway, near Tacoma, was a popular social center. Later, Pettus became one of the Northwest's most famous radicals of the Left, but in the early 1930s his co-workers saw him as a hardworking and capable newsman who shared the disillusion of many with the economic system. Where others who had joined the Guild had been unwilling or unable to devote much time to the new union, Pettus acted differently. He became convinced that the country's newsmen needed the protection of such an organization, and he made the effort to bring the new union to Tacoma. The assignment meant talking to his fellow workers, winning support from some, annoyance from others. It meant spending evenings and weekends arguing with and urging the hesitant and frightened. It meant losing a friendly relationship with management. To Pettus, organizing the Guild was worth the sacrifices. [3]

When a letter to the national Guild office from a jobless Tacoma reporter was forwarded to Pettus, he replied with characteristic intensity:4 He urged the prospect to become a Guild member-at-large rather than joining the new Tacoma chapter, since there was little hope of finding a job on that city's newspapers. The *Ledger's* staff, he wrote, was "cut to the bone. For several years the only persons hired were youngsters who work for nothing and work damned hard. The only ray of hope I see is the five-day week. It makes jobs for the experienced men who deserve them and who have been kicked in the face plenty." Pettus believed that the Guild could change all that. The organization would assure jobs for the men who had been used, then "booted out for the sake of more profits." 5

When the Tacoma chapter was chartered in November, 1935, the American Newspaper Guild was a few days short of two years old, and the colorful details of the union's short history were well known to Pettus. He had watched Heywood Broun, the idealistic columnist of the *New York World-Telegram*, who spurred and inspired his fellow reporters to form a newsmen's union. Broun, whose bulky figure draped in ill-fitting clothes was to be a familiar sight on Guild picket lines, affirmed Pettus's conviction that unions offered an answer for reporters' troubles. In his August 7, 1933, *World-Telegram* column, Broun had written:

The fact that newspaper editors and owners are genial folk should hardly stand in the way of the organization of a newspaper writers' union. There should be one. Beginning at nine o'clock on the morning of October 1, I am going to do the best I can in helping to get one up.6

Only six days before Broun's words were published, the Cleveland Editorial Employees Association, the germ of the union, was formed. The following December, the American Newspaper Guild was created. At the same time, the Roosevelt Administration was fumbling for a labor policy. Publishers had been invited to draw up a newspaper industry labor code under the National Recovery Administration. The publishers, not surprisingly, designed a voluntary code to make their own lives easier. Although one of the provisions set maximum hours and minimum scales for some papers, the NRA declared that reporters were professionals, excluded from such provisions.7

As reporters around the country followed these events in conservative trade organs such as *Editor & Publisher* or the liberal opinion magazines, Broun and the union focused discontent on the corporate "lords of the press." In the *Nation*, Broun attacked the notion that a code would bind the publishers.

It is utterly impossible to discuss employment conditions in the newspaper code or any other without facing the fundamental fallacy on which these codes are created and the monstrous manner in which they are interpreted.

When an employer speaks of the industry — usually with bated breath — he refers only to the property rights of himself and his fellow employers. He isn't even thinking of the right of labor and the rights of the public, if any. Into the NRA conception there has crept from time to time the word "partnership." The publishers thought that to mean a partnership of the employers. Indeed to them a code is a sort of land grant giving them complete and exclusive right to hunt, fish and exterminate Indians.

. . . The publishers construe the freedom of the press to mean that no governmental agency has any right to compel them to do anything whatsoever. If you ask a newspaper owner to put a rope on the fifth floor so that somebody may slide down in case of fire he may very well draw himself up and say, "How dare you interfere with freedom of the press?" Until there is a good newspaper code there will be . . . no good codes, because if you boil all the publishers of America down — a consummation greatly to be desired — you will find that you have in essence automobiles, textiles, steel, munitions, utilities and all the leading industries of the country. 8

Publishers, indeed, ran roughshod over the shaky labor legislation of the New Deal and the union found itself on the defensive almost at once. In San Francisco, Dean Jennings, for five years a rewrite man on the Hearst *Call-Bulletin*, was fired after he attended a Guild convention. The dismissal led the Guild into an extended confrontation with the publishers and showed convincingly that the publishers dominated the labor machinery of the recovery program. A momentary victor through a decision of the National Labor Relations Board, the Guild lost all when Roosevelt, responding to publisher pressure, removed the case from NLRB jurisdiction to the unfriendly Newspaper Industrial Board.[9]

While the Jennings case was pending, the Guild unit on the *Newark Ledger* precipitated the union's first major strike by asking its crusty publisher, Lucius Russell, to negotiate a contract covering wages and hours. Russell refused and on November 13, 1934, posted the following notice on the office bulletin board: "You can go to all the Regional Labor Boards you damn please and you will get no relief from *The Ledger*. . . . I will make it quite nervous for quite a number of *The Ledger* personnel if the thing ever reaches that point." The following day he added another bulletin: "I am going to discharge 25 percent of the staff in the next two weeks and after I return from Hot Springs I will discharge 25 per cent more." Three days later the Guild members walked out on strike and manned sound trucks to announce: "Lucius T. Russell, publisher of the *Newark Ledger*, is unfair to editorial workers. He violates the NRA." [10]

The strike gave the union its first symbols of sacrifice and dedication to worker rights. Broun called the Guild members on the Newark picket line "an army with banners," and the impression of a workers' crusade was heightened by the general dislike reporters and the public shared for the newspaper's publisher. Russell, in fact, succeeded in driving away any support he might have expected, including his readers and advertisers. The Guild was able to convince merchants to withhold their financial support, causing the stockholders of the newspaper to request a court appointment of two trustees to negotiate with the Guild while Russell vacationed in Hot Springs. Following this, Secretary of Labor Frances Perkins ordered a labor mediator to help settle the strike.[11]

By the fourth month of the strike, the harassed trustees turned to the courts for relief. On March 7, 1935, a court, in a sweeping restraining order, prohibited the Guild from picketing, from talking to "loyal workers," from distributing the *Guild Reporter* or any printed material carrying "misleading" information about the *Ledger*, from loitering near the paper, and from using radio to comment on the strike.[12]

The eighteen-week strike was settled on March 28, 1935, in part due to the intervention of the Roosevelt Administration and in part because Russell had decided to sell the property to S. I. Newhouse. The sale, two months later, resulted in the collapse of the Newark chapter. For only a moment, the Guild could hail the Newark experience as a "labor triumph." [13]

Meanwhile, a few papers were being won through negotiation. The first of these was the *Long Island Press*, owned by S. I. Newhouse. He reportedly commented to Broun on the signing of an agreement: "You've made a guinea-pig of the *Press*." Broun replied, "Well, you certainly walked right into our laboratory." [14]

The first major newspaper contract was signed without a struggle a year later by J. David Stern, liberal publisher of the *New York Post*. The Guild contract called for a closed shop, check-off of union dues, two-week annual vacation, and dismissal notice. It was one of the few closed-shop victories the union was to win.[15]

In comparison with the battles which lay ahead, the Guild victories before 1936 were small indeed. The big men in the field, the William Randolph Hearsts and the Roy Howards, had not been touched. Until these giants could in some way be brought to the bargaining table, the Guild had little chance of success. The union's attention was to be focused on building sufficient strength to battle one of the large chain newspaper owners.

Most Guild leaders assumed that William Randolph Hearst would be a union target once chapters had been formed on each of his newspapers. His newspaper empire was impressive and his opposition to the Guild was unrelenting.[16] Hearst's financial resources were extensive, though, and the union needed time to prepare for the contest. Behind Hearst's public rebukes of the Guild for trying to organize "professionals" lay an organization determined to stop unionism among reporters. Hearst, of course, was not alone in this view. He shared a hostility toward unions with many publishers and could count on their support.

In the meantime, without forcing a conflict with Hearst,

the Guild benefitted from the public's dislike for him. In Newark, the union had learned the value of community sentiment against a publisher. Hearst's words and actions were immensely helpful to the Guild cause.

By 1934, Hearst had turned from enthusiastic support of Franklin Delano Roosevelt to bitter opposition. In the midst of a great crusade to save America from the danger of communism, Hearst found Reds everywhere, particularly within the labor movement, and described the Roosevelt Administration as "more communistic than the Communists." He was impressed with what Hitler had done for Germany. He declared: "Fascism will only come into existence in the United States when such a movement becomes really necessary for the prevention of communism."[17] Hearst portrayed university campuses, labor unions, and other segments of society as hotbeds of communism, fed by the federal administration in Washington. Through his chain of newspapers he sought to ride to new power on an anti-Roosevelt, anti-communist, anti-labor crusade.

Many differed with Hearst. American campuses were an important center of the opposition as boycotts of Hearst newspapers, magazines, and newsreels were carried out. Some students even went so far as to burn the publisher in effigy, and Charles Beard, the historian, spoke out: "There is not a cesspool of vice and crime which Hearst has not raked and exploited for money-making purposes."[18]

Hearst responded to the criticism by drawing himself above the attacks. He advised his readers: "Whenever you hear a prominent American called a 'Fascist,' you can usually make up your mind that the man is simply a loyal citizen who stands for Americanism." [19]

In the Pacific Northwest, Hearst's red-baiting effusions fell on a citizenry used to and often sympathetic to labor-union militancy and the political radicalism that often accompanied it. While the *Post-Intelligencer* fanned Hearst's irritating charges throughout the region, Terry Pettus took a step that would lead to a new union on Hearst's Seattle newspaper.

As 1936 began, Pettus talked to two of the Seattle Guild members, Emerson Daggett and Lowell Wakefield, editors of the *Voice of Action*. The *Voice of Action* was started in 1933 in Tacoma as the organ of the Unemployed Citizens League, but almost from the start it was recognized as the voice of the Communist Party in the Northwest. Its young idealistic editors firmly believed in the labor cause and along with four members of their staff had joined the Guild in April, 1935. [20]

Wakefield became a member of the Communist Party in New York while he was a student at Columbia University. Later, as a writer for the *Daily Worker*, he had uncovered the Scottsboro case in Alabama which provided the party with one of its most celebrated causes during the 1930s. Wakefield was too independent to work without friction in the party, and the history of his membership was characterized by numerous conflicts and threatened withdrawals. He came from a wealthy Seattle family, and his attractive wife shared his party enthusiasm. [21]

Daggett was also a Seattle youth and had attended the University of Washington, where he became active on the school's radical fringe. He was a member of the socialist organization — the Thursday Afternoon Club — and edited its paper. When this production ceased, he transferred its second-class mailing permit to the *Voice of Action* and became one of the editors. Along the way he joined the Communist Party, but his commitment was short-lived, and he left to enter the public-relations field in the late 1930s. [22]

The *Voice of Action* editors informed Pettus that David Selvin of the Pacific Coast Labor Bureau was willing to help organize the Guild in Seattle. Selvin's apartment was available for such a meeting. They also said that Tom Potwin of the *Seattle Times*, Forrest Williams and Dick Seller of the *Post-Intelligencer*, and Fred d'Avila of the *Seattle Star* were interested in joining. [23]

Pettus immediately asked Selvin to set a date — a Sunday — for a meeting. Pettus admitted there were still some "holdouts" in Tacoma, but he thought that a chapter in Seattle might help break their resistance. "Only one charter in the Northwest makes us all vulnerable and does not make for a feeling of security on the part of the many to whom this sort of thing is strange." [24]

Selvin set the meeting for Sunday, February 23, in his room in the Baroness Apartments at the corner of Terry and Spring. [25] Pettus sent notices to Potwin, Williams, Seller, and d'Avila, asking whether or not they were interested in organizing a Guild. If they were, the time and the place of the meeting would be given. "Naturally," Pettus wrote, "any reply to this will be strictly confidential and in no way will your participation be allowed to jeopardize your position." [26] At least one of the four, Seller, already had indicated to the national Guild office early in 1934 that he was interested in a Seattle chapter. Seller had been wary then, writing to the Guild that: "Newspapermen feel that those who start the move will become a martyr to the cause, and reporters have seen too many martyrs get nothing but martyrdom to care for that." [27] Pettus tactfully respected the writer's concern when he approached Seller in 1936.

The February, 1936, gathering was the conception of the Seattle chapter, but little about the meeting foretold its significance. Only one of the four invited showed up at the meeting — Williams. In addition to Selvin, Pettus and his wife also were present. The results were discouraging, but those attending knew others were interested if only contact could be made. Pettus continued to push for organization.

He was helped by the knowledge that the Guild had struck Hearst's *Wisconsin News* in Milwaukee. On February 17, only five days before the Seattle meeting, twenty-two Milwaukee Guild members had ended a sleepless night in a downtown apartment by mounting a surprise picket line in below-zero weather. As the Wisconsin newsmen worked earnestly to build up public support for a strike that had little encouragement from organized labor, newspaper employees in other cities began to see more clearly that this was the beginning of the battle against Hearst. Some Guild officials hoped that Milwaukee might settle the matter. A vice president wrote: "I believe this strike will be a godsend to the Guild movement as sooner or later a typical American daily probably had to be struck on the paramount issue of the five-day week. This is no crazy Russell and no Harlem Weekly. Hearst is a tough baby. It will be one hell of a fight. But Milwaukee is probably the best spot." [28]

The Milwaukee strike lasted until September, 1936, and in running its course provided a number of useful lessons for the novice Guild strategists in the Pacific Northwest. Labor support was needed; the Milwaukee unit suffered because the Guild was not affiliated with organized labor. Community support was available; it only had to be mobilized. Hearst publishers could not negotiate freely; the word they gave one day might be cancelled the next by Hearst.

While Pettus and the others watched and learned from the Milwaukee experiment, other journalists took heart from the boldness of their Midwest brothers and sisters. A member of the staff of the *Washington Posten,* the weekly Norwegian language newspaper, closed a letter to Pettus: "God and Lenin bless you for Milwaukee — I worked for the *PI* for six months!" [29]

Such letters encouraged Pettus and his fellow Guild members. If they were taken ". . . in the aggregate they show more strikingly than all the talk in the world that editorial workers are not the individualistic asses the publishers want to believe we are," Pettus concluded. [30]

Organization in Seattle moved far too slowly for the impatient Pettus. Another setback came in the latter part of March when Selvin learned he was being transferred to San Francisco. He worried whether his replacement in the Pacific Coast Labor Bureau would be willing to play the same role in attempting to hold a Seattle "nucleus intact" until there was sufficient strength to grant a national charter. The group was still small, with only Everhardt Armstrong, the *Post-Intelligencer* drama writer, Williams, Daggett, and one or two others showing some interest. [31]

Organizing the Guild was touchy business in Seattle. Williams, who played a strategic role, probably was a bit more uneasy than most of the new recruits. He took such precautions as to refer to all individuals only by initials and to initial even his own letters.

Several meetings had been held by the first of May, but they were not as yet held weekly. During the first part of April the group had been looking for a new meeting place. Williams thought that a "middle-aged man" with the initials E. A. (Everhardt Armstrong) would make a good president of the Seattle Guild, and Armstrong had a musician friend who might allow them to use his downtown office for meetings. Williams feared, however, that management had some suspicion about the meetings and that the date should be changed to Saturday to prevent the wrong people from finding out about the organizing efforts. Armstrong heard from a reporter for International News Service, Hearst's wire service, that Ed Stone, night city editor of the *Post-Intelligencer,* was aware of the meetings and had heard that Pettus was coming over to organize the men in Seattle. Stone was believed to be unsympathetic and was suspected of having told all the *Post-Intelligencer* executives about the effort. Williams thought it probably would be best to "lay low" for a time. If Armstrong's musician friend didn't come through with a meeting place, perhaps a room could be rented at the Frye Hotel, where clubs sometimes met. [32]

Despite the tensions, there was some reason for optimism in Seattle. Interest was growing, and newsmen on both the *Post-Intelligencer* and the *Star* were proving to be "O.K." as far as the Guild was concerned. There were no members on the *Times*, a reflection of that paper's extreme opposition to the Guild. The group in Seattle also was starting to think in terms of interests shared by newspaper workers around the country. Williams, at least, was sending a dollar as often as he could to help with the *Wisconsin News* strike against Hearst.

While things were moving slowly in Seattle, events were taking place elsewhere which were to help weld a unit at the *Post-Intelligencer*. Pettus had made important contacts with the Northwest Printing Trades Federation, primarily through Wakefield, and in mid-April attended a Portland meeting of the Federation at Guild expense. Selvin was instrumental in getting Pettus in contact with Howard Grant, secretary of the Federation, and Grant's interest in the Guild was to pay off handsomely when the question of the printing trades crossing a Guild picket line was raised in August. [33]

While Pettus was in Portland, he also tried to recruit some Portland newsmen to the Guild. Among those he attempted to contact was a future United States senator, Richard E. Neuberger, whose name had been furnished by Clyde Beals, editor of the *Guild Reporter*. Neuberger failed to respond to Pettus's invitation to discuss the Guild. [34]

Early in April the Guild received word from its national office that Morgan Hull of San Francisco had been named an organizer and that he might visit Seattle soon. It was encouraging to know that Hull was an acquaintance of Charles Daggett, the new city editor of the *Seattle Star*. [35] Daggett, who was not related to Emerson Daggett of the *Voice of Action*, was a Guild member, and it was hoped his connection with Hull would bring positive results to the Seattle situation.

Seattle Guildsmen moved to raise funds for a national organizer and discussed the plan at their April 19 meeting at the Frye Hotel. There were some situations brewing which made good recruiting material for the Guild — the *Post-Intelligencer's* hiring of Jack Jarvis from the *Star* for $20 a week, a $5 raise, for one. To the experienced reporter, the wage was low and threatening. Some Seattle newsmen feared the same situation developing in Seattle as in Tacoma — young and cheap help hired in place of the experienced and higher-paid reporters. But Jarvis was considered a "good man, and . . . hot for the social club." 36

Events at the *P-I* were disquieting. Bart Guild, Hearst's West Coast efficiency expert, seemed to some Guild members to be bent on committing acts which could lead only to a rapid increase in Guild membership. He was accused of taking by-lines from *P-I* men who rated themselves "heavyweights" and generally had made himself irritating to members of the staff. 37

But while the prospects for recruiting seemed brighter, success was not overwhelming. Harold Mansfield, a *P-I* reporter, was approached and found to be cool to the social club. 38 Bernice Reddington, the home-economics editor who was about to be eased out of her job, was a bit fearful of attending any of the meetings. She thought the Guild sounded a bit radical. "I thought they might drop a pineapple or something." 39

And there was still the ever-present problem of finding a suitable meeting room. The Frye Hotel was charging $3 for the room, and Williams, at least, felt this could better be spent in supporting the Milwaukee strike. 40

The Guild was beginning to be noticed in Seattle by May — an eventful month for the new organization in the Pacific Northwest. The Tacoma Guild faced its first real showdown with management and was able to win the reinstatement of Rex Kelly, unit chairman of the *Tacoma Times*, following his discharge. The victory was important for the Seattle chapter, and that same month, on May 12, Hull, West Coast organizer for the Guild, issued a charter for the Seattle Chapter of the American Newspaper Guild. Twenty-two members signed the charter, but several attending the meeting refused to commit themselves to the organization. Slim Lynch decided to make a great show of signing the charter. Lynch walked to the front of the room for all to see and made so much of signing that he annoyed a few in the crowd. 41

Lynch's display probably was needed, for the Guild chapter which was organized that night had no great abundance of courage. The Guild was becoming more and more a topic of conversation around the newspaper plants, particularly the *Star* and the *Post-Intelligencer*. Newsmen joining the Guild were well aware that the organization was frowned upon by William Randolph Hearst, and great pains were taken to see that Guild membership was kept a secret from the *Post-Intelligencer* management.

On the *Star* the news that Hull had come to Seattle to help organize the Guild was greeted with open hostility on the part of the Scripps management. Editor Rodney Brink called his news staff together one afternoon in early May and proceeded to read an address which explained the Scripps's attitude toward the Guild. Although the message was couched in rather pleasant language, those listening clearly got the idea that the paper's publishers were "hostile towards organization of editorial workers and that they organized at their peril." Brink also made it known that he regarded Hull as an "incompetent newspaperman who couldn't hold a job." [42]

All these matters were discussed in great detail at the meetings of the Mutal Benefit Uplift Society, the new euphemism for the Guild chapter. Charles Daggett, city editor of the *Star*, was named president of the new chapter, a position which he had not sought but had accepted after he realized most other capable members were fearful of taking the post.

During the remainder of the month, Guild matters were fairly calm in Seattle. The members slowly adjusted to the idea that they now belonged to a union, and, to the surprise of some, no firings or other drastic action resulted from the formation of the Guild chapter. In fact, the *Post-Intelligencer* responded by giving raises to several Guildsmen, including Williams and Lynch, [43] who was at that time head of the photographic department.

At the same time, the *Post-Intelligencer* management sought to win loyalty by giving the security of contracts to selected employees. [44] The contracts, however, did little to improve the attitude of the employees toward the paper.

FOOTNOTES CHAPTER II

AN ARMY WITH BANNERS

1. Interviews with Mr. and Mrs. Terry Pettus, October, 1959.
2. For actions of the Tacoma Guild, see Newspaper Guild Collection, Archives of Labor History and Urban Affairs, Wayne State University, Detroit. Hereafter referred to as Newspaper Guild Collection.
3. Pettus interviews, October, 1959.
4. Frishman to Pettus, January 23, 1936, Pettus Papers (MSS in Manuscript Division, University of Washington Library). Hereafter referred to as Pettus Papers.
5. Pettus to Frishman, February 8, 1936, Pettus Papers.
6. *New York World-Telegram,* August 7, 1933.
7. Irving Bernstein, *Turbulent Years* (Boston: Houghton Mifflin Co., 1970), p. 134.
8. Broun, "The Industry," *The Nation,* CXL (February 20, 1935), p. 223.
9. Daniel Leab, *A Union of Individuals* (New York: Columbia University Press, 1970), pp. 182-190.
10. "Strike: Broun Defies," *Newsweek,* V (March 23, 1935), p. 23; see also Leab, pp. 153-168.
11. *Ibid.*
12. Broun, "Because the Judge Says So," *The Nation,* CXL (March 20, 1935), p. 336.
13. Broun, "White Collar into Plume," *The Nation,* CXL (April 10, 1935), p. 420; Leab, p. 164.
14. "The Newspaper Guild Attains Man's Stature," *Literary Digest,* CXVIII (July 28, 1934), p. 30.
15. "Gift on a Platter," *Business Week,* August 3, 1935, p. 22.
16. See Rodney Carlisle, "William Randolph Hearst's Reaction to the American Newspaper Guild," *Labor History,* X (Winter, 1969), pp. 74-99.
17. Arthur M. Schlesinger, Jr., *The Age of Roosevelt: The Politics of Upheaval* (Boston: Houghton Mifflin Company, 1960), p. 85.
18. *Ibid.*, p. 88.
19. *Ibid.*, For a view more favorable to Hearst, see W. A. Swanberg, *Citizen Hearst* (New York: Charles Scribner's

Sons, 1961), pp. 442-446, 468-471.

20. Emerson Daggett to American Newspaper Guild officials, April 20, 1935, Newspaper Guild Collection.
21. Lowell Wakefield interview, July, 1966. This also is covered in an early thesis draft prepared by Paul Anderson on the *Voice of Action,* University of Washington, 1966.
22. Emerson Daggett interview, March, 1966.
23. Daggett to Pettus, February 10, 1936, Pettus Papers.
24. Pettus to David Selvin, February 15, 1936, Pettus Papers.
25. Selvin to Pettus, February 14, 1936, Pettus Papers.
26. Pettus to prospective Guild members, February 15, 1936, Pettus Papers.
27. Richard Seller to Guild officials, April 10, 1934, Newspaper Guild Collection.
28. Don Stevens to National Executive Board, American Newspaper Guild, undated, Newspaper Guild Collection.
29. Lund to Pettis (*sic*), March 5, 1936, Pettus Papers.
30. Pettus to Lund, March 7, 1936, Pettus Papers.
31. Selvin to Pettus, March 24, 1936, Pettus Papers.
32. Forrest Williams to Pettus, April 5, 1936, Pettus Papers.
33. Selvin to Pettus, March 24, 1936, Pettus Papers.
34. Pettus to Richard E. Neuberger, March 31, 1936, Pettus Papers.
35. Pettus to Selvin, April 6, 1936, Pettus Papers.
36. Williams to Pettus, April 12, 1936, Pettus Papers. See also Bernice Reddington interview, May, 1959.
37. *Ibid.*
38. Williams to Pettus, April 14, 1936, Pettus Papers. Mansfield later became public-relations director of the Boeing Co.
39. Bernice Reddington interview, May, 1959.
40. Williams to Pettus, April 14, 1936, Pettus Papers.
41. National Labor Relations Board, "Transcript of Hearings in Case C-136" (Seattle hearings), pp. 349 and 851. Hereafter referred to as "Transcript" (Seattle).
42. Williams to Pettus, May 7, 1936, Pettus Papers.
43. "Transcript" (Seattle), p. 2021, testimony of Charles Lindeman.
44. "Transcript" (Seattle), p. 1405, testimony of Raymond Colvin.

CHAPTER III

A MARTYR EMERGES

For some time after the Seattle Chapter of the American Newspaper Guild was chartered, it appeared the organization might never meet again. Most members harbored no real commitment to the fledgling unit, and the absence during May of the two strongest supporters was felt strongly. Terry Pettus was ill for several weeks and had been too involved in the Rex Kelly case in Tacoma to pay much attention to Seattle. Then, on his recovery, he left for the Guild's national convention in Toledo. The other guiding force, Forrest Williams, took a vacation, on which he and a fellow newspaperman, Gordon Metcalfe, drove through eastern Washington. Williams felt that the efforts necessary to organize the unit had drained him of all his energy.

Others felt somewhat guilty about not meeting, but little was done. One of the officers talked about calling a meeting one afternoon, but then he proceeded to get drunk before any arrangements could be made.[1] The matter rested until the *Post-Intelligencer* management provided the nudge which launched the Seattle chapter toward the first major victory for the Guild and a defeat for William Randolph Hearst.

News of the organization of the Seattle chapter came to management through a circuitous route. The Guildsmen in Seattle prided themselves on their closed-mouth attitude toward the organization, and no announcement was made in the city of the formation of the chapter. However, Clyde Beals, editor of the *Guild Reporter*, was unaware of the need for secrecy and included a story in the *Guild Reporter* telling of organizing a chapter of the Guild despite strong opposition from the city's newspapers. The Guild organizer, Morgan Hull, who provided the story, painted the *Post-Intelligencer* opposition as unusually strong. The issue also dealt with the *Wisconsin News* strike and urged Guildsmen to boycott Hearst in every way possible.[2]

The two items created something of a furor among *Post-Intelligencer* executives. Charles Lindeman, assistant publisher, was upset to see national attention being given to a statement that the *Post-Intelligencer* unit had been organized despite "intimidation and pressure." Lindeman was walking toward his office on the day the *Guild Reporter* was circulated at the *Post-Intelligencer* and encountered one of the charter members, Mrs. Marion Badcon. She contended she was surprised by the statement and refused to admit that membership in the Guild was in any way disloyal to the *Post-Intelligencer*. [3]

Members of *Post-Intelligencer* management were beginning to ask questions about who did and who did not belong to the Guild. The general atmosphere of tension grew. Guild members were somewhat paranoid about their membership, which made the slightest unsympathetic view from management seem like a major attack.

But the Guildsmen need not have bothered with those slightly opposed to the Guild, for many employed by the *Post-Intelligencer* were openly hostile to the entire idea of labor organizations. To Hearst, the Guild and anyone who joined it were tainted by the Communist affiliations of some of its members. Hearst's management on the *Post-Intelligencer* was quite willing to accept "The Chief's" word on these matters and to follow his edicts as carefully as possible. [4]

Heading the *Post-Intelligencer* was Vaughn Tanner, rather an ineffective publisher in many ways but one who viewed his relationship to the staff as paternalistic. He devoted a good deal of his time to talking about justice, but no one was quite sure of what his actual views were. His role in ferreting out members of the Guild was minor compared to some members of management, but there was no doubt in anyone's mind where Tanner stood with regard to the Guild.

It was mainly the lower echelon of management who devoted time to determining who was and who wasn't in the Guild. Among the most active was Oliver Morris, day city editor. After the announcement in the *Guild Reporter* that a unit had been organized, Morris conversed frequently with the reporters and photographers in his attempt to determine the membership of this organization.

Among the persons whom Morris asked about Guild membership was Richard Seller, who later was chosen president of the chapter. Morris not only informed Seller of Hearst's opposition to the Guild but claimed that Hull, the

Guild organizer, associated with Communists. [5] Hull was in Seattle at the time to organize the Guild. Morris commented that Hearst never would recognize the Guild and was opposed to the whole idea of the organization.

In response to questions about whether he belonged, at first Seller claimed he did not. In Seller's words, "I was afraid to." [6] Later, he admitted his membership. Ed Stone, night managing editor, told Seller that he was a "God-damned fool for belonging." [7] In fact, Seller contended, he felt conditions were far worse on the *Star*, and he encouraged the Guild to use its efforts to gain better conditions on the Scripps paper. Seller even admitted that at one point he told Morris he was going to withdraw from the Guild rather than enter a fight against the *Post-Intelligencer*. [8]

But somewhere along the line Seller became a "good Guildsman" and one of the most vigorous in seeking a victory over Hearst. Seller's doubts about the Guild were gone by the time Edward Woods, the Hearst attorney, attempted to intimidate Seller in the National Labor Relations Board hearings. "So you set out, as I understand you, sir, to continue to take the money and still join the organization which Mr. Morris said to you was fighting the man that paid you?" Seller responded: "No, he said the man that paid me was fighting the organization that I joined." [9]

Jack Heise, a photographer, was the first Guild member on the *Post-Intelligencer* to admit his affiliation with the labor union and did so only after intensive questioning by Morris. "Yes, I'm a member of the Guild," Heise admitted. "Does belonging to it mean my job?" "No, Jack, not your job," Morris told him. "But, damn you, we just gave you a $2.50 a week raise, and this isn't the way to treat us. Hearst never will recognize the Guild, and you might as well be resigned to your fate. You won't ever go any further in the Hearst organization if you belong to the Guild, and there won't be any more pay raises."

Heise also began to feel the official cold shoulder from *Post-Intelligencer* management. Only a few days before, Heise had submitted a series of short-short-stories, the Mark Hellinger kind, to the city editor for use in the paper. Heise was told that the stories would start running in the *Post-Intelligencer* the next week and that he would receive $10 a week for them. He also promised that an effort would be made to have the stories syndicated. This agreement was important to young Heise, for he hoped that eventually he could give up his photography work and devote full time to fiction.

However, the day after Morris learned that Heise had joined the Guild, the stories were returned with the comment: "I am sorry, we haven't got the space or the inclination or the money to pay for them." [10]

The Heise case prompted Morris to have a conversation with Slim Lynch to see if the chief photographer could persuade Heise to quit his Guild membership. Lynch refused such an assignment and admitted that he also was a member of the organization. Morris was astonished and thought Lynch was "nuts" to get mixed up with such an organization. As Lynch later recalled, Morris said there ". . . would be no advancement, no pay increases, no favors done to anyone who belonged to the American Newspaper Guild." [11] *Post-Intelligencer* officials seemed to cool toward Lynch after this incident.

Morris told Forrest Williams that the Guild would fix salaries at a low level, and a man no longer would be able to get ahead on his own initiative. Williams refused to admit his membership. [12]

Art French, a close friend of Frank Lynch and his co-worker in the photography department, was not as reticent to admit his membership. Morris responded by calling French "a horse's rear end, and the son of a so-and-so . . . ." He claimed "anybody that belongs to it was just a dirty . . . ." Later that day French went by managing editor Arthur Dunning's office and heard Morris say, "By God, they all belong to the American Newspaper Guild," and Dunning answer, "I don't give a damn, we can get a whole . . . staff from California." [13]

Heise and Lynch were working in a sensitive area of the *Post-Intelligencer* at the time. Photography long had been a concern of Hearst executives, inspired perhaps by the Chief, who laid out his newspapers on the floor, paced around them, and occasionally stooped to scrawl a note to an editor about content or photography. [14] Hearst executives down the coast in Los Angeles were responsible for photographic quality, and the *Post-Intelligencer's* pictures bothered them.

In February, 1936, after looking at several copies of the Seattle paper, R. V. Edwards, production manager of the *Los Angeles Examiner*, typed a note to Bart Guild: "In looking over copies of the *Post-Intelligencer*, I am of the opinion that something is radically wrong with the pictorial content of the paper." Edwards suggested that the gray tone of the pictures was caused by inferior prints, lacking sufficient contrast for engraving. He also noted that *P-I* sports and society pictures too often were posed, "not what we term action pictures." 15

Lindeman and Ray Colvin, editor of the *P-I*, flew to Los Angeles on May 23 to discuss the photography problem with Edwards and Ray Van Ettisch, managing editor of the *Examiner*. By this time, the management was aware that Lynch was a Guild member.

A few days before the Los Angeles conference, Lynch and other photographers had been called in by Lindeman, Morris, and Dunning to discuss Edwards's criticisms, which Bart Guild had passed on to the *P-I*. Lindeman compared the Seattle paper with copies of eastern Hearst newspapers. The assistant publisher was amiable and sympathetic, offering additional help in the department if needed. Lynch left feeling it had been a fair talk and that Lindeman had demonstrated an understanding of the photography department's problems and had made some good suggestions. 16

In addition to the problem of printing, Morris referred in the meeting to the "inside situation." Hundreds of negatives had accumulated in the darkroom, unidentified and unfiled. Papers, chemicals, and other supplies were wasted, and there were haphazard out-of-pocket purchases of equipment and supplies. The printing from negatives and supervision of assignments had been handled poorly by Lynch. The candid camera, a favorite of Hearst, had not been used as often as Edwards and Morris wanted.

In Los Angeles, the Hearst executives discarded plans to send either French or Lynch to study photography on the *Examiner* in preparation for retraining the Seattle staff. Instead, they decided to send a man from Los Angeles to "instruct our (*P-I*) photographers, reorganize the department, and investigate it thoroughly." 17

Without advance notice, Samuel Sansone arrived in Seattle on June 6 to become manager of the photography department. Reporting for work on Monday morning, Lynch found a note on the darkroom door, informing the staff of his demotion. On June 12, Sansone sent a memorandum to Colvin and a more complete report to his superiors on the *Examiner*. His report mentioned poor arrangement of the darkroom; worn-out cameras; improperly-stored chemicals; unidentified negatives; poorly-kept records; and wastage of film, paper, and chemicals. Sansone noted: "It is evident that there has been little or no management." [18]

On this point Lynch certainly did not disagree. He readily admitted his had been a title only and that he operated much the same as any of the other photographers. Most of the time he was out on assignment like the rest of the photographers, and only a rare assignment offered much incentive to do an imaginative job. Much of the time Lynch was annoyed and bored by his job, and at times he was angry with the insignificance of his work. Sometimes Lynch's title of manager of the photography department seemed utterly ridiculous. "Hell! I was just a photographer." [19] Lynch readily admitted he was no photographic manager, and until May of 1936 the whole situation hadn't seemed too important. The staff got the pictures the paper needed. Even Sansone, for all his horror at the terrible situation in the photography department, had to admit that most faults were corrected within ten days after his arrival. [20]

The case against Lynch was put together in rapid form. Nothing about the photographic department in the *Post-Intelligencer* had been changed, but suddenly the management situation in the department seemed important to Hearst executives. No one had been concerned before that the negatives and print files got behind. The photographers had to do all their own darkroom work and filing, so the situation had not been viewed as serious. All the photographers had supplies of their own on the shelves, and some belonging to French were left over from an outside photo project which he had completed three years before. [21]

The only ingredient in the whole picture which had changed was Lynch — now he was a member of the American Newspaper Guild. This affiliation made him appear to be a different person even to some who had known and respected him for years. Morris, at the time Heise was hired on the paper, told the young photographer he was fortunate indeed to be working under one of the outstanding photographers on the coast. [22] Yet, now Lynch was not fit to be manager of the photographic department, and in a few days he would be found unfit to work on the paper at all.

Shortly after Lynch was removed from the managerial job, Heise was again pressured by management and asked to change the time of his vacation. He refused, resigned from the paper, and joined the staff of the *Seattle Star* with a raise in pay.

The Lynch and Heise cases began to make the Guild members feel uneasy, and a general meeting of the Seattle chapter was called for Wednesday evening, June 17. Members were told there were matters of urgent importance. Perhaps the chapter should begin a war chest as a hedge against future trouble. 23

The tension was building. During this same week, the entire library staff of the *Post-Intelligencer* openly admitted its membership in the Guild, and the strike situation on the Hearst paper in Milwaukee became more serious. Some Seattle members felt that interest shown in the *Wisconsin News* strike might be a good investment for the Seattle Guild, which might need help in the not-too-distant future. However, the Guild was having difficulty getting new members, and a membership drive was given immediate attention. Union leaders cooperated by demanding that all reporters covering labor events show a membership card in the Guild. 24

The weekly meeting of the Guild on June 24 saw a turnout of thirty-five members, and the take was $7 for the Milwaukee strike and $6 for the Auto Mechanics' strike in Seattle. Guild members were beginning to realize that local labor might be an important factor in case Hearst should force a showdown with the Guild.

Matters were building toward a climax. Two *Examiner* photographers were brought in from Los Angeles a few days after Sansone's arrival. Lynch, "sullen and disinterested," in the view of his superior, continued to take pictures and to become more and more bitter about his new position. Sansone's suggestion that "babies make wonderful pictures" received a nearly contemptuous greeting from Lynch. He commented years later: "Well, for Christ sake, that's like telling some kid in kindergarten to hold up his hand to go to the bathroom. . . ." 25

Sansone and his cohorts did little to win the support or respect of Lynch and his fellow Guildsmen in the photo department. Later in the month Edwards studied the *Post-Intelligencer* presses, indicating management suspicion that presswork might partially account for the quality of reproduction (earlier the stereotype metal had been tested on Edwards's order); then he visited the darkroom.

Sansone's report prompted Lindeman to call in the

department editors, including Dunning, managing editor; Morris; Colvin; E. G. Hiller, assistant city editor; Marion Strixrood, women's editor; and Sansone. Edwards told of finding tremendous waste, running possibly into several thousand dollars, and gross mismanagement of the department. It was decided to fire Lynch that day, July 6. [26]

Lynch was on assignment at the time of the decision. Sansone had informed Lynch that day that he was assigned to cover the race track, which meant night work over the weekend, and that he was going to have to work Monday on the late shift also. Lynch was supposed to have been off at 1 p.m. that day. Then Sansone asked about lighting for the Freddy Steele championship fight, and Lynch had to admit he didn't know the situation but would check. Lynch was carrying out this job when his wife informed him, by telephone, that Mel Sayre on the desk had called to say that Colvin wanted to talk to Lynch. When he arrived back at the office, Lynch found Colvin in the sports department. The two walked back to the editor's desk together, and Colvin asked Lynch for his keys, as the photographer would no longer need them since he was not working for the paper. Colvin was uneasy about the firing and seemed pleased to be able to tell Lynch that a check for four weeks' pay waited for him at the office — two weeks for his notice and two weeks for vacation. He could arrange with Sansone for turning in his equipment. [27]

If the Guild were looking for a cause, for an immediate test of its strength and purpose, the firing of Slim Lynch provided the group with just such material. But unfortunately, the Guild wasn't quite sure what it wanted, or what it could do, and another month of frenetic activity passed before the closing of the *Post-Intelligencer*.

FOOTNOTES CHAPTER III

A MARTYR EMERGES

1. Forrest Williams to Terry Pettus, May 19, 1936, Pettus Papers (MSS in Manuscript Division, University of Washington Library). Hereafter referred to as Pettus Papers.
2. *Guild Reporter*, May 15, 1936.
3. National Labor Relations Board, "Transcript of Hearings

in Case C-136" (Seattle hearings), pp. 291 ff. Hereafter referred to as "Transcript" (Seattle).

4. W. A. Swanberg, *Citizen Hearst* (New York: Charles Scribner's Sons, 1961), pp. 441, 477.
5. "Transcript" (Seattle), p. 1,117.
6. *Ibid.*, pp. 1,117-1,120.
7. *Ibid.*, p. 1,122.
8. *Ibid.*, pp. 1,136-1,138.
9. *Ibid.*, p. 1,148.
10. "Transcript" (Seattle), pp. 2,053-2,054, 2,056-2,057; Richard Seller to Betty Ballantine, July 23, 1936, Newspaper Guild Collection, Archives of Labor History and Urban Affairs, Wayne State University, Detroit.
11. "Transcript" (Seattle), p. 858.
12. *Ibid.*, p. 349.
13. *Ibid.*, p. 1,009 ff.
14. *Fortune*, XII (October, 1935), p. 43.
15. NLRB Exhibit R-51, February 3, 1936.
16. "Transcript" (Seattle), p. 853.
17. *Ibid.*, p. 1,357, testimony of Ray Colvin, editor.
18. NLRB Exhibit R-45, June 15, 1936.
19. Frank Lynch interview, May, 1959.
20. NLRB Exhibit R-45, June 15, 1936.
21. "Transcript" (Seattle), p. 816, and Lynch interview, May, 1959.
22. *Ibid.*, p. 2,062.
23. Williams to Pettus, June 14, 1936, Pettus Papers.
24. *Ibid.*, June 21, 1936.
25. Lynch interview, May, 1959.
26. "Transcript" (Seattle), pp. 1,310-1,311, testimony of Colvin.
27. *Seattle Times*, September 17, 1936.

CHAPTER IV

THE GUILD STRIKES BACK

Ed Weston was working in his office in room 109 of Seattle's Labor Temple on the evening of July 7, 1936. It was a little past six o'clock, and Weston, business agent of the Boilermakers' Union in Seattle, was hurrying to get ready for that evening's meeting of the Metal Trades Council. Weston was a powerful man in Seattle's labor scene, even though he was somewhat to the left of many of Seattle's labor leaders.

Weston was interrupted when a man stuck his head in the union office and asked: "I suppose you're the same kind of a guy I've been talking to all afternoon?" Weston had no idea what the man was talking about, and he asked whether or not the visitor was looking for trouble.

The man explained he was not. He was Slim Lynch from the *Seattle Post-Intelligencer*, and he had been discharged for his work in organizing the American Newspaper Guild. He had spent the day down at the Labor Temple talking to people, but no one seemed very much interested in giving help.[1]

Within a few minutes Weston had written a resolution to present that night to the Metal Trades Council and the next night to the Central Labor Council, requesting the *Post-Intelligencer* management to show cause why the newspaper should not be placed on the unfair list for its treatment of labor. Lynch approved the resolution wording and agreed to wait outside the Metal Trades Council meeting in case Weston needed testimony on behalf of the resolution.[2]

Lynch waited in the hall for word from Weston. The head of the boilermakers pleaded the Guild's cause, and finally the photographer was called before the group to plead for himself. This was the first time the emotional, affable Irishman ever had appeared before a labor group, and he was awkward and obviously frightened as he entered. Weston began to worry that he had made a mistake in asking Lynch to appear, because the Guildsman seemed to have frozen before the audience. Finally, Lynch broke through his nervous state and told the metal workers: "I want to tell you folks, I'm a hell of a lousy speaker."[3]

Union members were not at all certain a photographer or reporter ever could belong to a labor union, but Lynch seemed to be solid as he proceeded to tell the story about being fired from the *Post-Intelligencer*. The resolution was passed at the meeting, and the following night it went before the Central Labor Council under the sponsorship of the leftist metal trades. [4] Such endorsement usually meant that the right-wing unions, led by the Teamsters, opposed the resolution as a matter of principle.

As Lynch later admitted: "We were so naive about trade unionism. I thought it was something like the Mystic Knights of the Sea. They were all brothers, and I didn't know there was a left wing, a right wing; believe me, I just didn't know about it."[5]

This left-right fight somehow had to be minimized if the Guild were to have the support of all Seattle labor. The support of the Teamsters' Dave Beck for Lynch made the difference, for on July 8 the resolution came before the Central Labor Council, and was passed with scarcely an argument.[6] Even unions which had not been contacted to support the resolution joined in giving full backing, and before the evening was over the vice-president of the Council had pushed through a motion to have the Central Labor Council appoint a committee to advise, counsel, and aid the Guild in gaining Lynch's reinstatement.[7] The Guild had erred in talking first with the left-wing unions, but the Teamsters were willing to overlook the mistake. It was a useful lesson for Lynch and his colleagues.

Such pledges of support from the unions were encouraging, but so far no definite commitment had been made to the Guild. The Council had asked only that Hearst management discuss reinstating Lynch. The battle was more for a person than for a newspaper reporters' union, but there was talk that if the Guild should go on strike, the unions would lend support. Guild members were uncertain what all this meant. How far should Richard Seller and Forrest Williams, chairmen of the *Post-Intelligencer* unit, actually enter into this alliance with the Central Labor Council? Williams, in particular, was wary. It was "o.k., of course, for Lynch to speak, as he's already out."[8]

Lynch could and would do as he pleased. He was becoming more and more difficult for the Guild to handle as he threatened to take another job immediately unless the

Guild took action. If he did this, the Guild had lost a cause with which it could fight Hearst. The Guild scarcely could afford to lose Lynch, because sympathy for him was bringing new members to the organization. Six joined the day after Lynch's discharge, making a total of thirty-five members on the *Post-Intelligencer*, almost a majority of the editorial staff. Guild leaders reasoned the Guild then would be in a position to ask for collective bargaining, with the union representing the editorial staff of the paper. But despite some signs of encouragement, the Guild still was not a well forged organization. Its members appeared to lack commitment, and only sixteen from the *Post-Intelligencer* showed up for a July 8 meeting despite the urgency of the situation. Those present reluctantly contributed only a few dollars to the Milwaukee strike. Fred d'Avila, Guild secretary, took $4 from the collection, contending the Guild owed him that amount. No one present remembered why. The remainder of the money went into a fund to finance a local strike in the event the Lynch case forced the issue. [9]

The Guild committee named to file the formal protest against the Lynch firing included Seller, Williams, and Lynch. The letter asked for Lynch's reinstatement and indicated that the Guild wanted to meet with *Post-Intelligencer* management. [10]

Besides contacting the Labor Council, members of the Guild also had turned to that new, and only vaguely understood, creation of the Roosevelt administration, the National Labor Relations Board. The NLRB people were sympathetic and promised to do all in their power to see that Lynch received help.[11] The NLRB contacted the publisher, Vaughn Tanner, and wanted a full explanation of the Lynch firing. In addition, representatives from the Labor Council wrote to unions throughout the country, urging them to file protests with the *Post-Intelligencer* against the firing, and these also were beginning to arrive in Seattle.

With such interest in the Lynch case, Tanner scarcely could ignore the letter sent from the Guild. Tanner explained: "I will be glad to discuss this matter with anyone or any group of my employees, but I cannot obviously discuss it with anyone outside the *Post-Intelligencer's* employ."[12]

The Guild sent an answer to the Tanner letter immediately, pointing out that the union was the appropriate agency to represent Lynch and restating the contention that

Lynch was discharged for Guild activities. Tanner was asked to reply within a week, and if no reply were forthcoming, the matter would be referred back to the *Post-Intelligencer* Guild members for "whatever action they see fit to take." [13]

If Guild members hoped by this letter to persuade Tanner and the Hearst management to reinstate Lynch in his old job, they were disappointed. Instead, seemingly in response to the threat of the letter, the Guild found itself with not one but two martyrs to defend.

Shortly after Tanner received the second letter, another militant Guildsman on the paper became embroiled in a situation which led to his firing. Everhardt Armstrong had been with the *Post-Intelligencer* for seventeen years, and despite the pay cuts which the Hearst employees had taken during the depression, Armstrong still was making nearly $70 a week, one of the highest editorial salaries paid by the newspaper. Following the Lynch firing, Armstrong had taken charge of the Guild's recruitment effort on the *Post-Intelligencer*.

On Monday, July 13, Ray Colvin, the day managing editor, approached Armstrong in the composing room and asked how long it would take to familiarize an experienced man with the routine in the drama department. When Armstrong answered two or three days, he was told to take his vacation beginning Thursday. Armstrong was startled, not so much by the fact that he was to change his vacation from August to July, but from recognition of the fact that such an untimely vacation notice in the Hearst organization frequently was a prelude to dismissal. Armstrong was keenly aware of the demotion of the Hearst San Francisco critic, Redfern Mason, a Guild member, to the hotel register beat after he was sent on an impromptu vacation. Dean Jennings's dismissal from the Hearst *San Francisco Call-Bulletin* under similar circumstances nearly disrupted the participation of the American Newspaper Publishers' Association in the newspaper code of the NIRA. [14] Armstrong was told his replacement would be J. Willis Sayre, a non-Guild member.

Armstrong objected strongly to the whole situation, and, pretending to call his wife, conferred with the *Post-Intelligencer* unit strategy committee. Following this, he questioned Sayre and Colvin, who had issued the order. He asked if Sayre would continue in the job if Armstrong were fired from his job for Guild activity. Sayre didn't know. He did say, however, that he would not cross a picket line to take Armstrong's job in case a strike were called. Sayre accompanied Armstrong to Colvin's office, and there the drama editor was assured that he was not being fired, but rather helping out the paper by taking his vacation at this time. Sayre spoke up, and much to the embarrassment of Colvin, is reported to have said: "Why don't you tell him, Ray, this is all a Guild matter." Colvin denied this was the case and continued to press Armstrong to start his vacation July 16 and refused to give assurance that he would not be fired on his return.[15]

Armstrong next headed for the library, where he told Ray Holmes and Cliffe Erickson he would do whatever they suggested — either "go out and take a punch" at Colvin or accept the vacation date offered him. Armstrong pounded on the desk excitedly and when Mrs. Marion Stixrood, women's editor and not a Guild member, came in, Armstrong engaged her in a conversation about her attitude toward the Guild. Erickson, who by this time had become a militant Guildsman, shoved a Guild card at her. Armstrong demanded to know whether Mrs. Stixrood was for or against the organization.

Mrs. Stixrood said she never had been asked to join and denied that Mrs. Marion Badcon had approached her on the subject. And, although Mrs. Stixrood admitted she did read the *New Masses* and the *New Republic*, she would not belong to an organization which was hostile to her boss. With this, Armstrong said there were "rats" around, and the Guild members present knew who they were. As Mrs. Stixrood turned to leave, Armstrong talked about "scabs" and "stools."[16]

Toward the close of the day Armstrong, at the urging of some of the more cautious members of the Guild, agreed to take his vacation beginning July 16, and here the matter might have ended had not the Hearst management pushed the whole affair one step further. Tuesday afternoon Armstrong was summoned to Colvin's office and informed: "After talking it over with the management, we have decided to let you go right away." "Right away?" snorted Armstrong. "Well — now that I'm an ex-employee — I might tell you you lied yesterday when you said I wasn't being eased out." "You're fired for your defiant attitude and nothing more," Colvin declared.

With this move, the *Post-Intelligencer* management had

created the second martyr to the American Newspaper Guild's cause. Colvin moved from the newsroom toward the desk of his secretary, Edith White, with Armstrong in close pursuit. Armstrong grabbed Colvin's arm and after shaking the managing editor, said: "I am going to tell everyone about this. I am going to tell everyone what you have done." He then swung around facing the men in the newsroom, motioned for quiet, and announced: "Fellow employees, I want to tell you that I have been fired by Mr. Colvin for belonging to the American Newspaper Guild." Colvin denied the accusation, but this seemed to enrage Armstrong even more, and he turned to Colvin: "You are a liar; you are a liar, and you know it." Then, at Colvin's request, Edith White made out an order for three days' pay for Armstrong, and his seventeen years with the *Post-Intelligencer* were terminated without either dismissal pay or a hearing from the publisher. [17]

Tension around the paper increased sharply during the next few days as Guildsmen planned their actions against Hearst. Loyal employees strained to show the full measures of their devotion to their employers. At least three reporters decided to avoid the Guild, and apparently without the encouragement of management, signed a "manifesto" opposing the union. Carlton Fitchett, one of the three, acted because the atmosphere in the newsroom was "unfavorable" and "tense." Employees gathered in small groups for numerous conferences. There was a divisive feeling, and when Fitchett was approached by Lester Hunt and Fred Niendorff, two of the highest paid and most respected *Post-Intelligencer* employees, Fitchett signed the document. The manifesto read: ". . . we, the undersigned, . . . have not authorized the Seattle Chapter of the American Newspaper Guild or any other organization or group to represent us in the negotiations with the management regarding wages, working conditions, or anything else. . . ." [18]

Hunt and Niendorff talked about the manifesto on a Saturday fishing trip. After they drew it up, three others, including Ed Stone, the night city editor, signed it. The manifesto then was placed in Hunt's mailbox, awaiting his return from vacation, and seemingly died there. However, the sponsors of the petition were among the employees who did not strike and who frustrated Guild efforts to expand its membership on the *Post-Intelligencer*. [19]

Others who pursued an active anti-Guild role included the women's editor, Marion Stixrood, who called her department's employees together to explain why she was not joining the Guild. She felt it was wrong to belong to an organization which attacked her employer. She explained to the women on her staff that Charles Lindeman, the associate publisher, had asked her to call the meeting. She had considered belonging to the Guild, she explained, but she had not joined when she realized the present setup consisted of mostly office boys. She expressed her view that anyone who wished to join would have an excellent opportunity for martyrdom.[20]

She was certain no one would be discharged for Guild membership, but at the same time she could not favor anybody in the way of positions or salary who belonged to an organization fighting the man for whom she worked. She concluded by asking all who were not going to join the Guild to report to her.[21]

Later in the day she met Bernice Reddington, head of the newspaper's home-economics department. Lindeman's instructions had been misunderstood, Mrs. Stixrood explained. He had wanted her only to ask the women who were not going to join the Guild to report this information. Reddington, who had not joined the Guild but did not feel particularly loyal to Hearst, passed on the information in as "serious a way" as she could.[22]

The next morning Charles W. Hope, the regional representative of the National Labor Relations Board, asked Lindeman if Mrs. Stixrood had called a meeting to intimidate her employees. Lindeman sent for Mrs. Stixrood and asked for an explanation. He then explained the danger in what she had done and warned her: "This is not your business, and you must tell them at once that you don't care who belongs to the Guild or who does not." She complied.[23]

At this point, both the *Post-Intelligencer* and the *Star* units of the Guild were meeting to discuss ways of supporting a strike should one develop. By July 16, twenty-two members of the *Post-Intelligencer* unit had signed strike pledges with the understanding that the paper's executive council would call a strike only as a last resort after all negotiations had failed.

On July 16, Tanner sent a reply to the second letter which had been sent by the Guild. He offered to meet with a committee in his office at 3:30 to discuss the situation. Members of the Guild committee — Walter Rue, Seller, Erickson, Holmes, French, and Williams — gathered in the city room in view of the other employees before going to the publisher's office for a two-hour meeting.

Seller, spokesman for the group, explained that the purpose of the meeting was to bargain collectively for the reinstatement of Lynch and Armstrong. Lindeman promptly refused to reinstate either man, arguing that the firings had been based on adequate grounds. French, defending Lynch, charged that Samuel Sansone, Hearst's photographic troubleshooter, had failed to correct any of the darkroom problems. The discussion moved to intimidation of Guild members by Morris and Stixrood. Lindeman insisted that the editors spoke as individuals and did not represent the newspaper's position on Guild matters. When Seller suggested that the management post a bulletin-board statement to that effect, Lindeman agreed to consider the idea. The conference ended with Lindeman stating: "We have spent a couple of hours bargaining collectively, and on this particular issue our mind is closed." 24

If Hearst management had closed minds on the matter and considered it a closed subject, it was not taking into consideration the diverse groups which were becoming interested in the *Post-Intelligencer* and its relationship to the Guild.

On the morning of July 16, the matter of Lynch and Armstrong was brought before the convention of the Washington State Federation of Labor meeting in Vancouver, Washington. "Delegate Krenz" read a letter from the Seattle Chapter of the American Newspaper Guild. The letter, signed by Fred d'Avila, Guild secretary, said that the Guild had been granted a charter by the American Federation of Labor. (The affiliation with the AFL had taken place at its June convention in Toledo.) But d'Avila hastened to assure the delegates of the authenticity of the Guild as a labor union: "We members of this union are labor people in every sense of the word. We have organized to improve our working conditions, raise our salaries, reduce our hours of work, and protect ourselves from groundless dismissals." The letter said that the Guild would work in every possible way to advance labor's cause and would adhere rigidly to labor's policy of boycotting unfair establishments. "We want

41

to help other unions both with financial and moral support." [25]

The letter detailed the opposition of the *Post-Intelligencer* to the Guild and presented an account of the Lynch and Armstrong firings. After Krenz finished reading the letter, he appealed to the convention to give "moral and financial support" to the Guild in its fight with Hearst.

The plea for support did not go unheeded. The convention secretary recorded that Dave Beck, a delegate from the Teamsters Union, asked for a committee to settle the dispute without a work stoppage. It was a gesture characteristic of the Teamster leader. He moved that the State Federation Executive Board call a meeting of all crafts employed by the *Post-Intelligencer* "that might be affected in the instance of a strike with the *P-I* and the Guild. . . ." [26]

The convention also approved a resolution backing the Guild and endorsing the efforts of the Seattle Central Labor Council to win reinstatement of the dismissed employees. The committee, appointed as the result of Beck's motion, included James Taylor, state president of the Federation, and representatives of all the printing trades unions, the Newsboys Union, the Teamsters Union, and the Ferrymen Union. [27] Despite the state federation's interest, efforts to bring the Guild and the newspaper together centered in the King County Central Labor Council.

In Seattle, the Guild members were haunted by fears and uncertainties. The most militant pushed for an immediate strike, with little consideration for how this might be accomplished or its effect. Following the unsatisfactory meeting between members of the Guild unit on the *Post-Intelligencer* and publishers Tanner and Lindeman, plans were made to submit a Guild contract to Tanner, along with the request for reinstatement of Lynch and Armstrong. If these were rejected, a strike was to be called. Even the most cautious of the Guild unit expected that the new request would be made to Tanner no later than July 22. Such a direct plan of action worried the national Guild officers, as well as some Guild members within the *Post-Intelligencer*. The Seattle chapter just was not ready to support such a strike, particularly against one of the nation's largest publishers. Of the thirty-five members of the *Post-Intelligencer* unit, only twenty-two were considered active and willing to go out if a strike were called. There was no hope of closing the paper, and the fifty employees left working inside probably would not suffer at all from the strike. At the most, the Guild could succeed in causing Hearst embarrassment and perhaps some financial damage to his paper. [28]

Even small thrusts at Hearst were becoming important, however. Hearst became more and more the central issue in the campaign of the national Guild. The Guildsmen were restless and needed someone against whom their resentments could be directed. Armstrong, Erickson, and Lynch were becoming difficult to control, and some urged measures to keep the three out of the meetings completely. After all, they had nothing to lose from drastic action. Lynch and Armstrong were out of work, and Erickson cared little for his $12-a-week job as an assistant librarian. Erickson, treasurer of the group, was suspected of attempting to withhold a telegram from the national office which warned the Seattle chapter to go easy on any plans for a strike. Erickson was annoyed by such advice and urged the *Post-Intelligencer* unit to ignore it.

While Seattle labor leaders were planning for further negotiations after the threat of an immediate strike appeared to fade, the Hearst management also was preparing its case. Bart Guild was back in Seattle on his third trip to the city in a year. Guild members were sure that this trip had a lot to do with the threatened strike. For the time being, however, the heat appeared to be off. City room executives, for some reason, became "reasonably nice" to known Guildsmen, and Colvin, day managing editor, reportedly spoke to Williams for the first time in seven years. Morris, the city editor, fairly beamed upon another Guild member to whom "he hadn't addressed a word for weeks."[29]

Guild members continued to founder in their efforts to reach a sane and reasonable plan of action. The more experienced labor leaders of the city exercised the needed caution and moved ahead with plans for negotiations. Labor in Seattle already had committed itself to the Guild's cause and scarcely could afford to have a group of inexperienced and emotional newspapermen undertake action which might prove highly embarrassing to the entire labor movement. The conservative element in the Central Labor Council received an agreement from the Guild that no strike action would be taken until labor could do some further exploring and investigating of the case. The Guildsmen did not know exactly what plan the conservatives might have, but their union was nothing without the support of Seattle labor, and Seattle labor was telling the Guild to wait a few days before taking any action. Lynch backed this plan also, which strongly indicated that Beck was providing the thinking behind the move.[30]

Meanwhile, the Guild set up a "subsistence income" payment plan for Lynch and Armstrong. Members pledged contributions of five per cent of their salaries, which would yield an income of around $100 a month for Lynch and Armstrong. However, many members were $15-$20 a week reporters, and it would be difficult for them to continue to contribute.[31]

The Guild also devoted time to getting itself on a more solid organizational basis in case a strike should be called. Charles Daggett, president of the chapter, asked to be relieved of his Guild office in late July. The *Post-Intelligencer* employees understood. Daggett just did not want to be put in a position of having to go to a Hearst publisher to negotiate for a unit as weak as the one on the *P-I*, particularly when there was little or no hope of winning the negotiations. Seller, who took the lead in the crisis and, in the opinions of some, was about the only rational person around, was the logical man to succeed Daggett.[32] Finding a person to take over the presidency of the Seattle chapter at such a time was not easy. As a member of the Guild, Seller was not popular with Hearst management, but he was an able reporter and could get a job elsewhere if needed. As president of the Guild unit which might call a strike against Hearst, however, his would be a prominent and dangerous role.

In addition to these obvious problems, Seller had some of his own reservations. He was interested in labor and the labor movement, but certain elements within it bothered him. He had little understanding of the Communist element and was annoyed to see Morgan Hull, the Guild organizer who had issued the charter to the Seattle chapter, becoming closely associated with the union in Seattle. If trouble broke out again, Seller did not want Hull sent to represent the national Guild. Seller particularly was upset by Hull's association with Lowell Wakefield and Emerson Daggett of the *Voice of Action* during the time he was in Seattle in May. He felt such association with avowed Communists might be fine in New York, but it certainly had hurt the Guild in Seattle. Hull also had annoyed some Guildsmen by an appearance before the Central Labor Council in which he had excoriated Hearst at great length, which certainly had done little to quiet the persistent rumor that the Guild was bent on damaging Hearst.

Furthermore, Seller was annoyed by the announcement of the formation of the Seattle chapter which Hull had placed in the *Guild Reporter*. Seller disagreed with the assertion that the *Post-Intelligencer* unit was organized despite much intimidation by management. "At that time, the management had done little more than drop a word here and there that 'Hearst does not look with favor upon the Guild,' and the publication of that article precipitated a concentrated campaign against the Guild, and — some think — was the original cause of recent troubles."

These sentiments of Seller's became exceedingly important following Daggett's resignation. Seller saw the danger of the situation and was reluctant to place his head in the noose. A good deal of liquor flowed at the Guild meeting the night of the election before Seller finally agreed to accept the position. Bolder then, he placed one important restriction. If he accepted the office, Wakefield and Daggett would have to turn in their Guild cards, because Seller would not have the Guild identified with the Communist Party.[33]

The issue was becoming particularly important because of talk around Seattle that a left-wing element was about to start a labor daily. Labor had been without a daily newspaper to support its cause since the death of the *Union Record* in 1928. Now Harvey O'Connor, Anna Louise Strong, Wakefield, and Daggett were talking of a new newspaper and were claiming that Hull had supported the idea.[34] Terry Pettus, president of the Tacoma chapter, also had shown interest in the publication and had talked to Strong in Portland during the spring of 1936 and later had corresponded with her on the subject of the People's Daily.[35]

Wakefield further had annoyed members of the Guild by campaigning for the city council as a member of the Communist Party and the American Newspaper Guild. Guildsmen did not like the association.

All these matters were communicated to Jonathan Eddy, the national Guild's executive secretary, who until this time was amazingly unperceptive of the situation in Seattle.

He warned that the national officers concurred that nothing could be done with Hearst except through the cooperation of all the chain newspapers. However, he appreciated the militant way in which the young Guild in Seattle was reacting as long as it did not bring on a strike. The Guild in Seattle might have to back down, Eddy warned, but this would not kill the chapter. [36]

Now Eddy attempted to allay the fears over the Communist issue which both Seller and Erickson had expressed. Eddy had complete confidence in Hull's devotion to the Guild cause and pointed out that a union rarely went on strike without the red scare being dragged out. Guild President Heywood Broun and Eddy were used to being called Communists — all the militant had to bear the label. "When such figures as President Roosevelt and John L. Lewis are accused of being Communists, as they are in the Hearst papers today, I think it is about time we refused to let ourselves be deprived of effective workers in our own organization by failing to scrutinize carefully the evidence." [37]

Eddy's comments failed to still the fears of Seller, who proceeded by asking Williams to meet with the two *Voice of Action* editors and to request that they surrender their cards in the Guild. Williams did talk to Daggett but found the *Voice of Action* editor "did not take kindly" to the suggestion, and he was sure that Wakefield would not surrender his card. [38]

Word of the attempt to purge Daggett and Wakefield brought immediate protests from Tacoma, where Pettus was shocked by Seller's action. It was illegal, wrote Pettus, for Article I, Section 4a, said in part: "No eligible person shall be barred from membership, suspended, fined, expelled or discriminated against by reason of sex, race or religious or political convictions or because of anything he writes for publication."

Pettus was certain that Seller was wrong in making the request. The Guild would lose the backing of the left-wing unions, and those unions had given it the most moral and financial support. Pettus assured Williams that he was not a Communist and not particularly concerned with politics, but he did believe in the Guild and hated to see it broken up by red-baiting. Pettus also pointed out that the *Voice of Action* had devoted much editorial space to the Guild. The new union didn't dare get off on a red-baiting kick. "A large amount of disgust felt by intelligent persons towards Hearst is his 'red-baiting.' Christ, everybody is a Communist who disagrees with him and it will seem strange to have the Seattle Guild join with him in demanding the blood of Mr. Stalin's lads." 39

That same night Pettus wrote to Wakefield to apologize for Seller's action and to indicate his great disgust for the whole action. To Pettus it was "so damn stupid and such a shabby way to repay . . . the 'Voice of Action' staff for its help." Pettus asked Wakefield to believe that the Seller action did not represent the feeling of the entire Seattle chapter.

The Pettus letter to Williams appears to have effectively silenced the opposition to Daggett and Wakefield, but the two men ceased to play an active part in Seattle Guild affairs. It is ironic that later Seller was to be identified as a member of the Communist Party. 40

The Guild needed a leader, someone to give the fledgling unit some self-confidence, and it had that man in Seller. He was no fool, nor was he a radical at that time. He believed in the union and what it could accomplish. He was neither for an immediate strike nor did he fear a strike if it should come. He was willing to wait and exhaust all possibilities, but he wouldn't flinch if he were thrown into a strike situation. He was somewhat annoyed by national's caution, and he wrote a Guild executive:

This is a militant unit. Probably, eventually, the national will realize that we folks out here in the Pacific Northwest, are but only a few years removed from the pioneers. They may understand that only a half-century ago this was a wilderness up here, and that out of that wilderness, the Pioneers have built a little pioneer city of a half million people!

Maybe, they'll learn that, darn it, the people up here — like the crews we produce at our University — fight till they drop for a cause! There is hardly a member of the Guild, except two who withdrew to be replaced yesterday by two members . . . , who hasn't had his back arched for a fight!

Seller hoped the dispute with the *Post-Intelligencer* could be settled without a strike. If, however, the Hearst management chose to rebuff "state and city labor" in their efforts to give men a fair deal, Seller feared Hearst was going to have another strike. Seller was sorry that national was unable to give financial assistance, and he realized that national did not want to get tied up with any losing strike. But in Seattle, the Guild would not lose. "We Pioneers are pioneering this Guild now, and if it's tough, we'll like it better. I hope this doesn't sound like a school boy's dream!"[41]

Of course it was a school boy's dream, for how could thirty-five members, only twenty of whom were active, possibly hope to call a strike against Hearst and emerge with anything except a sound defeat? There was no money at all in the treasury for waging a strike, and, despite all the bravado which the Guild members had exhibited, they had not as yet even talked to the leaders of the printing trades' unions to see how the typographers, pressmen, stereotypers, and others might feel about a strike against Hearst. Guildsmen had vague promises from members that individuals would not cross the line on the basis that Hearst had to provide for their welfare and safety, but that was all.

Perhaps the Labor Council committee, once it started working, could find a way out of all this, but it had to be soon. Both Guild and personal affairs were becoming more desperate. Lynch particularly was in a dire situation. The illnesses of his wife and a child had raised his debts to more than $500, and he had two other children to support in addition to the one who was ill. Lynch had no money, and the Guild was trying to keep him going.[42]

With such personal situations plaguing leaders of the threatened strike, the urgency of the situation to these men was more apparent. The Guildsmen pushing for a strike realized that the longer the matter was delayed, the less likely it was that a strike ever would be called. The July 23 date for a showdown with Hearst had been changed to July 28. The latter date also came and went, and no telling action was taken.

The strike tempo began to increase on July 29 when Lynch and d'Avila were seated as Guild delegates to the Central Labor Council. The first action taken by Lynch and d'Avila was to ask that the *Post-Intelligencer* be placed on the unfair list. [43] Action on the resolution was postponed on August 5 for a week, to allow Council leaders to meet with the Allied Printing Trades Council.[44]

The Guild's appeal to the Central Labor Council resulted in a fortuitous alliance of labor's hostile elements. The Council-appointed committee included the secretary of the Council, the editor of the *Labor News*, and representatives of the Automobile Mechanics Union, the Operating Engineers Union, and the laundry and dry-cleaning branches of the Teamsters Union. At this committee's request the *Post-Intelligencer* agreed to meet with the Guild committee on the firings. When that meeting failed, the committee asked the *Post-Intelligencer* to show cause why it should not be placed on the unfair list. The committee's membership had been expanded, meanwhile, under the pressure of the conflict between the craft and industrial unions.

Seller appraised the situation this way:

. . . those who believed in industrial unionism — and this was quite a conflict — raised the question as to whether or not they should not be included on this committee, because the longshoremen said that they handled the paper that came over the docks, and the fleet engineers and waterfront workers said that they shipped this paper and the inland boatmen brought it from Canada. . . .

The committee was broadened with those advocates of industrial unionism who had the view that craft unionism ". . . was moribund and corrupt and that the craft unions wouldn't support each other. . . ." What was needed was a whole industrial alliance, the industrial workers argued.

Here was a key question on which the success of the threatened strike turned. Should all unions support the action against Hearst, this would be a great victory for the Guild. Several unions were particularly important. The decision as to what the Typographical Union would do was, of course, critical. If these union members crossed the picket lines, Seattle could be just another repeat of Milwaukee. Then there was also the powerful Teamsters Union. If Beck withheld his support, there was no hope that the Central Labor Council would back the Guild's threatened strike against the *Post-Intelligencer*.

Within the committee which had been appointed by the Central Labor Council to recommend action, support for the Guild position appeared doubtful during much of the proceedings. The typographical representatives reminded the group that they had a contract with the *Post-Intelligencer* which had to be respected. Pressmen took a similar position. It was the Inland Boatman's Union representative who finally stood up and said: "We have contracts with the paper, but we believe in industrial unionism, and if these people go on strike we won't deliver any papers." This was the nudge which Beck's Teamsters needed. Lynch had worked hard to persuade Beck that the Guild was worthy of Teamster support. The Inland Boatman's Union provided the rationale for supporting the Guild, and the Teamsters joined, bringing the craft unions with them. The Teamsters also had contracts for delivery, and should a strike against the *Post-Intelligencer* be called, the Teamster representatives promised: "We won't deliver anything."[45]

This position taken by the Teamsters was an important concession, because usually Beck's men would recognize only the picket lines of their own craft. Individuals from the printing trades promised their support, and letters Guildsmen wrote to friends outside Seattle were buoyant and enthusiastic. Guild members expressed not the slightest doubt that labor could present a united front against Hearst if he did not meet the Guild demands.[46]

National Guild officers felt no such enthusiasm about the printing trades. Eddy cautioned Erickson: "Every time we get into difficulties, it seems to be a sad but true fact that the printing crafts come out on the side of the employers. This is a product of the illogic of craft unionism which should not cause us to cease our efforts to work in unity with them." Eddy reminded Erickson that in Milwaukee the printers were working despite a reprimand from the Wisconsin State Federation of Labor convention.[47]

Eddy urged Seattle Guildsmen not to place too much confidence in the assurances that Seattle printers were different from other tradesmen in cities where the Guild had been involved in strikes. ". . . I suppose you know that from past experience you cannot expect them to walk out with you if their international can do anything on God's green earth to prevent it." The printers in Lorain, Ohio, had refused to cross the picket line, but Charles P. Howard, International Typographical Union president, ordered them to get a police guard and go through. They did. The sanctity of their contracts was given as the reason. In San Francisco during the general strike, Howard appeared before his printers, and

50

as a result the printing crafts were the only crafts that walked out "on their brothers." [48]

As the Labor Council waited to take action on the resolution to place Hearst on the unfair list, it was not only the Guild which courted the printers as ardently as young swains. The Hearst management was worried by this united front which labor seemed to be showing, and while there was comfort in the fact that the printers usually stayed loyal to the company, the fact that the typographers in Seattle were operating without a contract — only with an agreement — was cause for worry.

By August 4 the Hearst management forces acted to bring as much pressure as possible on the printing trades and on Beck to prevent any unified labor front against the *Post-Intelligencer*. Telegrams, over the signature of Harvey J. Kelly, Hearst labor negotiator and a former labor adjuster with the American Newspaper Publishers' Association, were sent to international printing trades unions to attempt to persuade them to stay aloof from the labor alliance which threatened the *Post-Intelligencer*. Among those who received wires were Howard, president, International Typographical Union; George L. Berry, president, International Printing Pressmen and Assistants Union; Leon Deveze, president, International Stereotypers and Electrotypers Union; Ed J. Volz, president, International Photo-Engravers Union; and Monroe Roberts, president, Mailers Trade District Union.

The telegrams singled out Dave Beck as the villain in the action against the *Post-Intelligencer* and claimed he told the State Federation of Labor convention that he would throw a picket line around the newspaper plant and would endeavor, by intimidation, to prevent union members from passing through. He also reportedly was trying to secure support from those not in accord with the union policy of contract liquidation that said members would allege fear of physical violence as an excuse for not reporting to work. Kelly also charged that Beck promised he would shut down the *Post-Intelligencer* plant even if it required bloodshed. Kelly said he personally discounted such allegations, but even if only partially true, serious consideration had to be given to methods for stopping an outsider from intruding himself and his associates into newspaper matters to promote a personal ambition to be a labor dictator.

This was Kelly's plan: First, Kelly assured the international presidents that the *Post-Intelligencer* would publish under any and all circumstances regardless of consequences. Also, establishment of picket lines by outsiders would result immediately in the establishment of able and ample protection for employees. Any employee refusing to cover his job would be subject to discharge for neglect of duty. Kelly thought trouble could be avoided if the international presidents would demand of Dave Beck the safe conduct through the picket lines for all members whose services were necessary "for liquidation of contract obligations." [49]

The situation which Kelly described indeed would have been menacing to the *Post-Intelligencer* if it had been true. The Guild was described as operating from a powerful position, but Kelly had overstated the situation. Erickson labeled the charges against Beck "wholly untrue."

We have never been officially told by any union head that there would be a picket line established so tight and menacing around the *P-I* that no one would get through it. No union man whose organization holds a contract with the *P-I* has been or will be threatened if his contract says he must work, irrespective of other unions being out on strike. [50]

Even so, elements within the printing trades began stalling the move for a strike against Hearst. One representative from the printing trades complained to the executive committee of the Central Labor Council that the Guild should have affiliated with the Allied Printing Trades Council before it sought recognition from the Central Labor Council. Because the Printing Trades Council had not been informed, the representative said, the printers hoped that action on the resolution could be delayed at least until the Allied Printing Trades had acted at their meeting on August 11. The printing trades' representative was accused of stalling. However, somebody at the meeting reminded the group that Beck was in California and would be back for a meeting before August 12. This, the executive committee agreed, was sufficient cause to delay the vote.

The Guild, by innocently overlooking affiliation with the Printing Trades Council, had stumbled on the best possible course of action as far as its own interests were concerned. If it had joined the Council, the Guild might have forced it to take an official vote on the matter of a boycott, and clearly the only vote the printing trades could give was against sanctioning such action.[51]

In addition to the telegram, the Hearst officials were busy preparing for any emergency which might develop from this dispute with the Guild. *Post-Intelligencer* officials pushed the signing of contracts with individual employees, which started in May, continued through the summer, and intensified as the threat of a strike increased. Hearst strategists hoped this would guarantee a loyal staff during any emergency. Then, in July, preparations began for enlarging the basement of the building so that an adequate newsprint reserve could be stocked.[52] As Lynch recalled: "They had the whole damned building full of paper up there so they could print for a long time. . . ."[53]

In the back shop, printers worked overtime to set "time" copy into type, with some estimates that three-hundred to four-hundred galleys of such material were set. This copy had no particular time value and could be thrown into the paper when needed. Printers were encouraged to work overtime to set the copy, although the whole thing seemed pretty silly to the printers; however, this was the depression, and the extra dollars would help in case a strike did result. These overtime sessions continued right up until the night before the strike.[54]

Now as the company and the Guild waited to see what action the Central Labor Council would take, company guards began to appear in the *Post-Intelligencer* Building. Some women employees complained that they were scared to walk past the men.[55] It was a most unnatural and unusual situation which prevailed on the *Post-Intelligencer* in the days before the strike, and no matter where loyalties lay, it was not a pleasant place to work.

The Guild called the Hearst guards who filled the building "Angels." They were a rough bunch, many brought up from California to help break a strike. Such a crew was a worry not only to the employees on the paper but also to the police of the city. Within a few hours after these men had been checked into a Seattle hotel, the police paid a visit and warned them against causing any trouble. These men were to see to it that anyone who wanted to go to work had protection. It did little to allay the fears that a strike on the *Post-Intelligencer* was imminent.

Individuals working on the *P-I* became more and more tense as the strike approached. One Hearst employee announced to Guild members that he was going to move his family out of town. Guildsmen were surprised that a fellow employee could think them guilty of terrorizing women and children. It was not the Guildsmen the employee feared, he explained, but rather the other people who might join in closing the *Post-Intelligencer.* [56]

By August 10, the strike fever was so high that even Williams was becoming convinced, although reluctantly, that this time everyone meant business. Orders had been sent for one-thousand paper picket ribbons and "unfair to labor" signs. By August 10, Seller was confident that the walkout would come Thursday, the day following the meeting of the Central Labor Council. The Guild was no stronger than it had been at the time the trouble started. Only about half the Guild members actually attended meetings or played any active part. The rest had joined because some close friend or associate had shoved a card under their noses and told them to sign. Such members added no strength to the Guild and could not be counted on to go on strike. Seller and the more militant Guildsmen argued the Guild would be united once the strike started.

Williams, always the voice of caution within the Guild unit, had taken on more of a position of power since he had been named chairman of the *Post-Intelligencer* unit. Three days before the strike Williams still was certain that a strike simply had to be avoided. He realized that Lynch and Armstrong would howl for his "assassination" if he made this position known. He might even get into a fist fight, but the idea of the strike didn't make sense to him. What was the object of the threatened strike, anyway? In his mind, it was only to punish the paper for what it had done to two friends. The result would be a minority strike which would drag on for months and might end with all the strikers being compelled to leave Seattle and go elsewhere to seek newspaper jobs — perhaps even change their names. "We may hurt the paper considerably," Williams reasoned, "but at the same time we'll damned near ruin ourselves. . . ." [57]

Williams had on his side the national Guild officers and many labor leaders who were becoming aware of the weakness of the Guild. Build the chapter, they urged, and then strike later.

This position was winning Williams no friends among the militant forces, and Seller threatened to resign in disgust over Williams's stand. But Williams was no sorehead and he knew he could be wrong in his position. "After I'm fired myself I'll probably be able to understand fully the feelings of the discharged Guild leaders who are pressing so hard for the immediate strike."

Williams realized he could not stay the tide, and on the day of the Council vote he sent the following telegram to Eddy:

GUILD LEADERS HERE FORCING STRIKE THURSDAY FOR REINSTATEMENT STOP APPEARS I CAN'T STOP SELLER LYNCH DAVILA STOP MEMBERSHIP STILL THIRTY TWO OUT OF SEVENTY STOP TYPOS UNCONCERNED STOP FEAR HEAVY ODDS BUT WILL GO OUT WITH THE BOYS STOP SELLER NOW MAIN STRIKE ENTHUSIAST STOP UNIT MEETS WEDNESDAY NIGHT

FORREST WILLIAMS [58]

That evening, August 12, 1936, the resolution condemning Hearst as unfair to labor again came before the Central Labor Council. Although the debate was loud and there seemed to be opposition to the move, even on the part of Claude O'Reilly, president of the Council, there was no real strength opposed to labeling Hearst unfair to labor. The vote was 347 to 3 in favor of the resolution. The three dissenting votes came from the printing trades, and while they were indicative of trouble ahead, it was not serious trouble. Seattle labor was taking on Hearst for a battle, and even the skeptical Williams was somehow swept along. While the Council voted, the *Post-Intelligencer's* presses rolled for the last time that summer. Half of a page of the next morning's paper proclaimed: "New York World-Telegram Explains Why It Cannot Sign Contract With The Newspaper Guild." The *Post-Intelligencer*, the article said, "is in accord with this position." [59]

A number of Guild members awaited the outcome of the vote in the city hall, where Forrest Williams, the city hall reporter, had an office. Williams's office was too small for the gathering, which moved out into one of the judge's chambers. The vote condemning Hearst was what the Guild wanted; yet somehow, when this was accomplished, no one

was quite sure what it meant. Suddenly it began to dawn on
the Guild members. They were about to strike. If they were
on strike, their pay from Hearst would stop. Some of them
had wives and families to support. What did all this mean?
Confusion dominated the gathering. Somehow they found
themselves facing a fact which they were not yet able to
accept emotionally. [60]

One of the more naive Guildsmen asked whether this
meant there was apt to be a strike, and Lynch responded:
"Hell, you are on strike." Fear more than elation greeted the
statement. A little more of the realization of what a strike
meant hit with an impact. As Lynch later recalled: "Jesus,
we were disturbed." [61]

It remained for a friend outside the Guild to bring
something resembling composure to the group. Eugene
Dennett, a member of the Inland Boatman's Union of the
Pacific, sensed the near panic. There was something nearly
catatonic about the state of the group when Dennett stood and
began to talk — not to anyone or about anything, particularly
— but he talked. No one listened, but slowly some of the shock
of the realization that they were on strike began to wear
away. Someone started talking about a picket line, and this
pointed up the need for plans and action to get the strike started the following morning. Somehow doing something made
the whole idea of the strike seem more meaningful and less
ominous. [62]

FOOTNOTES CHAPTER IV

THE GUILD STRIKES BACK

1. Ed Weston interview, April, 1959.
2. *Ibid.* and Richard Seller to Betty Ballantine, July 23,
   1936, Newspaper Guild Collection, Archives of Labor
   History and Urban Affairs, Wayne State University,
   Detroit. Hereafter referred to as Newspaper Guild
   Collection.
3. Frank Lynch interview, May, 1959.
4. Weston interview, April, 1959.
5. Lynch interview, May, 1959.
6. Central Labor Council minutes, July 8, 1936, Labor
   Temple, Seattle, Washington.
7. Seller to Ballantine, July 23, 1936, Newspaper Guild
   Collection.
8. Forrest Williams to Terry Pettus, July 8, 1936, Pettus

Papers (MSS in Manuscript Division, University of Washington Library, Seattle, Washington). Hereafter referred to as Pettus Papers.

9. *Ibid.*

10. *Ibid.*

11. Seller to Ballantine, July 23, 1936, Newspaper Guild Collection.

12. *Ibid.*

13. Seller to Jonathan Eddy, July 14, 1936, Newspaper Guild Collection.

14. Edwin Emery, *History of the American Newspaper Publishers Association* (Minneapolis: University of Minnesota Press, 1950), p. 229. See also Roger Allan Simpson, "The American Newspaper Guild and the Seattle Post-Intelligencer Strike of 1936" (unpublished Master of Science thesis in Journalism at the University of Wisconsin, 1961, pp. 43-44).

15. National Labor Relations Board, "Transcript of Hearings in Case C-136" (Seattle hearings), p. 628 ff. Hereafter referred to as "Transcript" (Seattle) or (Washington, D.C.).

16. Seller to Eddy, July 14, 1936, and Seller to Ballantine, July 23, 1936, both in Newspaper Guild Collection; Williams to Pettus, July 14, 1936, Pettus Papers; and "Transcript" (Seattle), pp. 678, 1,887-1,888.

17. "Transcript" (Seattle), pp. 1,887-1,888. As the Hearst attorney demonstrated to the National Labor Relations Board, dismissal pay sometimes was allowed by the *Post-Intelligencer* management. Lynch received four weeks' pay — two for separation and two for vacation. Helene Cole, dismissed in January, 1936, also received four weeks' pay. See "Transcript" (Washington, D.C.), pp. 183, 190.

18. "Transcript" (Seattle), p. 1,940.

19. *Ibid.*

20. *Ibid.*, p. 427; Bernice Reddington interview, May, 1959.

21. "Transcript" (Seattle), p. 1,709.

22. *Ibid.*, p. 427.

23. *Ibid.*, p. 1,711.

24. Stenographic transcript of the July 17, 1936, meeting is Exhibit B-35 in the National Labor Relations Board records.

25. Washington State Federation of Labor, *Proceedings of the Thirty-fifth Annual Convention*, Vancouver, Washington, July 13-16, 1936 (Seattle: The Trade Printery, 1936), pp. 71-72.
26. *Ibid.*
27. *Ibid.*, pp. 82-83.
28. Williams to Ray Torr, Hearst Chain Guild Committee, July 19, 1936, Newspaper Guild Collection.
29. Williams to American Newspaper Guild officials, July 25, 1936, Newspaper Guild Collection.
30. Williams to Eddy, Clyde Beals, and Torr, July 23, 1936, Newspaper Guild Collection.
31. Williams to American Newspaper Guild officials, July 25, 1936, Newspaper Guild Collection.
32. Williams to Pettus, undated, Pettus Papers.
33. Seller to Eddy, July 17, 1936, Newspaper Guild Collection.
34. Erickson to Eddy, July 24, 1936, quoted in Eddy to Morgan Hull, July 29, 1936, Newspaper Guild Collection.
35. Anna Louise Strong to Pettus, April 16, 1936, and Pettus to Strong, April 17, 1936, Pettus Papers.
36. Eddy to Seller, July 17, 1936, Newspaper Guild Collection.
37. Eddy to Erickson, July 29, 1936, Newspaper Guild Collection. Hull, who had joined the Communist Party in 1934, later handled public relations for the party. Daniel J. Leab, *Union of Individuals* (New York: Columbia University Press, 1970), p. 261.
38. Williams to Pettus, August 2, 1936, Pettus Papers.
39. Pettus to Williams, August 3, 1936, Pettus Papers.
40. Pettus to Lowell Wakefield, August 3, 1936, Pettus Papers. Regarding Seller, see Vern Countryman, *Un-American Activities in the State of Washington* (Ithaca, N.Y.: Cornell University Press, 1951), pp. 35, 44; Washington (State) Legislature, *First Report, Un-American Activities in Washington State, 1948* (Olympia: State of Washington, 1948), pp. 30, 93, 246.
41. Seller to Ballantine, July 23, 1936, Newspaper Guild Collection.
42. Seller to American Newspaper Guild officers, undated, Newspaper Guild Collection, and Lynch interview, May, 1959.

43. Central Labor Council minutes, July 29, 1936, Labor Temple, Seattle, Washington.
44. *Ibid.*, August 5, 1936.
45. Seller interview, May, 1959.
46. See letters for July and August, Newspaper Guild Collection and Pettus Papers.
47. Eddy to Erickson, July 29, 1936, Newspaper Guild Collection.
48. Eddy to Williams, July 29, 1936, Newspaper Guild Collection.
49. Harvey J. Kelly telegrams to Charles P. Howard, president, International Typographical Union; George L. Berry, president, International Printing Pressmen and Assistants Union; Leon Deveze, president, International Stereotypers and Electrotypers Union; Ed J. Volz, president, International Photo-engravers Union; and Monroe Roberts, president, Mailers Trade District Union, Newspaper Guild Collection.
50. Erickson to Eddy, August 9, 1936, Newspaper Guild Collection.
51. *Ibid.*
52. Williams to Pettus, July 18, 1936, Pettus Papers.
53. Lynch interview, May, 1959.
54. Floyd Larkin interview, May, 1959.
55. *Ibid.*
56. "Transcript" (Seattle), pp. 369-370.
57. Williams to Pettus, August 10, 1936, Pettus Papers.
58. Williams to American Newspaper Guild, August 12, 1936, Newspaper Guild Collection.
59. *Seattle Post-Intelligencer*, August 13, 1936, p. 2.
60. Lynch interview, May, 1959.
61. *Ibid.*
62. *Ibid.*

CHAPTER V

THE DAY THEY STRUCK HEARST

"Hearst Is Unfair to Labor!"

Somehow, on the morning of August 13, 1936, this small group of Hearst employees felt strongly enough about the statement to march back and forth in front of the publishing plant of the *Seattle Post-Intelligencer*. They wanted to make certain that Hearst's shortcoming was no longer known only to members of his newspaper family. The pickets parading before the entrance to the *Post-Intelligencer* building were a bit bewildered by the situation in which they found themselves. Few passersby could identify the strikers' armbands and knew little, if anything, about the American Newspaper Guild. Many had read the morning editions of the *Post-Intelligencer* without finding a word about the strike. And now a few men and women were shouting nasty names and making brash charges against a powerful publisher — William Randolph Hearst.

It appeared that such a pitiful protest hardly could have much effect; yet labor-conscious Seattle citizens could not help but admire the courage and conviction of such a foolhardy group. But neither could they help but notice that the newspaper plant bustled with activity as, during the early hours, loyal employees entered and went about their jobs. Except for the pickets on the outside and a few plain-clothes guards on the inside, the daily newspaper appeared to be following its usual routine. Curious employees peered from the large second-story windows at their ungrateful colleagues along Pine Street who had embarked on a protest seemingly destined for failure.

The employees on the picket line were hardly more enthusiastic about the success of the venture and felt uneasy under the scrutiny of the curious inside and outside the *Post-Intelligencer* building. These men and women were reporters, librarians, and key editors who the day before had been producing the newspaper. They wore their newly acquired symbols of the labor movement with about as much ease as the adolescent wears his first mustache — with pride, yet some embarrassment.

The pickets scarcely had time to adjust to their new

situation before they found themselves being elbowed aside as the more powerful and experienced labor elements of Seattle moved down from the hills, up from the waterfront, and out of the Labor Temple. Eugene Dennett of the Inland Boatmans' Union of the Pacific had done some advance recruiting, so that when Frank Lynch and Arthur French visited the waterfront on the morning of the strike idle longshoremen were ready to lead a march from the union halls. A phalanx of labor's more experienced fighters moved up from Skid Road to the respectable business district. There, joined by metal workers, lumber workers, and other members of the labor movement, they formed a line around the *Post-Intelligencer* plant. As the line grew, it startled a few shoppers walking toward the city's biggest department store, Frederick & Nelson, just across Sixth Avenue from the newspaper plant. Inside the big store, word of the picket line passed quickly; some of the shoppers left the store to watch, others to join the picket line. [1]

During the first hours of the picketing, when the number of participants grew from fewer than twenty to several hundred, Teamsters were notably absent from the picket line. Their old enemies, the longshoremen, dominated the scene. Although the drivers' union had provided the support the Guild needed the night before in the Labor Council meeting, Dave Beck's union had stayed aloof from much of the strike planning, perhaps because of the Guild's effort to line up support first with the left-wing unions. Beck, in 1959, said he did not recall meeting with Lynch about strike preparations, but he conceded that he may have counseled the photographer, in the same manner that many other union emissaries were advised by the Teamsters' leader about how to carry out a strike. Beck insisted he did not "supply any of the formulative thinking." [2]

By noon, however, Teamsters were pouring into the lines around the newspaper. The cry had gone out across the city that Harold Hiatt was inside guarding the Hearst plant, and the Teamsters had a score to settle with Hiatt. He was remembered as the guard who had shot and killed Teamster William Usatalo during the Northwest Brewing Co. strike in 1935. The Teamsters had fought for three years to wrest jurisdiction over beer drivers from the Brewery Workers Union. The Teamsters had solid labor support, but the Brewery Workers struck Northwest and other breweries to force the issue of jurisdiction. The Usatalo murder and disclosure that the brewery union was subsidizing the plant it was striking finally gave the Teamsters uncontested jurisdiction. [3] The Teamsters were enraged by the Usatalo murder, and the funeral became a demonstration of this volatile emotion. Instead of allowing the undertaker to cover the wound in the middle of the dead man's forehead, the wound had been exaggerated so that each person passing the open coffin vowed revenge for the dead Teamster. [4]

Hiatt and Peter Marinoff, the operator of the brewery, had been convicted of manslaughter by a jury in Pierce County. But then, in August, 1936, the Washington State Supreme Court would reverse the convictions after the two men had been sentenced to twenty-year terms at the state penitentiary. [5] The Teamsters were not as forgiving. Here was their chance to avenge their comrade who had lost his life for labor's cause. Hiatt was equally willing to confront his accusers as he almost swaggered out the front door of the *Post-Intelligencer* and started up Pine Street. Within seconds Hiatt was lying bloody and beaten, and a circle of policemen was fighting to keep him from being even more seriously injured.

Thus, violence came to the picket line, and the employees inside the building, who only a short time before had felt something akin to disdain for their colleagues in the street, now felt fear. They wondered how they might escape from the building without meeting Hiatt's fate. The prospect was stark. This was no strike of a few members of the feeble Newspaper Guild. This was a strike of the entire labor movement against Hearst. It was no longer some thirty-five members of the *Post-Intelligencer* staff fighting for the right to organize and protesting that two of their number had been fired for union activities. The martyrs of the American Newspaper Guild, Frank Lynch and Everhardt Armstrong, had become the martyrs of all Seattle labor. The enemies of the Guild — Hearst and the *Post-Intelligencer* — had become the enemies of all Seattle labor.

The early morning uncertainty and depression of the Guild strikers gave way to optimism and elation as each new labor element joined the picket line. The real aims of the strikers — the reinstatement of Lynch and Armstrong and the recognition of the Guild by Hearst — seemed less important than the emotional goals. Labor was confronting Hearst by surrounding one of his newspaper plants. The Guild strikers experienced a heady sensation.

Forrest Williams had worried that a handful of Guild strikers would make a silly band to be jeered by their colleagues working comfortably inside the building. Now, as more and more pickets joined the march, he wondered how he could have so misjudged the situation. The strike was succeeding. So great was Williams's enthusiasm that he refused to leave the line for nearly two days and even then had to be carried away in a state of near exhaustion. [6]

Dick Seller had prepared for the strike, even while Williams and others doubted it should take place. Art French, at Seller's direction, had ordered the printing of one-thousand ribbons to identify pickets and a sign company had been given an order for "unfair" signs. [7] But signs were relatively unimportant, for the impressive part of the picket line was the sheer number of participants. By noon the pickets were too numerous, at least 250, to be contained on the sidewalk, and the crowd overflowed into the streets. By some estimates, it was to grow to more than a thousand. Additional police had been called, but requests from the *Post-Intelligencer* to limit the number of pickets and to break the line went unheeded. Mayor John Dore was not about to start breaking up a picket line which was sanctioned by the entire labor front in Seattle, but particularly by Beck and the Teamsters. "Irish Johnny" Dore had won reelection the previous spring with the help of Beck and only a month before the *Post-Intelligencer* strike he had gushed to the delegates of the state labor convention that "I am going to pay back my debt to Dave Beck and the Teamsters in the next two years regardless of what happens." [8] That morning John Dore strode along the picket line, chatting amiably with the union members. He said later, probably wryly, that he "might have given money to some fellows on the street who asked for it." Police knew how to handle a crowd. As long as relative calm prevailed, they did not interfere. [9]

The Guild members needed the reassurance which the size of the picket line gave, for the strike was the work of the local unit and had received no sanction and little sympathy from the national office in New York. National officers had much of their time and effort already absorbed in the strike against the *Wisconsin News*. The national treasury was always empty, and it was only by the greatest effort that one strike could be kept in progress. Two strikes were impossible. Jonathan Eddy, the executive secretary of the Guild, had urged the Seattle officers to delay a strike as long as possible. Yet, when Seller wired Eddy that a strike was under way, Eddy could do no more than send his blessings and head for Seattle. If the Guild were going to get into a strike, someone with some experience had better be on hand to guide it. [10]

Three more telegrams went to the national Guild office the day of the strike. The first was sent at noon and demonstrated some of the dismay which the Seattle Guild felt at its own strength. The wire read: "Six reporters, four typos, forty per cent pressmen, stereotypers, mailers working. Picket lines of 300 keeping rest out. *Post-Intelligencer* plans to print at *Times*. Typos there will walk out if it does." [11]

The telegrams showed at least one uncertainty which had bothered the Guildsmen. By the time the telegram was sent the Guildsmen seemed certain that the paper's printers were not going to cross the picket line. But a rumor that the *Post-Intelligencer* was about to attempt to print at the *Times* was disturbing. In order to show its strength effectively, the Guild had to stop the Hearst paper from being printed any place.

In the *Seattle Times* composing room, printers were nearing the end of the afternoon shift when they were ordered to stay on overtime to set type. The International Typographical Union executive committee readily checked this move and sent an order that *Times* printers could not set *Post-Intelligencer* type. The ITU contract with the paper, the committee declared, allowed the union to specify which printers could do the work, and, consequently, *Times* printers could go home. [12]

Pickets in front of the *Post-Intelligencer* heard the rumors of the attempt to print at another newspaper plant, and the cry went up to send pickets to the *Times* and to the *Star* to prevent any such action. Swarms of pickets were crowded into Teamster-driven cabs, and within minutes new picket lines were formed around the *Times* and the *Seattle Star* plants. [13]

In the middle of the afternoon the second telegram of the day was sent to the national Guild office. This time the message carried a bit more assurance. There was already a measure of success for the Seattle Guild. "The *P.-I.* did not publish first edition first time in Seattle newspaper history. No hopes of publishing any editions *so far.*" [14]

Up to this time the picket line in front of the newspaper plant remained fairly well behaved and good natured. The enthusiasm for this newly initiated project was still high, and the pickets had not yet wearied of the activity. As the afternoon wore on and the chances of the *Post-Intelligencer* being published lessened, the mood of the picket line began to change, and the Hearst management within the plant became more and more worried about the safe removal of the loyal employees. At five o'clock one of the chief reporters for the paper, Les Hunt, walked from the plant unaccompanied by police. None of the pickets threatened or touched him in any way. However, Hunt could sense the mood of the picket line, and he was relieved to be outside the building. [15]

Other Hearst employees and officials shared Hunt's apprehensions, and the new headquarters of the Hearst management in the Benjamin Franklin Hotel was gripped by fear for the safety of the fellow workers within the building. These workers also showed concern as they realized it was not their fellow employees, the Guildsmen, who formed the picket line but hundreds of unknown union members and sympathizers from throughout Seattle, and labor violence was not an unknown thing in the city. At the same time that the Guildsmen were getting word that the national executive secretary was on his way to direct the strike effort, Hearst men got word that the chain's key labor negotiator, Harvey Kelly, was enroute from Chicago.

Kelly hadn't gotten out of the airport before he was confronted with vivid demonstrations of the strong feelings aroused by the strike. After claiming his baggage he rushed to the nearest cab stand and asked to be taken to the Hearst headquarters. The Teamster driver quickly demonstrated that some cab drivers in Seattle were not for hire for that sort of mission. The driver ordered Kelly from the cab and drove ahead to pick up another fare. Kelly waited a few minutes and then approached another cab and asked to be taken to downtown Seattle. He decided he could walk a block or two to the hotel. [16]

By the time Kelly arrived at the Benjamin Franklin, the new Hearst strike headquarters was not unlike a forward battle station during the war. Calls flooding the switchboard were coming mostly from the employees still within the plant, and the picket line was becoming more and more restless. The rumor was out that someone had delivered several kegs of beer to the pickets, and in the words of one eye witness, ". . . the mob was pretty well mellowed up. They were scrappy." Those familiar with picket lines could sense that an explosive situation was building. The mob was growling, but as yet, except for Hiatt, no one had been hurt.

Kelly heard the growl as he walked up from the Benjamin Franklin and started toward the Sixth Avenue entrance to the *Post-Intelligencer*. His way was quickly blocked as the pickets moved in and pushed him away from the building in much the same way as a "chip of wood is moved along on a turbulent brook."[17]

The irritability of the pickets increased as the evening passèd and as the Hearst employees attempted to leave the building. Before the evening was over, ten employees had been beaten. Donald Litchfield, an artist, left the building and started up the street when a gang of pickets grabbed and tossed him over a fence later estimated to have been twelve feet high.[18] Litchfield was badly bruised and cut but did not sustain serious injury. No one could identify the assailants, but Litchfield contended that the men wore the buttons of the Teamster and Longshore unions.[19]

Shortly after 10 p.m., C. H. Bingham, the publisher's secretary, attempted to leave the plant. He was no sooner out the door when he was seized, kicked, and chased until he entered a streetcar. Even then he was pursued as a group of pickets followed him in a car, and after he alighted he again was roughed up.[20]

Several circulation workers also heard the growl of the picket line as they attempted to leave the *Post-Intelligencer* plant late that evening, and all received strong evidence of the resentment and bitter feelings which the swarming pickets outside felt for Hearst and the *Post-Intelligencer* management. Among those injured were Joe Resnick, J. H. Obertueffer, George Chew, H. C. Newbom, Thomas Short, Harold F. Fackler, and I. O. Fowler.[21] None of the workers was injured seriously, but there was enough display of fisticuffs to give credence to the stories of violence on the picket lines. Those opposed to the strike were to make much of this, and cries went up immediately for Mayor Dore to take action.

One of the more serious injuries took place early the

next morning. Anthony Almado, an employee whom Hearst had imported from Los Angeles the previous week, was parking an auto in the *Post-Intelligencer* garage when a group from the picket line seized and beat him. He suffered a minor concussion, fractured jaw, and bruises on other parts of his body. [22] As a result of the Almado incident, five men were arrested. Two were truck drivers and at least one a logger. The *Seattle Times* reported that the men were released shortly after arrest on the order of Mayor Dore. [23]

At the time of the Almado incident, nearly two hundred pickets were still surrounding the *Post-Intelligencer* building, a considerable number for five o'clock in the morning. However, this was quite a drop from the hundreds who had surrounded the plant in the late afternoon. By midnight police estimated there were still about one thousand men and women on the picket line to celebrate the end of the first day of the strike and to share in the triumph which accompanied the realization that a Hearst newspaper had been shut down. A weary Guildsman, perhaps Williams, left the picket line to send a note to New York to allow the national headquarters to share in this accomplishment. The telegram read: *"P.I.* missing fourth straight edition. Still no hope of their publishing tonight. Seattle Guild putting strike sheet on street at 6 a.m. Friday." [24]

After the opening hours of the strike, most Guildsmen spent their time on the news sheet. It was a welcome activity into which the strikers could throw themselves and avoid thinking too much about what the whole undertaking meant. The Guild news sheet was another immediate goal which could bring easy and quick rewards and help the Guildsmen keep their minds from the ultimate consequences of their actions. Many strikers were beginning to realize that the triumph they were experiencing might be a costly one indeed. Williams was certain that he never would be able to work in the newspaper industry again, but nothing could be done now that the strike had begun. Those consequences would have to be considered later. [25]

The Guild kept its promise to the national office and the following morning issued a news sheet entitled the *Guild Striker*. It was the only way the Guild members believed the public would receive labor's side of the strike against Hearst.

The *Guild Striker* which went on sale Friday morning scarcely could be considered a newspaper — at least one of any quality. It was hurriedly thrown together, badly written, and poorly edited. Its dominant characteristic was a nearly juvenile enthusiasm for this moment which the Seattle Guild had helped create, and the reporters were breathless to tell the world of triumph. Seller, the Guild president, termed the issue a product of a bunch of kids gloating over having accomplished something they really did not think was possible. [26]

Little in the news sheet explained why a strike was taking place or how the whole closure of the *Post-Intelligencer* had come about. The *Striker* was not written to inform but rather to convince both the Guildsmen and their readers. No one really could understand what the Guild hoped to achieve, for not even the Guildsmen could tell this. The more thoughtful puzzled over the situation and wondered if the whole strike were taking place simply because two men had been fired from the *Post-Intelligencer*.

Those who searched for other answers found one the same day in the *Seattle Times*. C. B. Blethen, publisher, never had been afraid to use a bit of emotionalism if it served his purpose. He wrote that he was startled to see a daily newspaper employing some 650 persons shut down by the labor element within the city. This was something more than an issue of freedom of the press. It was unconstitutional. It was a revolution. Blethen took his case to the people in his *Seattle Times* on August 14.

Surely Blethen couldn't admit that a large and powerful newspaper had been closed down by a union whose membership was only some thirty-five persons out of the 650 employed by the paper. Such a pitifully small organization hardly could be pictured as a threat to the very life of the city of Seattle. To Blethen, the real villain was labor, which threatened to take over the city and the nation, and the leader of labor in Seattle was a pugnacious, shrewd, and powerful Teamster named Dave Beck. He had risen to power as a laundry truck driver on the streets of Seattle, where he built the strongest union in the city. His drive for power was strong and unrelenting as he organized truck drivers, brewery employees, laundry workers, dry cleaners, and other workers of the city and area. Rumors of the ruthless labor leader, his goon squads, violence, and racketeering accompanied his rise to power in Seattle and the West Coast. This was a power which many in Seattle were beginning to fear and which many insisted could not go unchallenged. Beck's Teamsters had cast the vital votes needed for the Central Labor Council to put Hearst on the unfair list. Beck was the power behind the strike, Blethen concluded, and his front-page editorial disclosed this fact to the city:

Yesterday was written the most shameful page in Seattle's history.

By order of a labor leader, *The Post-Intelligencer*, Seattle's oldest newspaper, was compelled to suspend publication.

Out of the quiescent fingers of a complacent mayor and chief of police, slipped the government of this once great city. Today it rests in the firm hands of Dave Beck and his brawny crew of teamsters, loggers and longshoremen.

Gone is constitutional government. Gone is majority rule and freedom of speech.

Seattle is now the plaything of a dictator. Practically without an hour's warning a newspaper has been put out of business. Perhaps all will be — unless Beck's whim leads him to keep one for his own purposes.

If a newspaper — why not a department store? Or a bank?

Seattle definitely has been on the downgrade for some years, just because of our labor situation. Our city for a long time has been on industry's blacklist. Our progress has been stopped.

The suspension of the *Post-Intelligencer* is more likely than not to mark the place where Seattle lies — dead.

Dave Beck and his following comprise a very small fraction of the city's population. But one bandit can hold up a whole roomful of people.

How do you like the look of Dave Beck's gun?

The shame of it!

General Blethen had fired a cannon and in some ways defined the whole nature of the struggle. Beck rather than the Guild was to be the acknowledged enemy.

Both Blethen and the Teamster official understood the

situation far better than did many of the Guildsmen who were exulting in their "power." Several months earlier, Seattle's biggest businessmen, banded together as the Washington Industrial Council, Inc., had decided to fight Beck's efforts to organize automobile warehousemen. Beck had won that battle and the war then moved on to the newspapers. Beck saw that the Guildsmen were actors in a drama much larger than they imagined. "If the Teamsters were successful in organizing, because of their key position in industry, it would mean not only the success of the Guild strike, but it would mean definite organizational progress throughout the entire Northwest area." [27] The moment was critical; the Teamsters and Longshoremen were contesting jurisdiction over workers in many industries. [28]

Not only was Teamster power growing, but the Teamsters were the key to complete union organization of the newspapers. The crafts, the persons who produced and distributed the papers, already were organized. Now the publishers saw union organization spreading into new areas, the newsroom and circulation and advertising departments, to affect white-collar people who never before had belonged to unions. Retail executives watched the newspaper with apprehension, for they, too, had large numbers of poorly paid, unorganized workers. The world was changing rapidly and one man, Beck, not only understood the changes, but seemed to be responsible for many of them.

Beck was usually reluctant to involve the Teamsters in strikes; he preferred to persuade businessmen that union and employer had mutual interests.

Through the process of time and the evolution that accompanied organization, a certain percentage of businessmen found that the stability of their labor forces was an asset actually to their business. And in the instances where they did not denote that as such they at least felt that they were better off to be doing business with labor than to be in continual friction with labor out of which arose strikes and out of which arose controversy — all of which handicapped production in their own particular industry. [29]

But sometimes, because the stakes were so high, or the employers had drawn battle lines that common sense could not dissolve, strikes were necessary. Beck decided that this strike was necessary.

The Guild, in gaining Beck's support, had taken him on as an ally with all the advantages and disadvantages implied.

FOOTNOTES CHAPTER V

THE DAY THEY STRUCK HEARST

1. Ken Turay interview, September, 1975.
2. Dave Beck interview, April, 1959.
3. J. B. Gillingham, *The Teamsters Union on the West Coast* (Berkeley: Institute of Industrial Relations, University of California, 1956), pp. 46-47; *Seattle Times*, August 14, 1936; *Seattle Star*, August 14, 1936.
4. Ed Donohoe interview, May, 1972.
5. State of Washington v. H. H. Hiatt, *et al.*, 187 Wash. 226 (1936).
6. Mr. and Mrs. Claude Smith interview, August, 1960; Forrest Williams to Jonathan Eddy, August 10, 1936, Newspaper Guild Collection, Archives of Labor History and Urban Affairs, Wayne State University, Detroit. Hereafter referred to as Newspaper Guild Collection. See also the *Guild Daily*, August 15, 1936.
7. Williams to Jonathan Eddy *et al.*, August 10, 1936, Newspaper Guild Collection. There also is a copy in the Pettus Papers (MSS in Manuscript Division, University of Washington Library). Hereafter referred to as Pettus Papers.
8. Washington State Federation of Labor, *Proceedings of the Thirty-fifth Annual Convention*, Vancouver, Wash., July 13-16, 1936 (Seattle: The Trade Printery, 1936), pp. 5-8.
9. *Seattle Star*, August 14, 1936. According to Beck, Dore had been attorney for the same Brewery Workers who had fought the Teamsters so bitterly for jurisdiction. Yet when Dore ran for mayor of Seattle, Beck supported him over Arthur Langlie, "who was above reproach as to personal character but whose administration did not coincide with the thinking of the Teamsters. . . ." Beck interview, April, 1959.
10. *Guild Reporter*, September 1, 1936.
11. *Ibid.*
12. Mr. and Mrs. Floyd Larkin interview, May, 1959.
13. *Ibid.*
14. *Guild Reporter*, September 1, 1936. Actually the *Post-*

Intelligencer did not publish during the Seattle general strike on February 5 and 6, 1919.

15. Lester M. Hunt interview, April, 1960.
16. Harvey Kelly interview, April, 1959.
17. *Ibid.*
18. Larkin interview, May, 1959.
19. National Labor Relations Board, "Transcript of Hearings in Case C-136" (Seattle hearings), p. 311 ff; *Seattle Times*, August 15, 1936.
20. *Ibid.*
21. *Ibid.*
22. *Ibid.; Seattle Times*, August 14, 1936.
23. *Ibid.*
24. *Guild Reporter*, September 1, 1936.
25. See the Williams letters to Pettus during this period in the Pettus Papers and in the Newspaper Guild Collection. Also Richard Seller interview, June, 1961.
26. Seller interview, June, 1961.
27. Beck interview, April, 1959. In August, 1936, Beck was International Representative of the International Brotherhood of Teamsters, Chauffeurs, Stablemen and Helpers of America.
28. Indeed, in that month, the Teamsters organized warehousemen in the automotive industry and a month later, the Longshoremen began their march inland by signing up workers in several industries. The Teamsters won a favorable division of jurisdiction from the American Federation of Labor executive council and were able to expand their organization rapidly. Gillingham, p. 58.
29. Beck interview, April, 1959.

CHAPTER VI

BALLAD OF THE RED MILL

The strike against the *Post-Intelligencer* had something of the air of a musical comedy from its very beginning — a comedy filled with Damon Runyon characters acting out a fairy-tale plot. There were the heroes and the villains, the popular and the unpopular, the just and the unjust, the persecuted and the persecutors.

The setting was particularly appropriate for the standard musical comedy. One adversary was housed in the castle on the hill — the Benjamin Franklin Hotel, one of the city's largest and finest. This was the headquarters set up by the Hearst management, and the place was alive with activity as the loyal members of the *Post-Intelligencer* staff reported to work on radio scripts damning the American Newspaper Guild and Dave Beck. These scripts were used daily over Seattle stations and were important in the appeal for support which Hearst made during the strike.

A typical script in the early days of the strike not only blamed Beck for closing the *Post-Intelligencer*, but also called on Seattle citizens to rally to the defense of American liberties against the rapacious "labor dictator."

Where are you going to stand in this fight, Mr. and Mrs. Radio Listener? If you don't take a firm stand at once it may be too late. For the last five mornings you haven't received your morning newspaper because Dave Beck said, "no." Tomorrow it may be your bottle of milk of which he elects to deprive you, or your local bread, your meat, your vegetables. Let him continue in his mad career and he may soon be telling you where you can or cannot worship, when and where you can sleep and eat, what your children shall be taught in school, if indeed he decides to permit the schools to remain in operation. We will be with you again at 10:15 this evening. 1

In such a musical comedy, the headquarters for the opposing forces had to be nearly completely lacking in ostentation or splendor. It had to be the kind of place which signified the plea of the worker for his right to his job, his right to earn a living, his lowly position in society. Although selected quite by chance, the headquarters for the American

73

Newspaper Guild forces could not have been better chosen.

Guild activities centered around a location in the Alley Oop ballroom of the Red Mill Tavern, a saloon at Sixth Avenue and Union Street, two blocks from the *Post-Intelligencer* building. It had many advantages. It was close to the newspaper plant and provided the Guildsmen with the opportunity to keep a constant watch on the picket line, which remained at a full force of forty during the early weeks of the strike. Then, its roominess provided space for the numerous friends and well wishers who dropped in throughout the strike. Also, kitchen facilities were available to provide food for those busy with strike activities. And most important of all, it was free. The owner of the tavern, a Republican who never had been a particular friend of labor, was won over completely by the underdog position of the Guild, and in a moment of generosity he volunteered the back rooms of his tavern for the Guild headquarters. [2]

The activity originating in the Red Mill during the early days of the strike was frantic and frenetic. Guildsmen still little understood the situation in which they found themselves and were bewildered as to what was expected of them. They were jubilant that they had closed the *P-I*, but wondered where they would go next. They later laughed at their first hours in the picket line and the complete naivete' with which they had approached the problem. [3]

Abe Cohen, one of the most loyal Guildsmen, presented a most ridiculous figure during the early hours on the picket line when the Guildsmen were walking it alone. Cohen, from the library staff, had returned just recently to the *Post-Intelligencer* at the time the strike troubles began. Now he was out in the street in a long raincoat and a sandwich board supported by his small frame. His impression was anything but that of a threatening picket. [4]

Other Guildsmen were scarcely more threatening during the early hours. They had seemed rather embarrassed as the loyal members of the staff reported for work and walked unchallenged into the *P-I* building. However, once the longshoremen appeared on the scene, the picket line assumed new character as the Guildsmen began taking lessons in striking. If the place were to be closed, people could not be allowed to go inside the building, Guildsmen learned. Longshoremen instructed that when someone started toward the building, pickets had to push forward, bump him, and stop him, asking where he thought he was going. Then, after the entrant was stopped, the picket started bumping into the loyal employee and backing him away, giving distinct notice that no one was entering the building. By evening, with the benefits of such instruction and the fortification of some liquor, the picket line was neither meek nor mild, but after the first day, neither was it particularly threatening. [5]

Even the police entered the spirit of the strike and viewed the picket line, after the first day or two, with something approaching amusement or even sympathy. Both police and pickets had the definite feeling that there were no enemies in this struggle, and attractive young women on the picket line were not unappreciated by the men responsible for maintaining law and order in the city. Few policemen failed to notice Mrs. Terry Pettus, who accompanied her husband to the picket line from Tacoma every weekend. She also learned how to walk the picket line, but the police rather than the longshoremen gave her instructions. Inexperienced in such matters, on her first day on the picket line she was dressed in a new sailor hat, high-heeled shoes, with her long, blond hair bouncing off her shoulders. She walked determinedly at a good speed back and forth in front of the plant. After two or three trips, a policeman stopped her. She protested that she was following all the laws. Indeed she was, said the kindly officer, but at the rate she was going, she wouldn't last ten minutes, and he immediately demonstrated to her the techniques for preserving energy so she could walk a full duty period on the line. [6] Such incidents early indicated if the pickets behaved themselves, there would be no trouble with the police.

The Guildsmen also learned during the early hours of the strike that it took more than men and signs to carry out a successful strike. It was the Maritime Federation forces which provided this important advice and instruction. A Mrs. Dumbra, a familiar name on the waterfront, offered her assistance and advised the strikers that victories were not won on the picket line alone. The only way to win a strike was to give the men enough to eat, and if the Guildsmen were going to eat, they couldn't do it on the strike benefits. That money had to go for rent, for transportation, and for the picket line. The food had to come from the strike kitchen. In a few hours Mrs. Dumbra and her friends had established one of the important adjuncts to any strike, the kitchen, and had given the necessary instructions so that the young, inexperienced wives of the Guildsmen were ready to feed the hundreds of people needed to carry on a successful strike.

Within a few days, however, the women of the Guild, the members, the wives, and the girl friends largely had surrendered the cooking duties to one of those characters that every strike attracts. He had no connection with the Guild, but he had learned to enjoy the excitement of a strike. He liked strike people, and he found that his former training as a cook gave him an easy entree to this exciting atmosphere. This brought the man known to most of the strikers only as "Sparrow" to the Red Mill, and it was Sparrow who provided meals — good meals — during the fifteen-week strike. And, when food was scarce around the kitchen, it was rumored — but Sparrow would neither confirm nor deny — that some of the turkeys and other food which fed the pickets and strikers were sneaked in the back way by sympathetic policemen. [7]

Sparrow was only one of that strange breed which characterized the labor strife of the 1930s — the strike followers. The speakers' bureau attracted a collection of orators representing all hues from the political spectrum and all walks of life. There were university professors, labor leaders, Democrats, Republicans, liberals, and conservatives. No one was certain where anyone stood on issues, but the strike followers were attracted by the excitement of the strike and became regular patrons of that big center in the back of the Red Mill Tavern. There was food, interesting conversation, and always action, which seemed to indicate that a good deal was being accomplished, but no one was quite certain just what.

Much of the activity in the Red Mill consisted of publishing the *Guild Daily* — the name given the Guild newspaper after the first day. The *Daily* was hardly an example of good journalism, but it was a saucy, sensational little sheet, usually four pages, published to keep the city informed of the Guild's position during the strike. It was neither well written nor well edited, nor were all the facts published in the paper well founded. Both national and local news filled the front page and a lively sports section dominated the inside. What it lacked in coverage, it made up for in opinions. It was a costly proposition, and as an advertising medium, it was a near failure. But the *Guild*

Daily provided therapy for the confused and uncertain strikers during the fifteen weeks. [8]

The Hearst management also was busy during the opening days of the strike preparing for whatever direction events might take. Reinforcements to the Hearst guards, "the Angels," quickly were flown into Seattle by private plane, and by August 17 some seventy-two were housed in a warehouse within four blocks of the *Post-Intelligencer.* The number was increased almost daily during the early phases of the strike. [9]

There was no doubt as to the presence of the Hearst forces, but there were unconfirmed rumors that the men were armed. There was information that four Thompson sub-caliber machine guns were held by the group, but information also suggested that the force was not ready to move until after August 20. [10] The men never did take an active part in any Hearst attempt to break the strike.

Mayor John Dore responded to Hearst's threat of force by publicly ridiculing the "Angels" and at the same time reasserting his contention that the police would not be used as strike breakers. In a speech at the Ballard Eagles' Hall, Dore warned:

I'm telling you (neither) William R. Hearst nor any other person is going to turn gunmen or gorillas loose here. The first day they do I'll turn loose our police department and they'll think they've had a touch of hell on earth. The day is over when the police are going to use guns and gas to break strikes. . . . [11]

The Hearst formula for breaking the *Post-Intelligencer* strike wasn't particularly novel; endless variations of it were used in the 1930s by corporations of all sizes and types. Employers had mastered the techniques for fighting unions in several decades of labor strife, and by 1936, the battle was fought with a high degree of sophistication. It was a striking coincidence, but probably no more than that, that the National Association of Manufacturers published, only a few days before the *Post-Intelligencer* strike began, a detailed plan for breaking strikes. Almost to the letter, the NAM's so-called Mohawk Valley Formula spelled out the steps Hearst would take in Seattle.

The Mohawk Valley Formula, named for the locale of the Remington Rand strike of 1936, attempted to apply "scientific methods" to handling strikes. Its underlying aim was

> to win public support by branding union leaders as sub-
> versive and threatening to remove the affected industry
> from the community if local business interests stood by
> and allowed radical agitators to (influence) workers
> otherwise ready and anxious to cooperate with their
> employers.[12]

Somehow, the formula didn't quite work in Seattle. However, the management strategy might have been more effective if its planners had known a bit more about the nature of Seattle labor. As it was, Hearst's attempt to discredit the union leaders couldn't have helped the Guild more if it had been planned by Seller, Lynch, and Armstrong.

Lynch, by blundering into the Labor Temple in search of help wherever he could find it, had discovered the deep rift in Seattle labor. Before the strike, a clear division existed between the leftist industrial unions, such as the longshoremen, and the conservative craft unions, led by Beck's Teamsters. The strike had united those two elements for a brief moment, but the essential philosophical differences remained. With its eyes closed to this basic fact, the *Post-Intelligencer* management, through press releases and broadcasts, branded all the participating unions as part of a Communist-led conspiracy. Linking Beck to the Communists was ridiculous; one doubts that many persons took the Hearst charges seriously. But by bludgeoning all labor, Hearst made it difficult for Beck and his allies to bring any influence to bear on the Guild. If the business-like Teamsters were enemies of the newspaper, just as the radical longshoremen were, Beck was not about to go out of his way to help the *Post-Intelligencer*. As one businessman noted:

> So, the situation is just stymied, the *P.I.* remains
> picketed and the town goes on about its business with
> Hearst propagandists fanning the air and blasting the
> country with anti-Seattle dynamite. [13]

The Seattle Chamber of Commerce, at least, listened to the Hearst propaganda and found in it cause for alarm about the harm the strike was doing to the city and its image. The Chamber on September 15 took up the "grave situation" with regard to labor relations in Seattle. A special committee was appointed to call on *Post-Intelligencer* management, offering the support of the business community in the strike. This same committee was asked to convey to General Blethen of the *Times* its congratulations on the stand which he had taken against the strikers and Beck. [14]

Hearst was not without his supporters in Seattle, although they were relatively ineffective throughout the strike. By making Dave Beck a villain in the strike, Hearst won the support of many who had strong feelings against this young labor leader who had fought his way to the top of the Seattle labor hierarchy. Beck had risen to the top of the Teamsters' union in the area and through his energetic organizing efforts had widened considerably the recruiting area for Teamster members. By 1936, he was the key force in the Seattle Labor Council. This position had not been gained without creating many enemies within both the business and the labor circles, and Hearst had fertile ground in which to plant an anti-Beck campaign. Beck fit the stereotype of many conservatives who feared the rising force of labor. Union power was viewed as a great threat to the rights and privileges of property, and with the world afire with conflicts between classes and among philosophies, the unrest in large parts of the city population was easy to understand.

The fears of such persons were heightened by the news of the 1936 presidential election campaign. [15] Many felt the liberal Franklin D. Roosevelt and the conservative Alfred Landon symbolized the opposing forces. Others were certain that Roosevelt's talk of a new deal for labor was nothing more than a thinly-veiled page out of the book of Karl Marx. Newspapers helped spread the word that President Roosevelt was closely tied with the Communist movement. [16] Some feared the country was headed straight for a dictatorship, unless Roosevelt could be defeated. Somehow labor, communism, and Dave Beck all seemed to be welded together in this great conspiracy. How Beck and the Communists could be placed in the same scheme never was fully explained. [17] It was just simpler to lump them all together and fight them as a single enemy.

Opposing this threat were Landon, the governor of Kansas, and the man who had strongly urged Landon's selection as the Republican candidate, William Randolph Hearst. [18] Few were really very taken by Landon, for he was not the type to extract undying loyalty from his followers. Probably fewer still had any great sympathy for Hearst. But many did sympathize with the cause which they perceived these two men waged — Americanism against communism, freedom against dictatorship.

The Seattle situation, as viewed by those frightened by the rising force of labor, was especially threatening because of the presence not only of Beck, but of Mayor Dore and Governor Clarence Martin, both favorable to labor and seemingly unwilling to do anything to meet the imminent threat which many saw in Seattle during the fall of 1936. Blethen beat the tom-tom of doom in frantic front-page editorials in the *Times*, but few responded. He was appalled at suggestions that the dispute between the *Post-Intelligencer* and the Guild be submitted to arbitration.

One or two misguided civil organizations and a more than misguided governor have suggested that the *Post-Intelligencer* "arbitrate its troubles with the union." What utter rot.

Blethen concluded:

No. You cannot arbitrate the Constitution of the United States. Nor starvation. [He contended that families were starving because they were deprived of jobs by the picket line.] Like Hearst or not, if the *Post-Intelligencer* is destroyed merely because certain labor leaders will it, chaos is at hand and Seattle is doomed. [19]

Mayor Dore was a pudgy Irishman who had been born and educated in Boston and did not at all object to being compared with his colorful fellow Bostonian, Mayor James M. Curley. Dore came to Seattle as a news reporter and spent eight years working in journalism. During his newspaper days Dore studied law and without any formal education in the field was able to pass the state bar examinations to practice law in Washington. [20] In the spring of 1932, Dore entered politics as a candidate for mayor against a nondescript field. He was known as the business-man's candidate, and this may have been the point which distinguished him enough from the rest of the field so that he was elected. [21] By 1934, the business community was disillusioned with Dore and its support was withdrawn, resulting in his defeat. Dore sought a replacement for this support and found it in labor, and particularly in Dave Beck.

Dore somehow made the switch from the businessman's candidate to Beck's by 1936, and it was while he was flying the Teamster boss's flag that the American Newspaper Guild struck the *Post-Intelligencer* plant.

If Dore had the reputation of being Beck's man, it was his own fault, for after his election he had said that his victory was due to the support of Beck, and as mayor, he would not forget this. [22] Beck feigned embarrassment by the statement, but he made the most of it. Dore lived up to the reputation throughout the strike and followed Beck's cues. When Beck supported the strike, so did Dore. There was no police interference with pickets and no threats of such action. When Beck began to grow weary of the strike and feared labor might suffer from too long or too open action, Dore threatened to use police to allow the printing trades' people to enter the plant. This would have ended the strike, and most of labor did not care to see the strike end on such a note. [23] For the most part, Dore earned the reputation of strongly supporting the strike, and following Hearst's blunt refusal to consider Dore as a proper arbitrator in the case, Dore became one of the most active speakers for the Guild's cause. [24]

Governor Martin, on the other hand, had no real connection with the strike. In fact, he strongly advocated letting Seattle settle its own problems. He had enough of his own. He was seeking re-election and had trouble both within his own party and from the Republicans. The Washington Commonwealth Federation had one of its leading spokesmen, "Radio Speaker" John C. Stevenson, seeking the Democratic nomination against Martin in the primary, and Martin wanted no excuse to alienate either the liberal or the conservative elements of the state. [25] Stevenson, one of the colorful politicians of Washington in the 1930s, had risen to prominence in the Federation through radio talks and made the most of his position as a county commissioner in King County. The Federation would have liked to have seen him in the governor's mansion in Olympia in 1936, but outside King County, Stevenson was not well enough known, nor were the politics radical enough to carry Stevenson through. [26]

On the Republican side, Roland Hartley, a conservative Everett businessman who reputedly led the forces against the Industrial Workers of the World in the 1916 Everett

Massacre, again was seeking the governor's office. Hartley had as his campaign writer one of the *Post-Intelligencer's* top reporters, Lester Hunt, a man antagonistic to the Guild. Hunt knew the background of the Guild strike and stayed loyal to Hearst. He made the most of the situation during the campaign to attack Martin and his failure to act in the strike. (Subsequently, Hunt became an editor of *International Teamster* magazine.) 27

Beck, Dore, and Martin were the objects of most charges made by Hearst and his supporters, for management scarcely could bring itself to attack the few members of the American Newspaper Guild who were on strike. The *Post-Intelligencer* made much of its assertion that only a few Guildsmen who were actually on strike were keeping 600 people from working. The number of employees varied greatly, depending on who was using the figure and for what purpose. Therefore, it behooved Hearst management to turn the strike into a gigantic conspiracy against the people of the city and state and to gain as much support as possible through political circles.

The Guild claimed that Hearst had other organized efforts working in his favor. One of these was an attack on Beck and what was termed labor racketeering in Seattle. According to the Guild, loyal *Post-Intelligencer* employees were put on daily telephone duty calling firms "and acquaintances" to aid in "this fight against union racketeering." Phone workers were warned not to mention the *Post-Intelligencer* in any way when they asked people to stop their laundry services and to do their laundry at home; to stop the milk delivery and to buy milk at the corner store; to stop patronizing bakeries that delivered and to buy goods in their local bakeshops. By doing this, solicitors explained, they were striking at the "biggest labor rackets in Seattle" and the "roots of labor racketeering," and thus "we (the *P-I*) are improving our position." 28

This solicitation was taking place at the same time that Hearst was living up to Guild Executive Secretary Jonathan Eddy's prediction that the publisher would threaten to quit Seattle unless the strike were settled. The announcement on September 16 by the associate publisher, Charles Lindeman, said that Hearst intended to liquidate assets unless a settlement were reached immediately. The *Seattle Times* reported that a group representing the Chamber of Commerce had asked that the decision be delayed until the matter could be considered by all interested parties. 29 The *Guild Daily* played the story in a much more sensational manner and brought out an eight-column banner to announce "HEARST QUITS." 30 As if to prove the seriousness of the threat, mechanics showed up at the *Post-Intelligencer* building and received safe passage through the pickets, with the expressed idea of helping to dismantle some of the machinery to be shipped to San Francisco. However, few if any machines actually were taken apart, and within a few days the mechanics left.

In the meantime, a businessmen's committee was working in the background with a labor committee, directed by Beck, which sought to end the strike. Many unions, including the printing trades, which up until this time had been willing to go along with the Guild, now seemed anxious for a settlement. An emissary from Beck attempted to sell the Guild on the idea of ending the strike, but Guild members were able to gain sufficient support from other unions to prevent this. 31

Many factors which Hearst counted on to work in his favor yielded opposite results. First, management seemed certain that labor would not unite to close the plant, and with this in mind, Publisher Vaughn Tanner had arrogantly refused to appear before the committee of the Central Labor Council to show cause why the *Post-Intelligencer* should not be placed on the unfair list. Then, too, Hearst had expected the printing trade unions to honor their contracts and to cross the picket line. Instead, the printing trades, while showing the proper amount of regret that they could not report to work, generally had supported the strike, with some printers donating time on the *Guild Daily*. Bitterness remained from a strike of the typographers and mailers in 1924, and the typographers particularly remembered a "straw boss" Hearst had sent in to run the shop. Although some of the printing trades' people supported a return to work, for the most part they were willing to go along with the Guild. 32

Who could have imagined the extent of the latent anti-Hearst sentiments which existed in the city? All Seattle, at times, seemed to be vying to outdo itself in supporting the

Guild. Some 2,500 turned out on August 25 for an "anti-Hearst, pro-Guild" demonstration. Although the *Seattle Times* claimed the demonstrators were mostly Democrats, the cast appearing at the rally was impressive. Mayor Dore, who had been rebuked in his efforts to negotiate the strike, came out swinging, and his popular suggestion was to drive Hearst out of the community and to bring in another paper. As Dore saw it, "The question is whether this man Hearst is going to run this town or whether the people are going to run it." To Dore, Hearst was unfit to own a newspaper, and the mayor made much of the publisher's "personal immorality." The Mayor concluded: "The trouble with Seattle's newspapers is that they are run by men whose chief claim to fame is that their fathers were born first." [33]

Also appearing at the rally was Warren G. Magnuson, county prosecutor, who assured the Guild that the Democrats were with the new organization. Jonathan Eddy reminded the audience that Hearst soon would announce plans to remove the *Post-Intelligencer* from Seattle, but he cautioned people to ignore this. The crowd found the idea of the Hearst paper leaving Seattle an appealing one and loudly applauded the suggestion.

Also expressing ideas popular with the crowd was Deputy Prosecutor Edward E. Henry, who sharply attacked the Law and Order League, which represented the business and industrial interests of the city. To Henry, the League was nothing more than the unpopular Industrial Council which had gained the enmity of labor during the longshore strike in 1934. Typical of the spirit of the rally were Henry's comments that "Hearst's only hope is Fascism, your (the Guild's) only hope is Democracy." As proof of Hearst's Fascist connections, Henry accused the publisher, who was then visiting Rome, of being in the Eternal City to consult with Mussolini, the Fascist dictator. [34]

There were other speakers: the Reverend E. Raymond Attebery, pastor of Grace Methodist Episcopal Church; Howard Costigan, executive director of the Washington Commonwealth Federation; and Ed Weston, secretary of the Metal Trades Council, who first brought organized labor into the picture in the Guild's fight against Hearst. Weston probably best characterized the sentiment of the rally when he announced: "Everyone wants to lick Hearst." [35]

Outside the auditorium, as the *Seattle Times* pointed

out, solicitors sought funds to help the strikers, and newsboys sold the *Guild Daily*, the *Moscow News*, the *Daily Worker* and the *New Masses.* [36]

Many other meetings were held. In Everett, Mayor Dore addressed a group of sympathizers, and in Ballard, West Seattle, and other areas of the city, Dore, Lynch, Armstrong, and other important symbols of the attack on Hearst helped to rally support and to earn funds to keep the strike going. Eddy joined these speakers for out-of-town appearances in such cities as Tacoma and Portland.

But those opposed to the rising strength of labor and supporters of Hearst were not without their organizations and their methods of influencing people. Shortly before the beginning of the strike, a group was organized in Seattle, primarily growing out of the Industrial Council and following much the same line of thought. This was the Law and Order League led by industrialist Kirk Hillman, owner of Hillman Manufacturing, a heavy equipment company. The League was organized on the premise that it was unlawful for labor to show such united strength as it had demonstrated during the *Post-Intelligencer* strike and that the rights and privileges of the population were threatened by the rising force of labor. It was formed to keep men from having to join the unions and to protect society from the unions. Plans for the League were made by a group of businessmen who met at Seattle's most exclusive business club, the Rainier Club. Among those active in the League at the beginning were J. E. Wickstrom, a real estate broker; S. L. Savidge, Sr., an automobile dealer; Robert Bronson; Mrs. Elizabeth Selvin, and Hillman.

The League was supported by full-page ads from the Washington Industrial Council which urged citizens to fight for "law and order," and by September, meetings were attracting up to 1,000 persons. F. R. Singleton, the hired secretary of the League, announced that people were joining the organization at the rate of 500 a day. [37] The League's aim was to recruit at least 25,000 members. [38]

All this was a minor annoyance to those supporting the strike, but the League exerted no particularly effective role and was not really feared. However, it caused many rumors, and active union men of the city expressed concern. A questionnaire reprinted in the *Guild Daily* showed that League members had been polled to ascertain the number of firearms each possessed. Rumors also circulated that members were having evening target practice, but exactly what the League planned to do with this armed force was unclear. 39

The League did provide Mayor Dore with some of his best material for his tirades at the various public meetings supporting the Guild. He referred to one leader of the League as a "half-wit," while another earned the epithet of "old scabherder." Still another was described as living off "a house of prostitution he's got down on Seventh Avenue." Dore promised the audience he would close the house down the following week. One of Seattle's leading citizens, Dore contended, missed the organizational meeting of the League. He ". . . must have been out on a party the night before or he'd have been there." 40

A group which grew out of the League eventually attracted the most attention and for a time appeared to be an effective force working for Hearst. By mid-September the Republican women of the state were organizing pro-America groups to support Landon's candidacy. Few of these meetings adjourned before the women had condemned Dore, Martin, and the strike against the *Post-Intelligencer*. At the same time, these leaders of the GOP, who cast themselves in the role of preserving America from such evils as labor unions and leftist organizations, warmly praised that loyal Republican, William Randolph Hearst. No mention was made of the fact that in 1932 the Hearst chain had supported Roosevelt.

By the middle of October, a new League arose to oppose the strike. Members of the League of Seattle Housewives were local clubwomen who picketed the Labor Temple in support of the *Post-Intelligencer*. Armed with American flags and sandwich boards, the women proclaimed: "We Want the P.I. Reopened," and "Save Seattle from Shame." Although the group announced that 150 women would participate, only about a dozen showed up. Despite their determined announcement: "We left our breakfast dishes in the sink and will stay here until our feet (give out) . . ." the women were gone within a couple of hours. They were treated with the utmost courtesy, and the Guild offered lunch for the women on the basis that Hearst was not taking good care of his pickets. However, the women returned home to finish their dishes before the sandwiches were delivered by Guildsmen. [41]

The following day, spurred on by the publicity given the League of Housewives, a new pilgrimage was announced by Mrs. Edwin Selvin, wife of the publisher of the *Business Chronicle* and an active member of the Law and Order League. Mrs. Selvin announced she would lead the women of the state in a march on Olympia to demand that Governor Martin purge Seattle of "racketeering." The march, obviously inspired to discredit Martin, attracted wide attention in Seattle newspapers and encouraged fifteen loyal women employees of the *Post-Intelligencer* to stage their own march. Their picket line was formed in front of the Teamster headquarters, where the women demanded "Down with Beckism." They were treated courteously despite the fears of Teamster leaders that some of the union members might provoke an incident, and the women left shortly after they were offered a keg of beer ("Dave'll be glad to buy it."). [42]

The big rally for the pro-America women came on October 13, when a group of 500 went to Olympia to protest racketeering in Seattle and, among other things, the closing of the *Post-Intelligencer*. The women demanded that the governor rid the state of the Beck influence. Governor Martin, considered rather impolite by the pro-America group, kept the women waiting for several minutes. When he finally greeted them, they had been joined by a pro-Martin group, supporting the American Newspaper Guild and the strike against Hearst. This group was led by State Senator Mary Farquharson, wife of a University of Washington professor. [43]

The Guild had rallied its own booster group after learning that the pro-America women intended to demand that Martin re-open the *Post-Intelligencer* by using state troops, if necessary. A Martin assistant suggested that the Guild send its own women's group to the state capital simultaneously with the pro-America group. Thus, said the canny aide, the governor could assert that since it was impossible to please both sides, he would have to maintain his neutrality in the strike. The Guild heeded the advice, scoured the city of Seattle on the night of October 12 to gather women from unions and Democratic clubs, then organized the trek to Olympia the next day. [44]

When Mrs. Selvin and her Women of Washington arrived at the capitol the next noon, they were not alone —

and neither was the governor. Standing on the steps also were Seller, Lynch, and French, busily photographing the Women of Washington and enjoying the irony of the moment. Some of the women recognized Lynch, and the photographer did not escape without a sound lecture on the evils of labor, the Guild, Dave Beck, and the Democratic Party. [45]

Mrs. Selvin and her group were made famous by Mayor Dore, who ridiculed them as "Fur Clad Hussies" and "Perfumed Hussies." But the women had aroused some interest, and not even Dore's remarks could discourage Mrs. Selvin and her Law and Order League supporters. The Republican candidate for governor, Roland H. Hartley, carefully tutored by his *Post-Intelligencer* speech writer, Hunt, made much of the Women of Washington and their march on Olympia. [46] And Blethen came forth with another front-page editorial which said, "The women went to Olympia! Where were the MEN?" [47]

By the following week, Mrs. Selvin and her group had stepped up their attack on labor and the Democratic Party. After Dean Herbert Condon of the University of Washington denied the Young Democrats the right to ask Beck to speak on campus, the Women of Washington demanded that the University also deny Dore the right to speak on campus the following Friday. Hartley agreed with the women, and Dore responded by calling the women nothing more than "scabherders." [48]

As the women continued their drive with a threatened boycott of Seattle, Dore's Irish temper and wit both were in action:

But now, my friends, he (Hartley) is running on this anti-labor ticket along with these dear girls that went to Olympia, saying they came from Seattle and other places. And you know what I think of them. In fact, I think a little more of them than I said of them. But next Tuesday or Wednesday they all will be crawling in their holes. They won't be bothering anybody. [49]

A few days later Dore told the waterfront unions that he might have been a bit ungracious to Mrs. Selvin and her women, but then, he admitted having been prone to difficulty with the female sex. [50]

The Women of Washington staged another Seattle rally

which attracted, according to *Seattle Times'* estimates, 5,000 women. [51]

Mrs. Selvin's last efforts in connection with the strike came in late November, when a petition with twenty-six signatures was presented to the city's legal department demanding Mayor Dore's recall. This feeble effort was a bit short of the 25,186 signatures needed to bring the recall to a vote. [52]

For the most part, the work of Mrs. Selvin and the Law and Order League was futile. Dore continued as mayor; Martin was given a tremendous vote of confidence at the November 3 election; and the *Post-Intelligencer* plant was not opened until Hearst had negotiated an agreement with the American Newspaper Guild. In addition, Mrs. Selvin was the subject of a sensational article in the *Guild Reporter* which claimed she and her husband were living in Seattle under false names so that he could avoid supporting three children by a previous marriage. If such reporting were a bit below the belt, reasoned Morgan Hull, Hearst had no one to blame but himself—he had taught the striking reporters how to do such writing. [53]

Hearst had support also from other newspaper publishers. The American Newspaper Publishers' Association protested the refusal of the printing trades to cross the picket line and feared that this endangered the sanctity of future contracts. Even the strong support of Washington Newspapers, particularly the *Bellingham Herald,* seemed to have little impact on public opinion in the state, and no mass movement behind the Hearst cause developed. [54]

Some of the newspapers in the state were concerned with the reports that a new daily newspaper would be started in Seattle and that the famous "lady in red," Anna Louise Strong, was to be connected with it. The *Spokane Spokesman-Review* was particularly upset about the newspaper and the connection which it might have with communism. [55] There was some basis for the concern of the newspaper, for on August 27 a group headed by Richard G. Tyler, professor of engineering at the University of Washington, announced plans to start a new morning newspaper within sixty days. Backers hoped this paper eventually would merge with the *Guild Daily* and replace the *Post-Intelligencer* as Seattle's morning newspaper. Editor of the paper was to be Harvey O'Connor, former church editor of the *Union Record* and writer for the *Post-Intelligencer*. He since had left Seattle to do considerable writing concerning the growth of the labor movement in the United States. O'Connor was at that time in New York, but was expected to return to Seattle in the fall of 1936. Members of the executive committee for the new paper included Ed Weston, executive secretary of the Metal Trades Council; Earl Gunther from the Seattle Central Labor Council; the Rev. Fred Shorter, Church of the People in the University District; Mrs. Alice Sterling, Washington Commonwealth Federation; Howard Grant, Northwest Printing Trades; and the Rev. Sidney Strong, father of Anna Louise. The announcement admitted that Miss Strong had been offered the editorship of the new publication, but she had refused the position in order to return to Moscow to study Russian culture. The announcement further pointed out there would be no connection between the new newspaper and the *Voice of Action*, the reputedly-Communist weekly published by Wakefield and Daggett. 56

By October 2 the chances for the new paper seemed remote indeed as the publication date was delayed, and it was announced that O'Connor had resigned as editor. The same *Times* story reported that the *Voice of Action* was about to fold because of financial difficulties. On October 10 the official announcement of suspension of the *Voice of Action* was made. The circulation list was turned over to the *Commonwealth News*. 57

This ended the effort of the "extreme left" in Seattle to found a daily newspaper, but stories circulated that other papers might start. At one time Dore raised the question of making the *Guild Daily* a permanent morning newspaper. Rumors suggested that such leading Democrats as James Farley were interested in such a plan, but nothing developed. 58 All this indicated that many feared that the *Post-Intelligencer* might have suffered such a serious blow that it would be unable to recover. Those who reasoned thus failed to calculate the extent of Hearst's resources, and except for the *Voice of Action*, Seattle ended the strike with the same newspapers it had at the beginning.

Whereas many of Hearst's efforts failed, the Guild received more breaks than any one organization had the right to expect. It was something of a miracle to have won the united support of the labor front in Seattle by getting

EXTRA — VOL. I, No. 1.

THE GUILD STRIKER

5 Cents

Friday, Aug. 14, 1936 — Published by Seattle Chapter, American Newspaper Guild

P-I NEWSMEN STRIKE

Arbitrary Action of Hearst Paper Forces Walkout

More than thirty-six members of the Post-Intelligencer editorial staff went on strike yesterday after the Seattle Central Labor Council declared the morning Hearst newspaper unfair to organized labor.

A majority of the editorial employes of the P-I, accompanied by more than 600 pickets recruited from the ranks of labor, threw a picket line around the P-I building at Sixth and Pine Streets. The action was taken by the Seattle chapter of the American Newspaper Guild, which was demanding reinstatement of two veteran employes fired from the P-I for joining the Guild.

Because of the backing of the Central Labor Council and the immediate action of pickets, the first three editions of the P-I failed to come out. Printers employed at the Hearst paper failed to go through the picket lines and Publisher W. Vaughn Tanner admitted that the P-I editions would not be on the streets.

Seattle Labor Brands Hearst P.-I. 'Unfair'

The Central Labor council voted unanimously Wednesday night to declare the Seattle Post-Intelligencer unfair...

G. O. P. HEAD SIDESTEPS LABOR PLANK

Picked Up on the Picket Line

I was a picket in front of the P-I. yesterday.

All morning, most of the afternoon and a large part of the evening I strode back and forth before the swinging doors, where for the past ten years I had made my daily returns to work.

For ten years I faithfully served a master who was now serving me in the typical Hearst manner.

With but four hours' sleep I pulled myself from bed at 7 yesterday morning and went to join my fellow editorial workers on the picket line. Already on the job was my immediate superior, Raymond Holmes, militant librarian of the P-I. during the past sixteen years.

Parading in a picket line was an experience for a new paper man! Covering strikes and reporting back to the office knowing full well that what he would like to write will not be printed is an old game to him.

ON THE JOB!

An Open Letter to the P-I Management

Open letter to W. Vaughn Tanner, publisher; Charles R. Lindeman, associate publisher; Arthur Dunning, managing editor; Ray Colvin, day managing editor; John Callaghan, business manager; Oliver Morris, city editor and Eagle Freewater, advertising manager.

Remember, gentlemen, that you are in a tough spot. The Lord of San Simeon who has dedicated himself to immense profit-taking will hold you responsible for your failure last night to get that paper on the streets.

He'll be mighty wroth when advertising sinks to a new low—even for the Post-Intelligencer; he'll fume and rage when he learns that circulations has fallen so alarmingly. Profit for William Randolph Hearst is his only creed.

This is a bird letter. You know how the "Chief" is when he gets sore. And you know where he'll put the blame. He won't put it on the P-I. editorial men who quit. He can't. He'll put it on you. You won't like it, but gentlemen, you just can't lump it!

—Seattle Chapter,
American Newspaper Guild.

DEPOSED MEMBERS OF GUILD TELL CAUSE OF DISMISSAL

By EVERHARDT ARMSTRONG

Ray Colvin, managing editor, said my "defiant attitude" was responsible for the Post-Intelligencer's sudden eagerness to drop me from the payroll—after seventeen more or less "defiant" years on the staff.

My ultimate defiance, it seems, consisted in expressing willingness to forego a vacation rather than leave my desk at a time when the very existence of the Seattle Chapter of the American Newspaper Guild was menaced by Hearst's campaign of insult and economic terrorism in the Post-Intelligencer editorial department.

Mass Meeting Over Strike Tomorrow

PICKET LINE CARRIES FIGHT AGAINST P.-I.

More Than 500 Men and Women Join Forces to Fight Unfairness

With the confidence that they are carrying on a fight against the cash-nervy of labor, more than 500 pickets joined the picket line yesterday around the Post-Intelligencer to continue their struggle against the unfair tactics of that newspaper.

Walking until their feet were sore and their backs weary, the determined unionists surrounded the Post-Intelligencer yesterday morning to continue their steady vigilance throughout the day.

Beginning with about seventy men and women, including lawyers, teachers, writers, longshoremen, teamsters and metal workers, increasing numbers of union pickets joined the P-I. Guild members in their fight against Hearst's anti-labor dictation.

The ranks swelled to 100, then 200, and finally about 5 o'clock, the deadline for the P-I.'s first "green" edition, more than 300 lined the streets.

NOTORIOUS GUNMAN HIRED AS P-I GUARD

Harold Hiatt, Tacoma ...

Harold H. Hiatt, notorious gunman with a prison record ...

Post-Intelligencer Quits Publication, Says Management

The Seattle Post-Intelligencer last night suspended publication of its newspaper "indefinitely."

Climaxing a series of desperate efforts to publish the strike-bound paper, the circulation department of the publication last night announced that ...

The dramatic action, climaxing the most ceaseless activity by Hearst newspaper Guild's successful efforts to prevent the P-I. reaches the first four section in the Post-Intelligencer's ...

The action was announced by the department executives ...

NOTICE

Post-Intelligencer Printers

Members of P.-I. Chapel will hold a Special Meeting in Room No. 202, Labor Temple, Friday, 2 p. m.

J. M. L...

Live News For Morning Paper Readers ----- National, Local, Sports

Weather Forecast
For Seattle and vicinity: Fair Saturday and Sunday but overcast in the mornings. Little change in temperature.

THE GUILD DAILY

5 Cents

VOL. 1, NO. 2 SATURDAY, AUGUST 15, 1936 Published by Seattle Chapter, American Newspaper Guild

P-I RUSHES THUGS HERE

Zioncheck's Kin Blames Hearst

Picked Up on the Picket Line

[I]t looks like the bum joke of a local Hearst boss blew back on [hi]m and his pals.

The boss in question, on the [fi]rst day of the history-making re[po]rters' and editors' strike, passed [b]y a young copy reader, pacing [ba]ck and forth with his badge of [ho]nor—an oilcloth sandwich [po]ster.

"Well, it looks like you're quitting the newspaper business," the boss observed sarcastically.

It now appears that the whip [cr]acker and the rest of his ilk [a]re, temporarily at least, "quitting [th]e newspaper business."

* * *

Police tried to clear out the alley [be]hind the P.-I. building as pickets [pa]trolled to prevent any attempt [to] sneak scabs into the rear en[tr]ance. They did clear it for [a w]hile, and it may have re[m]ained clear had not a spunky [a]mateur picket stood up for his [ri]ghts.

He called up the city hall and [m]ade sure the alley was public [pr]operty, then came back and in[si]sted that pickets be allowed to [re]turn.

* * *

A young striking reporter, sell[in]g the Guild Striker to crowds [ac]ross the street from the picket[ed] "battle zone," amused pass[er]s-by with his cry:

"Extra—buy the leading morning newspaper. If the P.-I. [w]on't give us a break we'll put [ou]t our own paper."

* * *

No drinking was allowed on the [pic]ket line. Two cases of beer, [sen]t by a well-meaning sympathis[er,] arrived shortly after noon. It [go]t as far as the alley.

"Hey, stop that junk right now!" [a] longshore picket shouted. And [it] was stopped instantly and sent [aw]ay.

* * *

The pickets, along with the ma[jo]rity of right-thinking Seattle [pe]ople, weren't taken in with the [so]phistic arguments of the jittery [ol]d maid of Fairview Avenue—[em]pty arguments, worn thin and [ph]ony in repeated attempts money [ha]s used to beat down workers.

"Yeh, it sure is somethin' to get [w]orried about when the horrid [w]orkers cut off the morning pa[pe]r," a picket remarked as he [re]ad the pained howl of the [T]imes.

"But the Times didn't think it [wa]s so awful when they cut off the [fo]od of the mailers' and printers' [fa]milies they locked out a while [ago]. Matter of fact, they didn't [pr]int a line about it," he con[clu]ded.

* * *

An unusually wide assortment [of] unions was represented in the [ra]nks of the pickets last night at [th]e Post-Intelligencer strike zone. The list of crafts included longshoremen, ferryboatmen, motion picture operators, timber [w]orkers, marine firemen, wipers, [oi]lers, boiler tenders, cooks and [st]ewards and teachers. The picket [li]ne numbered about 250 men at [1]0:30 p. m.

* * *

The various institutes of re[s]earch which are forever probing [h]uman conduct and performance [to] find the dimensions of stamina [in] the human frame would be in[te]rested in the pickets who are [ai]ding the Guild. These fellows [do]n't care much about sleep.

Dozens of these friends of the [G]uild have been "pounding the [pa]vement" around the Post-Intel[li]gencer for stretches of twenty[-o]ne to twenty-five hours, taking a [na]p of two hours and then re[tu]rning to their post for another [st]retch.

Tells How Victim Was Hounded to Suicide by Jibes

Nadeau Says Publisher Also Doomed McKinley

Blame for the death of Marion Zioncheck was last night laid directly at the door of the Hearst newspapers by William Nadeau, brother-in-law of Washington's tragic young congressman.

"It was the constant badgering, deliberate misrepresentation and ridicule of the newspapers of the country, led by the Hearst string, that drove Marion to desperation and death," Nadeau declared.

"They never let him alone. Constantly and maliciously they distorted his statements, stamped his ideals as Communism, scorned every ideal he strove for, and aggravated his state of mental depression until they left him hopeless.

HIS BITTER PLIGHT

"He could see nothing ahead. He could not turn back.

"He would not repudiate the ideals he had striven for and he could see nothing in the future but the bitterness of misunderstanding and malignment.

"Rather than go back on the things he had spent his life striving for, he took his own life."

Nadeau pointed out that Zioncheck was not the only victim of the Hearst newspapers.

"Remember how Hearst was held morally responsible for the death of President McKinley?" he reminded. "How in Hearst newspaper columns there was the constant intimation that McKinley was a menace and something should be done about it? An assassin answered that with a bullet. But no murder charge could ever be laid against Hearst.

CAUSE OF A WAR

"And Hearst is generally held responsible for the Spanish-American War!

"I believe Zioncheck's death is the result of Hearst persecution.

"I'm calling on all my friends, on all the public who believe in fair play and decency and the right of a man to live and fight for his ideals without being damned and condemned for it by the press, to cancel their subscriptions to the Post-Intelligencer—if the P.-I. ever publishes again—and to stop their subscriptions also to all Hearst publications including his battery of magazines."

Resolutions in tribute to Zioncheck, passed at the last meeting of the Seattle Central Labor Council, read in part:

"Whereas, our beloved congressman, Marion A. Zioncheck, fought a valiant battle in behalf of the people whom he represented . . . his labor record in congress is a monumental achievement for the program of organized labor . . .

THE PERSECUTION

"Whereas, because of this unequivocal position he was subjected to the most unscrupulous and despicable persecution by those whose interests are inimical to that of the people of this nation . . . and whereas the organized labor movement recognizes that their persecutors must be held accountable as causes contributing directly and indirectly to the untimely death of our representative.

"Therefore be it resolved, that the Seattle Central Labor Council

(Continued on Page 3, Col. 1.)

GUILD OFFICER FROM N. Y. IS ON WAY HERE

Jonathan Eddy, Executive Secretary, Will Arrive at Boeing Field Sunday

Jonathan Eddy, executive secretary of the American Newspaper Guild, with headquarters in New York City, will arrive in Seattle tomorrow to confer with officers of the Seattle Guild chapter on strike plans and strategy.

This word was received yesterday by H. Richard Seller, local Guild president, who has directed the newsmen's fight for reinstatement of the two Guild members discharged by the Post-Intelligencer.

BROUN IS NOTIFIED

Eddy is en route to Seattle by airplane, and will arrive at Boeing Field Sunday morning.

Before the Guild strike was called at 7 a. m. Thursday, Eddy, National President Heywood Broun and other members of the national Guild's executive board were informed that all efforts to negotiate with the Post-Intelligencer management had failed.

Since the first picket line was formed around the Post-Intelligencer plant, the Guild's national officers have been fully advised of all important developments on the strike front in Seattle.

COMING BY PLANE

When informed Wednesday that Seattle Central Labor Council had placed the Post-Intelligencer on the unfair list after the Guild had reached an impasse in its efforts to deal with the Post-Intelligencer, Eddy assured Seller "the national Guild is with you 100 per cent."

The local Guild had followed Eddy's advice to call a strike only after all efforts to negotiate had failed.

— Be American —

High Worker Hurt In 15-Foot Fall

BALTIMORE, Md., Aug. 14.—Skyscraper window cleaning never worried Robert Beard, seventy-two, who has spent a lifetime at this work.

Today he was in a serious condition in a hospital after he fell fifteen feet while cleaning a window in his rooming house.

WHOSE IS THE SHAME?

(EDITORIAL)

On the front page of yesterday's Seattle Daily Times there appeared an editorial.

It was titled "This Shameful Page" . . .

There it was to greet the eye—first the paper's name, "Seattle Daily Times," and then the editorial heading, "This Shameful Page," right under the Times' name . . . two lines that at one glance spoke the truth, however accidentally. The Times described itself in blackface type!

For The Times became a shameful page with the printing of the editorial text that followed. (The signature to the editorial was conspicuous by its absence.)

The editorial charged that a labor leader had compelled the Post-Intelligencer to suspend publication. Shame on such a charge!

ONLY THE POST-INTELLIGENCER'S OWN UNFAIRNESS TO TWO VETERAN EMPLOYES IT FIRED WITHOUT CAUSE EXCEPT GUILD MEMBERSHIP CAUSED THE "P.-I." TO SUSPEND.

The editorial charged that Seattle's city government rests today "in the firm hands of Dave Beck and his brawny crew of teamsters, loggers and longshoremen."

Laugh with the rest of the town!

The editorial then weeps great crocodile tears: "Gone is constitutional government" . . . "gone is freedom of speech" . . . That editorial almost credits Beck with Hearst powers! AND Hearst ambitions and inclinations!

More tears follow. Seattle, according to that editorial, is going into a decline, "has been on downgrade for some years" . . . and the "suspension of the Post-Intelligencer is more likely than not to mark the place where Seattle lies—dead."

Well, somehow, Seattle lived and thrived and grew before Hearst took over the Post-Intelligencer and changed it from a conservative, fair-minded daily newspaper, respected and honored in the community, into what it is now—or rather was.

There are a good many citizens in Seattle who think the city may still survive even though the Post-Intelligencer has suspended publication "indefinitely."

Seattle, many think, may live even to days when men dare ask that labor be dealt with in all fairness and justice to employer and employe without a shameful news sheet crying half-truths in its headlines, and using its editorial columns to attempt to warp the judgment of its readers.

Let the shame fall where it belongs. The Times told the truth inadvertently when it carried those two lines so close together: "The Seattle Times — This Shameful Page."

THREE MEN IN A QUANDARY

Publisher Bringing Strong-Arm Men To Break Strike

POST-INTELLIGENCER REMAINS 'SUSPENDED'

Squads of thugs and strong-arm men last night we[re] speeding toward Seattle, imported from California [to] break the strike now existing on the Post-Intelligence[r] according to a dispatch from San Francisco.

The message read:

"Two carloads circulation strikebreakers left here today for Seattle in charge men named Thone and Nicoletti. Fairbanks of Examiner circulation staff [s]ent by plane. Five slugg[ers] from North Beach hired toda[y]. Another gang former pugs d[e]clined jobs when situation [ex]plained.

Other developments in t[he] strike called Thursday morni[ng] by editorial employes of the Po[st-]Intelligencer were:

1—Gangs of strikebreakers, [al]ready on ground und[er] Hearst executives' orders, we[re] quartered in Seattle hotels.

2—Harvey J. Kelly, former e[x]ecutive secretary of th[e] American Newspaper Publisher[s] Association and now Hearst's l[a]bor relations man, conferred [in] Seattle with heads of unions a[f]fected by the strike.

3—Joseph Howard, member [of] the National Labor Relatio[ns] Board, was en route by pla[ne] from Great Falls, Mont., prepar[a]tory to presiding at the hearin[g] of the board's complaint again[st] Hearst, the Post-Intelligencer an[d] affiliated companies in the di[s]missals of Frank (Slim) Lync[h] and Everhardt Armstrong, whic[h] precipitated the strike.

4—The Post-Intelligencer, by i[ts] own admission, remained "in[]definitely suspended." Subscrib[]ers, telephoning to cancel the[ir] subscriptions or to inquire wh[y] the morning paper had not bee[n] delivered to the door, met onl[y] a perpetual busy signal on Mai[n] 2000.

5—The Post-Intelligencer buil[d]ing at a late hour la[st] night, was completely dark an[d] the Sixth Avenue entrance wa[s] boarded up.

6—The picket line around th[e] Post-Intelligencer remained undiminished as scores of sym[]pathizers joined the striking members of the Post-Intelligenc[]er editorial staff.

7—Jonathan Eddy, executive secretary of the America[n] Newspaper Guild, was en route from New York City to Seattl[e] by plane to confer with mem[]bers of the Seattle Newspape[r] Guild.

—BE AMERICAN—

FEDERAL AGENT SPEEDS HERE TO PROBE STRIKE

Labor Relations Man to Study Cause of Dispute

On the first lap of his plane trip to Seattle, Joseph Howard, member of the national labor relations board, is scheduled to arrive here today preparatory to holding a hearing on the board's case against William Randolph Hearst, the Post-Intelligencer and affiliated companies.

Hearst and the Post-Intelligencer are charged in a complaint served on them by the board with dismissing Everhardt Armstrong and Frank ("Slim") Lynch for union activity, such dismissal being in violation of the national labor relations act.

COERCION CHARGED

The complaint sets forth the fact that the Post-Intelligencer is distributed in interstate commerce, thus bringing the unjustified dismissal of its employes within the scope of federal law.

"By their discharge of said Frank Lynch and Everhardt Armstrong," the complaint charges, "the respondents (Hearst and the Post-Intelligencer) have interfered with, restrained and coerced . . . their employes in the exercise of the rights guaranteed in the national labor relations act."

Hearst's agents are ordered to appear at the board's inquiry on

(Continued on Page 2, Col. 3.)

LONGACRES RESULTS

FIRST RACE—5 1-2 furlongs:
Premier Jim, 107 (Adams) 5.30 3.30 3.20
Play Money, 107 (Gray) 3.50 3.40
Glad Star, 104 (Bite) 3.50
Time, 1:07. Mammy's Miss, Restful, Nymel, Merry Day, Miss Willada, Silver Toes also ran.

SECOND RACE—6 furlongs:
Speedy George, 120 (Ellms) 10.70 4.20 3.60
Moonnybrook, 120 (Skeltz) 4.20 3.10
Leland, 105 (Baumgarten) 3.60
Time, 1:12 4-5. Wild Lily, Bonnie Francis, Shortage, Wyoming Daisy, Scout Manners, Awkward, Golden Gulf, Sweet Mayme also ran.

THIRD RACE—1 1-16 miles:
Marco, 104 (Bite) 13.70 4.40 2.40
Inauguration, 109 (Simmons) 2.90 2.10
Slogan, 109 (Josephbin) 2.10
Time, 1:47 2-5. Conquered, Spanish Citizen, Finnegan, Royal Crystal, Electron, Crystal Pier also ran.

FOURTH RACE—5 1-2 furlongs:
Karessa, 113 (Adams) 18.50 5.30 4.20
Ban Red, 116 (Grey) 6.40 4.40
Harlands, 113 (Merritt) 4.20
Ben Hamburg, Sky Bronze, Tom Watch, Gloria G., San Anselmo, Rowdy Andy also ran.

FIFTH RACE—6 furlongs:
Kings, 108 (Baumgarten) 6.30 3.80 3.30
Bank Shot, 108 (Bite) 7.80 4.40
Pasilipo, 107 (Leonard) 3.90
Beau Belmont, Trueback, Ascot, Sadar, Brilliant Gown, Crystal Lake, Blind River, Willie Klein, Pupee also ran.

SIXTH RACE—6 furlongs:
George Bair, 113 (Sinlaff) 7.50 2.70 2.60
Maryon, 113 (Grey) 2.80 2.50
The Trainer, 108 (Bite) 6.50
Laterga, Jane Packard, Lady Edith, Sea Fare, Jose Mac, Dickie Binder, Faftsan, Lord Yale also ran.

SEVENTH RACE—1 mile:
Rustle, 110 (Garrett) 46.90 17.00 6.70
Bleak Girl, 100 (Grey) 15.10 6.10
Lido, 113 (Simmons) 2.70
Time, 1:38 3-5. Wee Drop, High Delight, Elanar, Skeeter Rank, Bee B also ran.

EIGHTH RACE—1 1-4 miles:
Printemps, 110 (Simmons) 18.70 8.50 6.00
Severe Circle, 105 (Litzenberger) 9.50 5.10
Wabamet, 115 (Grey) 3.20
Time, 2:05. Bessy, Peter Russell, Rochester Bay, Chaffery, Credo Bay, Lucinander also ran.
Quinella—$87.50

The Guild Daily to Fill Vacuum in Morning Field

Yesterday . . . "The Guild Striker" . . .

Today . . . "The Guild Daily" . . .

From this day on, as long as William Randolph Hearst fails to give the citizens of Seattle a morning newspaper, the American Newspaper Guild will!

Every day — excluding Sunday — the Guild will publish this newspaper. It is the hope, of course, that it may be enlarged and improved from time to time—that if Hearst "quits," the Guild may carry on.

Such a program came only because the Guild learned how badly Seattle wanted such a publication from its first experience in issuing the "Guild Striker" yesterday . . . a publication which "sold out" its 20,000 copies to a public avid for news! So, today, and every day The Guild Daily!

Boy, Five, Falls 12 Feet While Playing

While playing on the roof of his home, 2005½ 2nd Ave., Ray Burke, five, fell twelve feet and was taken to King County Hospital last evening.

The youngster received a head injury but was reported in good condition. He is the son of Mrs. Betty Burke.

WEATHER FORECAST
For Seattle and Vicinity—Generally fair today and tomorrow; near normal temperature; gentle northwest wind.

The Guild Daily

SEATTLE'S ONLY
MORNING PAPER

Vol. 1, No. 11   WEDNESDAY, AUGUST 26, 1936   Published by Seattle Chapter, American Newspaper Guild   5 CENTS

DAVE BECK SUES TIMES!

5,000 Cheer Attacks On Hearst Policy

Labor Official Asks $250,000 In Libel Action

OVERNIGHT HANDICAPS

Editorials and News Article Cited; Strike Order Is Denied

Dave Beck, widely known Seattle labor official, yesterday sued the Seattle Daily Times for $250,000 for libel, filing him in the course of its attempts to break the *Post-Intelligencer* newspaper strike through editorials and news stories carried in its own columns.

Beck, described by the attorneys daily as a labor "dictator," filed a superior court action based upon a lengthy news story and two editorials, in which the Times attempted to picture him as a labor tyrant holding sway over the Post-Intelligencer strike.

EDITORIAL IS QUOTED

In one editorial quoted to full in the legal complaint, the Times, after allegedly inferring that Beck had usurped the powers of the city government and made the city too socialistic, in which the Times attempts to picture him as a labor tyrant holding sway over the Post-Intelligencer strike...

"Dave Beck and his following comprise a very small fraction of the city's population. But are bandit can hold up a whole roomful of people. How do you like the look of Dave Beck's gun? The union leader's complaint declared the editorial was intended by the Times to lead its readers to believe and did lead them to believe that he, Beck, "had ordered the strike, had established the picket lines, and was responsible for acts of violence, that he was a labor racketeer and radical racketeer, intent upon overthrowing by force, violence and other unlawful means, the authority of the lawfully constituted officials of the city of Seattle, and stifling the constitutional right of free speech and right to do business in only cific..."

CORRUPTION INFERRED

The editorial, Beck further declared, inferred that he was in charge in an unspecified way "to natives that were 'salfish and corrupt,'" that the Post-Intelligencer "had been compelled to suspend publication by his order," and that the suspension of the newspaper would be followed "by other similar acts on his part."

Beck, international representative of the International Brotherhood of Teamsters, Chauffeurs, Stablemen and Helpers of America...

(Continued on Page 2, Col. 2)

DESPONDENT AUBURN MAN ENDS HIS LIFE

Farmer Hangs Self in Garage; Body Discovered by Son

Slipping from the fender of his automobile after he had tied a rope to the garage rafters and slipped a noose about his own neck, Robert Wooding, middle-aged Auburn farmer, committed suicide at his home yesterday, Deputy Coroner Earl Nevin said.

Wooding's body was found by his son, Kenneth, twenty-one, while the latter was searching for his father. The elder Wooding had been missing, then sometime.

According to Nevin, he learned Wooding had been despondent over financial and family trouble. The body was taken to Hart's Mortuary in Auburn.

BANDIT GETS $30 AT GAS STATION

A curly-haired bandit who, at the point of a black pistol, forced R. H. Wiseman, attendant, to lie on the floor while he "looted the till, fled with $30 cash last night from the gasoline service station Wiseman operates at 12th Ave. and E. Cherry St.

Wiseman, who lives at 4298 E. Madison St., said he did not begin whether the holdup man escaped on an automobile or on foot, as he could not see from his prone position. The money was all in silver and currency.

Quest for Death by Gas Proves Failure

Gus Erickson begged "Let me die," when firemen revived him after a suicide-by-gas attempt last night.

His wish to die met an unfulfilled fate attendants at King County Hospital said last night that his condition has shown some improvement and is now "satisfactory."

The elderly man was taken to the hospital from his home, 3627 W. Park Ave. after the unsuccessful quest for death.

She Gets Divorce After Eight Years

After lying "suspended" for eight years, the divorce action filed in 1928 by Mrs. Jennie C. Hatch was carried to a successful conclusion yesterday.

Mrs. Hatch, 2447 W. Passaic, was granted a decree by Superior Judge Roscoe R. Smith from W. Isert J. Hatch, engineer fisherman, who married her at Roche Harbor in 1917.

3 Pedestrians Hit by Autos

Two Laborers Are Taken to Swedish Hospital After Mishap

Three pedestrians were injured by automobiles last night, one of them seriously.

Phil Oliver and Chris Jobb, both aged laborers, were struck down at 8th Ave. and Lenora St. in an automobile driven by Owen W. Roberts, 4224 Dayton Ave. They were taken to Swedish Hospital, where attendants said Oliver was in serious condition from chest and head injuries. Jobb received a compound fracture of the left leg.

Both were taken to the hospital, where officials reported the pair were crossing in the middle of the block.

Dee Wood, 3242 8th Ave. E., was taken to his home after being struck by an automobile driven by Ordin Odwell, 5857 17th Ave. S., who said Odwell stopped in front of his machine, but he was not seriously hurt.

Police Seek Mystery Box Origin

Ballard police last night were checking the origin of an empty cash drawer, found yesterday in the thick woods surrounding Fort Lawton, by John Grant, son of Joseph C. Grant, insurance company general agent, 6125 Bright St.

Grant, seventeen, reported finding the cash box, with the drawer wide open but empty, and turned it over to police. He said it had been placed there during the previous night, as he had not seen it the day before.

The drawer, of steel was three feet long, one-and-one-half feet wide and three inches deep. Police suggested it may have come from some section with a recent burglary.

W. C. F. Will Confer With Candidates

Members of the executive board of the Washington Commonwealth Federation and all candidates backed by WCF and their campaign managers will hold a conference at Federation headquarters, 2925 Union Ave., at 8:30 p. m. Wednesday. Strategy of the campaign and other important matters will be discussed.

Gas Leak Revealed at Eerie Fire

Fire which broke out of the ground about fifty feet from the Seattle Gas Company's storage tank at 13th Ave. S. and Eddy St. last night enabled the firm to locate a leak which has been vexing for the two weeks, Battalion Chief J. A. Stevenor said.

The blaze, while not spectacular, presented an eerie scene as it leaped from the ground in blue versions one foot high, burning over an area of about 100 square feet.

TWO NARROWLY ESCAPE DEATH IN BOAT BLAST

Men Painfully Burned as Fire Sweeps Craft; Lumber Plant Peril

Narrowly escaping a flaming death as an explosion set fire to the twenty-eight-foot cabin cruiser that struck Mid Ballard yesterday, Amos Spalding, twenty-seven, and Arthur Abramsen, thirty, are active, there in Ballard General Hospital last night, painfully but not critically burned.

A third man, Harold Abramsen, escaped injury.

Spalding and Arthur Abramsen saved themselves by leaping overboard.

A large boat shed in which the cruiser was stored was set afire by the explosion and a few moments later the flames spread to a nearby lumber in the Simmon sawmill company's adjoining plant at 2138 Vernon Place.

STUBBORN FIGHT

Firemen under Battalion chief Levi McCombie made a stubborn and successful fight to save the two-story million-dollar prop crafts and the adjoining smoking plant from a possible blaze and firms.

Spalding, who lives at 5127 14th Ave. N. W., had planned a fishing trip with the two Abramsens, who are cousins. He and Arthur went to the engine to start the engine while the third went to cast off the lines of the cruiser which was tied to the dock.

As Harold stepped off onto the other side, the burner started and turned between the cruiser and the lumber shed.

CLOTHES AFLAME

As Harold swung over the dock, he heard a deafening explosion and saw the other two, their clothes flaming, throw themselves overboard. He ran to the road and turned in a fire alarm. Meanwhile, a passing police prowler car crew picked up the burned boys and rushed them to the hospital.

Had the wind blew stronger, Chief McCombie declared, the flames would probably have swept underneath the docks on which large piles of lumber were stored. As it was, firemen were barely able to control the conflagration.

The cruiser was valued at $600, the shed at $3,000 and the contents of the shed at $250.

Accident Victim Is Fighting for Life

With "nothing his own," hospital attendants declared, in a grim race of war between life and death, John P. O'Donnell, twenty-five, 444 18th Ave. S., remained in Providence Hospital last night after accidentally shooting himself with a rifle Sunday while practicing with his rifle at Three Tree Point.

Pawnshop Episode Ends in Jail Cell

Mike Petkoh, sixty, Jugo-Slavian laborer, was being held in city jail on an open charge last night after Detectives Ernest Jewette J and J. R. Little insert, they arrested him in the act of offering to a pawnshop a black and tackle rumored stolen August 17 from McRae Bros., contractors, 614 5th Ave. S.

Speakers At Guild Mass Meeting Denounce P-I's Refusal To Settle Strike

CROWD OUTSIDE HEARS SPEAKERS

While several thousand cheered applauded and sang in Senator Auditorium at last night's affair mass meeting, additional hundreds who were unable to gain admittance held an overflow gathering on the sidewalk on both sides of Union St.

A loud speaker, mounted on the roof of an automobile, carried every word of the speakers from inside the building to the crowds outside. Cheering and bursts of song rose from the overflow meeting in sympathy with the demonstrations inside.

Further audience even included light screen beaming from upper windows of Union St. homes.

Only One in Court on Gambling Charge

Of ten persons haled into police court yesterday following recent gambling raids, one was fined and the rest each forfeited bail.

William McGee, charged with possession of gambling paraphernalia, was fined $25. Harry Larson, charged, forfeited $15, and C Campbell and Bert Randolph, charged with being in a gambling place after they were arrested in the same raid, forfeited $10 each.

Jack Jones forfeited $25, and Mike Cohen, E. Kloene and C Odson forfeited $15 each, all four for possession.

John Alexander and Howard Sipple forfeited $25 on charges of gambling.

Bids on 8 Road Projects Called

Bids on eight highway construction contracts have been called for by L. V. Murrow, Washington State highway director, and will be received at 10 a. m. September 15, in Olympia.

The projects include work on state roads in Spokane, Stevens, Yakima, Skamania, Grays Harbor and Adams Counties, and on city streets in Tacoma and Snohomish.

Milk Price Increase Goes Into Effect

Milk prices in Seattle jumped one cent yesterday to compensate for increased deliveries to producers.

Standard grades sold for 10 cents over their own counter, and 11 cents delivered.

Premium grades were selling at 12 cents to the store, and 13 cents delivered to the door.

The price increases were an attempt to compensate dairymen for the wage gains delivered by the Seattle Milk Dealers Association.

Audience Pledges Aid in Fight for Right to Organize

Five thousand persons declared war on William Randolph Hearst for his attitude toward organized labor last night in a mass meeting at the Senator Auditorium, and at the close of the meeting hundreds congregated outside.

At the conclusion of the meeting, interrupted by frequent applause, the audience rose to its feet and gave a pledge to constitute itself as a citizens committee for the purpose of defending the rights of the Post-Intelligencer strikers.

WILLING TO COMPROMISE

Public officials, including Mayor Dore, and chief spokesmen for the Guild, stressed repeatedly the evidence at hand in the present struggle to show that the latter is a public issue affecting the rights of all labor here.

When Jonathan Eddy, national secretary of the American Newspaper Guild, and Mayor Dore remarked that Hearst might establish or be ejected from this arena by the public taxes, tremendous applause came from the listeners.

Establishment of the citizens committee, which was prosecuted by Howard Costigan of the Washington Commonwealth Federation, came as a reply to the recent resignation in Seattle of the so-called Law and Order League. The speakers variously had portrayed the peril of the Law and Order group, manifestly inspired by special interests. It totally, they pointed out, were directly in "breaking the law and destroying the order" of the city.

DORE BRINGS APPLAUSE

Mayor Dore produced a roar of assent that lasted several seconds when he said:

"If Hearst brings any gunmen to club down and gas bomb the workers of this town we'll give them a reception that will—"

His words were drowned at this point by applause, and he continued after a pause—"We'll stop them in their tracks."

He went on to say that the police department would protect the city from violence.

Eddy, appearing as the first chief speaker, was first to suggest the idea that Hearst might announce in three days that he would leave the city flat.

The audience broke up this remark with a prolonged expression of approval.

"Wait a minute," Eddy about...

Church's Clothing Not Safe---Even in Church!

Carl V. Church, 5847 Woodland Park Ave., found yesterday that his clothing wasn't safe from thieves, even in a church auditorium. He reported to police yesterday afternoon that while he was painting afternoon that while he was painting at the rear of a church at 14th Ave. and E. Union St., his coat, the visitor, of black sealskin, contained 27 cash, painters' union card, driving license, liquor permit and an automobile certificate of ownership.

'Cop' Had a Badge and a Siren, But Not a Ticket!

A man who stopped a motorist, flashed a badge, threatened to give him a ticket for speeding and then left without giving the ticket was prowling a puzzle to police last night.

There to a stop. When the man threatened to make out the ticket but later, then asked for it. The man, who was not in uniform, left the car driving a car bearing Illinois license plates.

Police believe the man was a bluffing civilian without police credentials.

Portland Wins Over Seattle in Series Opener.....See Sports Page

WEATHER FORECAST
for Seattle and Vicinity—Fair today and Thursday; somewhat warmer; gentle to moderate winds, mostly northerly.

The Guild Daily EXTRA!

l. 1, No. 29   5 CENTS   WEDNESDAY, SEPTEMBER 16, 1936   Published by Seattle Chapter, American Newspaper Guild

HEARST QUITS

Curley Far Ahead In Massachusetts

New Dealer Leads Wisconsin Senatorial Vote

(Special to the Guild Daily)
Boston, Mass. Sept. 15.—Governor James M. Curley is leading his competitors opponent, Mayor Robert G. Greenwood of Pittsburg, in the race for the Democratic nomination for senator in the Massachusetts primary.

Curley, while campaigning as a Democrat, is not considered close with the White House. He is indorsed by the Republican Labor, he is disliked by pro-labor trade unionists because indorsed Italian Fascism and he indorsed Senator William Curley. For almost half of Milwaukee County the lead was 7,200.

The state Republican vote was heavier, two candidates polling 39,000 to 29,000 for two Democratic candidates. Progressive governor Phillip LaFollette totaled 35,000 without opposition. The straight ticket rule was believed to be taking some Farmer-Labor progressive Federation votes in other columns temporarily on local nomination contests, giving LaFollette prospects of topping the organization at November.

Labor's concerted drive to return gave the indication a roll-out vote confined opposition in four districts, a bar in three and a good showing in one.

ABOUT IN MAINE TONIGHT

A recount loomed tonight in the election with Gov. Louis H.J. conservative Democrat to the 1,500 votes behind Republican Senator Wallace White Jr. the voting reveals a strong inward restoration of prestige which is traditionally dry for the Republican slate.

Massachusetts liberals today are boiling over the indorsement in Boston Massachusetts Central Labor group of Governor Landon. Pres.

Coast Guard to Help Drag for Body

The coast guard will join the navy today for the body of John J. Jenkin Beach, lo estate who died when his lease made the overturned during in Lake Moulton. Lewis harbor patrolmen recovered yesterday.

Re harbor patrol dragged for Monday and yesterday, but the effort to recover the lost sailor had rightened the boat and was drowning after a paddle which had swung away.

The Shirley Point, Portland, with York, was served by a naval master setting.

Central Labor Group Indorses Democrats

The political welfare committee of the Seattle Central Labor Council last night unanimously adopted motion to recommend the endorsement of the state and active candidates of the Democratic Party this council when it meets to ratify the action.

In taking this position building Filip the general convention of the state convention of the Washington State Federation of Labor, meeting this week, also indorsed Gov. Clarence D. Martin and Lieut. Gov. Victor A. Meyers for reelection.

Indorsements of candidates are as follows: First District, Warren G. Magnuson; Second District, Mon C. Wallgren; Third District, Martin F. Smith; Fourth District, Knute Hill; Fifth District, Judge Charles H. Leavy; Sixth District, John M. Coffee.

Members of the executive board were instructed to urge members of the council to act as representatives as to be best in note, as the final is strengthened recommended on session of the majority of Washington, meeting final.

The committee also voted to ask temporary candidates to with the state the political move and various council positions to direct every recommendation and political endorsement building Franklin the.

(Continued on Page 2, Col 8)

STRIKERS TURN DOWN HEARST ULTIMATUM

8-Point Memorandum Seen as Call for Abject Surrender

Two events which served as prelude last night to the Hearst swan song wherein it was declared the Post-Intelligencer was through forever, were first an ultimatum from the P.-I. to the strikers, and second, an memorandum which could not be complied with.

The Guild unit, served with the Hearst ultimatum to settle on the P.-I.'s own terms, rejected the terms by overwhelming vote. There were only two dissenting ballots.

The ultimatum stipulated two chief requirements and six other points of agreement, all of which resolved themselves into a demand for abject surrender, strikers said. Plainly, the strikers were invited to return to work without management, reading Guild as accept as to mean "be picked but of also."

TO RETURN AS INDIVIDUALS

The third point was a P.-I. agreement to take back all strikers at the same rate of pay as heretofore prevailed. The fourth point stipulated that the strikers were to apply to their former superiors as individuals for reinstatement.

All these and the four unnecessitating points were conveyed informally to the assembled Guildsmen by J. M. Lemmon, president of the Typographical Union of Seattle. Lemmon read the formula from notes which he described as a memorandum which could not be reduced to contractual form and which the P.-I. would not sign.

Lemmon had a solemn air as he reached this point to speak relatively of the delicacy he had in hand.

HE URGED ACCEPTANCE

At the conclusion of his thought he reminded the Guildsmen that he remarked:

"I urge acceptance of this proposal. I feel that it is a final offer.

"They told me, that in the event of a rejection of these terms they would immediately remove every new linotype machine, and thereafter as rapidly as possible they would dismantle the plant. It sounded to me as if they meant it to Post-Intelligencer would be junked."

It became known as answers flowed back and forth that the ultimatum, the first to come from the publishers, was a culmination of two weeks' effort at mediation by Litardo and several LaFollette professional and associates of the printing trades. They dealt with Harvey J. Kelly, Hearst employment director, and Al Williams, general manager.

NO MILWAUKEE CONCESSION

"What about the Milwaukee agreement?" Guildsmen asked over and over, during some of the previous brief working conditions and wages had just recently been granted to Hearst to striking editorial workers in Milwaukee. They were shocked to know that one new line of contract concession had been mentioned or implied in the "double measure" offer that. Litardo shook his head in reply.

"I understand the Milwaukee plan," he said. "But they will not apply that plan here."

In addition to the four essential points that resolved themselves into a demand for the instatement of the striker who were proceeding from fear the entire plant wise proceeding from Litardo and a Federal Labor Council mandate which strongly declared the paper could never be regarded labor.

Non-Guild staff members approved the action

(Continued on Page 2, Col. 7)

EXIT MR. HEARST

[Editorial]

Hearst, vanquished by the might of organized labor and aroused public opinion, has fled the Seattle newspaper field!

Or has he?

In any event, this morning's announcement that the Post-Intelligencer plant is to be dismantled will wring no sighs from enlightened citizens who have long felt the need in Seattle of journalism of a more dignified and trustworthy type than any Hearst paper has ever offered.

In his fight to crush the local chapter of the American Newspaper Guild, the arrogant millionaire publisher challenged not only the forces of organized labor. He challenged every principle of fair play that Americans cherish. The determination of editors and reporters on the Post-Intelligencer to form a union evoked a campaign of economic terrorism culminating in the dismissal of two veteran employees for union activity. All attempts at negotiation with the union management failing, a strike was called—a strike that has silenced the voice of Hearst in Seattle, apparently, forever.

Nor will that snarling, scurrilous voice be missed. Seattle will not be left without a morning newspaper. Employment will be found for the 450 Post-Intelligencer workers, even whom no many crocodile tears were shed in frenzied radio broadcasts directed against the Guild. Already 113 persons, all enthusiastic over their new jobs, are employed in producing and distributing the Guild Daily and as that paper grows that number will rapidly increase.

There is a place in Seattle for a brightly written and sanely edited morning newspaper—a newspaper in which accuracy is not sacrificed to crude sensationalism; a newspaper that does not insult its readers day after day with rabid "policy" editorials and special articles that crowd legitimate news from its columns.

The staff we have to produce such a paper and we believe that Seattle will furnish the good will without which no publishing venture can ever flourish.

A new and fairer day is dawning.

Adieu, Mr. Hearst!

History of Strike

Climaxing with dramatic suddenness the month-old strike of the Seattle Guild, which new effort for unionization thrust aside by the P.-I. management, the latter last night announced permanent suspension.

The P.-I. strike had its inception in the abrupt and arbitrary action of the management in firing, first, Frank O'Bryan's Lynch and a few days later, Philip Eberhardt Armstrong, head photographer and drama critic, respectively.

The P.-I. held it had fired Lynch for inefficiency and Armstrong for insubordination. The Seattle Chapter of the American Newspaper Guild maintained they were discharged for Guild activity.

The firing of the two men took place shortly after the management learned of their work in behalf of the Guild. The Guild itself had been organized in May.

EMERGENCY MEETINGS

Lynch was fired on July 4. However, a few days after Oliver Morris, city editor, had learned of Lynch's Guild connection, Lynch was demoted from his managership and a recent 15 weeks pay increase was taken away. In the interim, before Lynch's firing, three non-Guild photographers had been imported from the Hearst Los Angeles Examiner.

Armstrong was next to go, and was let out July 14, eight days after Lynch.

Emergency meetings of the Guild were called after each dismissal. On July 14, the day after Armstrong's dismissal, a vote was taken authorizing the calling of a strike "when such action became necessary to settle the difficulty."

PEACE OFFERS IGNORED

The National Labor Relations Board was appealed to, and that body called a hearing to charge the P.-I. with unfair practices. Despite peace offers from the Guild, the P.-I. management continued to attempt to intimidate non-Guild members, and to destroy the union.

Finding itself against a stonewall of publisher opposition, the Guild called the strike on August 11, simultaneous with a Central Labor Council mandate that union mouths declared the paper could never be regarded labor.

Non-Guild staff members approved the action

(Continued on Page 2, Col 7)

Whaler Aground in Aleutians

The steam whaler Westpoint ran aground on the rocks at Reef Bight near Akutan Island in the Aleutian late Monday night, according to word received by coast guard officials last night.

The message sent by Commander R. W. Dempsey of the Bering Sea Patrol stated that the entire fleet, or was proceeding from Unalaska to the rescue.

Word of the ship's plight was brought to civilization by two members of the crew who walked twenty-five miles, the length of Akutan Island, to seek aid. The Westpoint's master and the remainder of the crew remained aboard, but the ship could not be refloated

P.-I. to Be Dismantled; Publisher Announces Permanent Suspension

SEVERAL GROUPS IN FIELD FOR SEATTLE PAPER

Various Coast and Eastern Interests Look Over Situation

A rush to enter the morning newspaper field left vacant by the permanent suspension of the Post-Intelligencer was seen early this morning, when it was learned that a half dozen different groups are considering the establishment of a new morning newspaper.

Local interests assure to the San Francisco office are said to be covered by three million dollars in a power and a large interest here and have to contemplating publication of a morning paper.

In addition, several Eastern groups have had their agents here to size up the situation. A first tried group has also been involved. As early as the first day of the Newspaper Guild strike on August 11, when the Post-Intelligencer suspended temporarily, several interests began plans to move into Seattle if and when the newspaper became permanent.

SPURS PLANS

Most complete of all the plans were those of Paul Richard C. Tyler and associates. Tyler declared last night that his group saw no aim to publish within forty-eight hours. Harvey O'Connor, brought from the East to edit the new paper, is now on the Atlantic Seaboard. Isitor as financed for the venture.

"The"action of the P.-I. management will pave the way for the publication of a permanent paper," Tyler said last night. Tyler declared that the new paper already has United Press service, and is practically ready to commence publication.

Maj. Archie F. Logan, president of Col. J. H. Brown, publisher of the Seattle Times, declared last night to any member of not the Times staff enter the morning field.

The American—

HULL GOES TO SAN FRANCISCO

Morgan Hull, international manager for the American Newspaper Guild left nearly by plane for San Francisco to attend financial aid for striking members of the Post-Intelligencer Guild unit.

Hull has been in Seattle for the past week, having come here a day or two after the departure for Kiwi of Jonathan Eddy, Guild international executive secretary. The purpose of both men here was to aid in bringing about morale change to end the strike.

Hull will remain in San Francisco for some time, planning a return to Seattle to resume efforts to settle the strike.

(Continued on Page 2, Col 7)

GUILDSMEN REJECT SURRENDER DEMAND

(Especially to the Guild Daily)

The Seattle Post-Intelligencer last night announced permanent suspension of publication.

Linotype machines and other mechanical equipment will be moved out of the P.-I. Building this morning. The plant is to be dismantled.

Local Hearst executives who have contracts probably will leave Seattle and accept positions on other newspapers in the Hearst chain.

Two startling disclosures were made to the Guild Daily last evening by Charles B. Lindeman, associate publisher of the Post-Intelligencer.

The announcement of Hearst's surrender in the face of united stand by union labor for fair treatment of striking Post-Intelligencer Guildsmen was made after the strikers had rejected what they termed "an unacceptable peace ultimatum."

The ultimatum came through J. M. Litonius, president of the Seattle Typographical Union, who urged its acceptance even though the Post-Intelligencer refused Guild recognition.

Litonius headed an Allied Printing Trades committee which was authorized by the P.-I. to make the proposal.

First hint of the P.-I.'s intention to quit came from Litonius. In urging acceptance, Litonius declared the P.-I. management had said Hearst would abandon his Seattle paper the Guild didn't vote favorably.

The Post-Intelligencer unit of the Guild turned down the ultimatum by an almost unanimous vote. Twenty lone men, or the unit were present when the vote was taken. It served ballots, and twenty-two voted against it. Eight other members were absent, the majority being out of the city.

The Post-Intelligencer offered to take the strikers back under the following conditions:

1—That the Guild call off the strike.

2—That pickets be removed from the Post-Intelligencer plant at 6th and Pine St.

3—That strikers accept positions on the paper at the same rate of pay as prevailed when the strike was called.

4—That the strikers apply for their jobs individually.

5—That they accept the word of the Post-Intelligencer that there would be no discrimination.

6—That a statement be issued by the Post-Intelligencer that the new newspaper would be acceptable to both parties.

7—That all conditions on the newspaper remain the same before the strike.

8—That the management will hire and fire at its discretion.

The management refused to recognize the Guild and refused in even consider the cases of Everhardt Armstrong, dramatic critic, and Frank Lynch, photographer, discharged from the paper for Guild activity.

A national labor relations board hearing on the Lynch and Armstrong cases is now in progress in Seattle, but the P.-I. has not agreed to abide by the board's decision.

Lindeman was asked explicitly last evening if the Post-Intelligencer would abide by the decision of the board.

He said:

"I can't say for certain, but I imagine we will appeal the case. It seems to be going in your favor."

In view of previous refusals of the management to let the board decide, Lindeman's statement was construed by Guild officers as another cleverly worded refusal to arbitrate either the two.

The P.-I. unit of the Guild went on strike after even reasonable attempt had been made to gain recognition under fear of discrimination and intimidation. Besides the reinstatement of Lynch and Armstrong, the Guild is seeking recognition and the right to collectively bargain for better hours and working conditions.

The Post-Intelligencer had in its propaganda and product of ideas from the Hearst press on first the American Newspaper Guild upon unionism appeared last night, when the door of the paper.

"We are closing by because we can't stand the gaff, and we want you to know we never were more union," he declared.

The P.-I. was again paying his former 24,000 and 9,000 a week he last 12 day pay tend... to the beginning of the strike. and we don't stand it he should "about it

"Until such time as the Post-Intelligencer not only liberally but actively dismantles its plant, fully actively prints with be able to believe even the latest announcement, one of the striking

(Continued on Page 2, Col 7)

Snoqualmie Forest Opened to Campers

Opening of closed areas in the Snoqualmie National Forest to camping by permit has been announced by A. N. Heine Forest Service.

The Guild Daily

FRIDAY, SEPTEMBER 25, 1936

5 CENTS

Seattle's Only Morning Newspaper in General Circulation

Published by Seattle Chapter, American Newspaper Guild

VIGILANTE CALL REVEALED!

Here's Facsimile of Fascist Summons to Arms

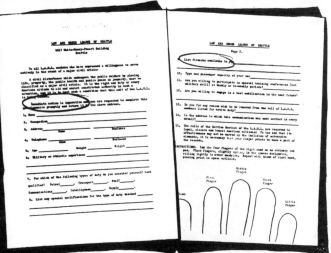

It CAN Happen Here—Above is a reproduction of the questionnaire sent out by the Law and Order League in its efforts to raise an anti-labor army in Seattle. Armed minute-men of John must, hourly mobilized will roll through Seattle streets at the league's bidding

if the plan goes through.

Blood will flow in Seattle unless this anti-social movement by a group of self-constituted community saviours is stopped.

While the call to arms goes out, a group of bankers and industrialists who give the movement its impetus are sitting smugly by.

They will not be at the front if bullets fly. It will not be the Fascist bankers who stagger backward, choking and with streaming eyes as the gas bombs are hurled.

Law and Order League Musters Armed Recruits

Virtual Army Is Planned by Bankers and Industrialists of City

Seattle's vigilantes are arming!

Today the Guild Daily presents on this page exclusively a reproduction of the call to arms as issued by the Law and Order League of Seattle from its headquarters at 5517 White-Henry-Stuart Building.

"List firearms available to you," is one of the vital queries in the league's questionnaire to actual and prospective vigilantes.

"Immediate action is imperative," says another sentence.

A "civil disturbance" also is predicted.

Former Ku Kluxers, Silver Shirts, Black Legionnaires and a host of hotheads may be expected to rally to the call.

SHADOW OF FASCISM

Just why the bankers and industrialists who constitute the Law and Order League want to raise an army is the question puzzling sober Seattleites.

That the Post Intelligencer strike and the potential difficulties on the waterfront are the reason most generally assigned.

Fascism is abroad in Seattle as indicated by the league's summons observers declared yesterday. The rise of Hitler in Germany at its inception did not have a more promising start that that accorded by the Law and Order League from its extensive and well organized headquarters.

MILITARY PHASES

Students of military organizations were quick to note yesterday numerous phases in the questionnaire which point to the raising of a virtual army.

An intelligence service, transport, communications and supply units all are provided for in the form of questionnaires.

Fingerprinting of all armed men in the Law and Order League's army was pointed to as a typical fascist or nazi method.

COUNCIL WILL DISCUSS BUDGET OF PARK BOARD

Fortified with a detailed recommendation for spending $400,000 for the park department in 1937, the city council this morning will meet with the park board, which largely compiled the budget, to iron out the various controversial elements. The budget calls for $400,185.10 for 1937 to $600,000 in all efforts to decrease the deficit which is still lacks the city next door.

The detailed recommendation sent from the council battery and grounds committee, composed of Councilmen Mrs. F. F. Powell, chairman, and Councilmen David L. Lockwood and James Scavotto.

Besides providing for augmented salary increases for city employes, the expenditure plan allows for substantial sums for improvements at the following parks and playfields:

West seattle golf course, $30,000; Cascade playfield, $5,000; Madrona Park, $5,000; Pritchard Beach, $6,000; Broadway playfield, $15,000; Madison Beach, $8,000; Van Asselt playground, $2,000; Colman play ground, $2,000, and Highland Park playground, $2,000.

The council, which did not wish to be deemed responsible for curtailment of these services, ordered the barbers and grounds committee to prepare the advisory estimate. The council cast devastating total amount to be spent by the board but has not supplied needed work of repairs or the expenditures, committee declared.

Heavy criticism of the board's action in eliminating certain specific improvements because it did not provide a higher yearly rate the size of the $173,123.26 allowance in 1936 was voiced yesterday before the council by J. D. Stanger, president of a local interest guild who is really sincere out in need of improvements to Broadway play field, which is located in a district that has a bar rate of dollar money among taxes to share of work in the cities are known to be prime Judge William G. Long.

PUYALLUP FAIR DRAWS RECORD SEATTLE CROWD

Thousands of Seattleites flocked to the Western Washington Fair at Puyallup yesterday in an attempt to set a new all-time attendance record. The day before Tuesday had given them a mark in short of a 40,000 paced through the turnstiles on Tuesday.

With Marion McKenzie leading the procession more than two hundred automobiles left here in a state auto caravan. Over one thousand Seattleites were in the procession.

SEATTLEITES WIN PRIZES

To date, several Seattleites have won prizes at the fair. Among them are Jacob Kludin, first, and G. H. Anderson, second, in the professional division of the art department; Anna R. Bedebe, professional color miniature edit; Edgar Shrieber, first, and Vera Drake, second conservative color salon, Fifth and Vincent Gilbert, third, moderated water colors; Stanley Pratt, University of Washington student, took a sculpture award

Injuries... 2 Boys

County's traffic toll for year rose to 115 last night the deaths of eleven-year-old Oliver of Mount Tolmie, as of Harry moter, and Warner, four.

Oliver boy was injured at 4th and Dr. B. September, a collision between his and his car and one driven by C. Black, Vancouver, B. C.

Late News FLASHES

TRAIN INJURES MAN
Trying to jump from a moving freight car today, Robert Burns, twenty-five, 311 Washington St., caught his foot in a metal brace and was dragged head downward along the ground for some distance before trainmen saw him. He was taken to King County Hospital with a back injury which hospital attendants said was not serious.

The accident occurred at 2nd Ave. S. and Holgate St. as the freight car was being switched.

LEAGUE SPURNED
ROME, Italy, Sept. 24.—Premier Benito Mussolini today declared that Italy would remain out of the League of Nations so long as the league persisted in recognizing Ethiopia as a sovereign nation, which, he says, does not exist.

MERRIAM TO AID
SACRAMENTO, Calif., Sept. 24 —Referring to the Salinas lettuce strike, Governor Merriam today expressed confidence his program for the settlement of the labor trouble would be accepted. He said he would submit his proposal to both sides tomorrow morning.

ADVISOR INSTALLED
Miss Freda Shepherd of Queen Anne High School will be installed as worthy advisor of the Queen Anne Temple at 1 o'clock tonight.

Marine Unions Refute Employer Statements

SAN FRANCISCO, Sept. 24—The Chamber of Commerce today sent an appeal to President Roosevelt asking him to intervene in the threatened maritime tieup and avert a possible repetition of the 1934 disorders. The present agreement between the waterfront employers and employes expires September 30, and all efforts to continue the agreement in force until through that the Maritime Federation of the Pacific.

"We are now operating under a set of conditions for which many of our brothers died in 1934 and, we are not going to abandon them for the last conditions that existed prior to the peace," Matt Meehan, district secretary, stated last night in making clear the position of the longshoremen.

"The hiring hall has already been declared and negotiated," Meehan said, "and there is no reason for further discussion of that issue."

As far control of the hiring hall by a so-called neutral board Meehan declared that it was merely an attempt to operate from the "old black list."

Meehan charged that the employers had been preparing for a lockout ever since the 1934 settlement and that a transport tax had even been levied against shippers for the purpose of building up an armed fund.

(Continued on Page 2, Col 1)

LEGION FAVORS CAPITAL DRAFT FOR WAR TIME

CLEVELAND, Sept. 24—(Guild Wire)—The universal service act providing for the drafting of capital and industry as well as men in the event of war was approved in a resolution by delegates to the American Legion's eighteenth annual convention. Another resolution adopted was one calling for neutrality in world affairs.

By unanimous acclaim, Harry Ualbert, Topeka, Kan., was elected national commander. Following the election, the convention adjourned, until New York in convention city for 1937.

CONFIDENCE IN PERSHING

The delegates gave a vote of confidence to Gen. John J. Pershing's World War policies to a extent to David Lloyd George's recent criticism of the American war strategy and command.

Five national vice commanders were also elected. They are Fred Johnson, Alabama; Belvedere Chandler, California; Leonard Fink, Tennessee; Leo Trainor, South Dakota, and Jack Crocker, Vermont.

Harry Ransom, Milwaukee, was elected grand chief of the 40 and 8 in replace Fred H. Parker, detroit, Washington state editor and retiring grand chief.

Mrs. Lavern Stoltz, Wayne, Neb., was elected national president of the Legion auxiliary.

Petitions Ask Strike End

Petitions calling on William Randolph Hearst and the management of the Seattle Post-Intelligencer to recognize the Seattle chapter of the American Newspaper Guild and make a closed-shop with the striking editorial employes of the newspaper will be placed in circulation today by the Seattle Citizens' Committee.

Thousands of names, it is believed, will be readily obtained to the petitions. The petition sheets, with spaces for the names and addresses of signers, read:

"To William Randolph Hearst and the management of the Post-Intelligencer:

"We, the undersigned citizens of the state of Washington, request you of the many positions taken and published in the Hearst papers in favor of Americanism, the guaranteeing of the American workers in their strike against your paper and urge that you reinstate the editorial employes which your employes on strike to the point that you gain collectively to order to win and maintain decent working conditions and an American standard of living."

ROOSEVELT SWEEPS U.S.

The Guild Daily EXTRA!

WEATHER FORECAST
For Seattle and vicinity: Mostly cloudy today and Thursday; little change in temperature; gentle to moderate south to east winds.

4, No. 71   PRICE 5 CENTS   WEDNESDAY, NOVEMBER 4, 1936   Published by Seattle Chapter, American Newspaper Guild

MARTIN AND MAGNUSON WINNERS

Atwood and Showalter in Close Race

Wand Hartley Snowed Under By Incumbent

-Supported Candidate Trounced

Magnuson Far Out in Front

Young Prosecutor Leading Over Wettrick

SCHOOL POST LEAD ENJOYED BY DEMOCRAT

Republican Incumbent Trailing by 5,000 in County

He's Still at Helm

FRANKLIN DELANO ROOSEVELT

CONGRATULATIONS MR. PRESIDENT

(An Open Letter)

Hon. Franklin D. Roosevelt,
President of the United States,
The White House,
Washington, D.C.

Dear Mr. President:

President Reelected By Greatest Electoral and Popular Vote in History

Landon Carries Only Three States; G. O. P. Candidates Wire Congratulations to Victor

STATE RESULTS

President Franklin D. Roosevelt was reelected yesterday by the greatest electoral and popular vote in the history of the nation.

Citizens Voted According to Conscience, Says Hamilton

Labor Showed Its Strength, Lewis, C. I. O. Head, Says

Roosevelt Piling Up Lead of 2 to 1 in All 48 States

Knox Wires Congratulations to Franklin D. on Reelection

Landon Congratulates Roosevelt on His Victory

Lehmann Reelected to New York Governorship for Third Time

Landon, Like Taft, Retires by Consent of All the Nation

Guild Daily Asks Hearst What He Thinks of It All

WEATHER FORECAST

The Guild Daily EXTRA

L. No. 81   **PRICE 5 CENTS**   **MONDAY, NOVEMBER 16, 1936**   Published by Seattle Chapter, American Newspaper Guild

A. F. OF L. WASHES HANDS OF P-I
FOR BREAKING STRIKE AGREEMENT

TOM SMITH NAMED W.C.F. PRESIDENT

Two-Day Session Closes After Adopting Comprehensive Legislative Reform Program

Tom Smith, county commissioner of the North End, was unanimously elected president of the Washington Commonwealth Federation at its convention yesterday.

The sessions, which opened Saturday, were attended by 648 delegates and approximately 300 visitors.

John Fox was elected first vice president, Dean Richard G. second vice president, and J. Gunther, third vice president.

A ringing progressive program drawn up by the convention, supporting labor's rights benefiting the farmers of the state, was smashed through by immense vote.

Other items were included in the platform, and all were greeted a hearty applause. No liberal-saving plank was omitted, everything from a plank for public ownership of public utilities to a smashing attack on the unjustified powers of the supreme court of the nation was met with the delegates' approval.

NO DEBATE

The shortened sessions of the convention came over the proposal to reduce the slogan "production" over the platform. A decision which lasted for fifty-three minutes ended with the delegates voting to omit it from the platform.

Howard Costigan, executive secretary, said he favored dropping the slogan and adopting instead the clear-cut, definite program which could not be distorted. The delegates, by a large majority, supported his contention when the issue was put to a vote.

A resolution asking the removal of William H. Cole, director of the state highway patrol, for his part in the McCleary terrorism, was passed.

Another resolution requesting the investigation of the Silver Shirt camps in this state by the sheriffs and other authorities was approved.

The following planks composed the platform adopted by the convention:

1. Public ownership of all natural resources, public utilities, banks and monopolies.
2. Protection of civil rights to workers.
3. Rights of labor to bargain collectively and to picket; repeal of the criminal syndicalism act.
4. Union wages in private and public employment and abolition of child labor.
5. Protection of farmers from the

(Continued on Page 2, Col. 4.)

YEGGS CARRY OFF SAFE WITH $9,000 IN CASH

Burglars Saw Through Iron Bars of State Liquor Store

Sawing their way through iron bars into the University District State Liquor Store, Seattle's daring safe-cracking gang early yesterday morning carried away the store's heavy safe filled with nearly $9,000 in week-end receipts.

After breaking through the iron-grilled windows, the yeggmen entered the store, located at 4605 Roosevelt Way, several hours after E. W. Nelson, store manager, had finished counting one of the largest week-end receipts of the year.

THEY CLIMB LADDER

Detective Lieuts. Richard F. Mahoney and George McKnne said the gang climbed up a fourteen-foot ladder to the second floor of the building. They sawed the iron bars that guarded the window and then broke the glass. The yeggmen then went down a stairs and found the safe.

Lugging the safe several yards, they got it to the back door of the liquor store. The yeggs then took a crowbar and broke down the heavily bolted back door.

The safe weighed 400 pounds. It was believed the gang backed a truck to the rear door and lugged the safe into it.

LARGE DAY'S BUSINESS

The burglary was discovered by Nelson when he came to the store yesterday morning to finish up some work. Nelson said because of the homecoming game Saturday the store did one of its largest day's business in history. He said at some time during the day the people were lined up outside of the store waiting to get service.

According to Detective Lieut. Mahoney, this is the largest "job" pulled since the Cairo and Shaw safer ckling when a gang which was later captured, got away with $25,000.

It was the same time last year that the safer cking operations in Seattle began. So far, the general yeggs have failed to meet all their attempts, detectives said.

P-I'S ACTION AMAZES LABOR BOARD OFFICIAL

Regional Director Recalls Moment When Pact Was Reached

Expressing surprise at Hearst's legal counsel, Harvey J. Kelly's repudiation of the agreement made with the local chapter of the American Newspaper Guild, Charles W. Hope, regional director of the National Labor Relations Board, said last night he would continue use of his offices to bring about a mutually agreeable settlement between the Post-Intelligencer and the Guild.

It was obvious Hope that the agreement which was later repudiated by the P-I was made possible. Hope first conferred with E. B. Fish, labor relations manager for the P-I, and later at Fish's request—called Dave Beck, Teamsters' Union head, into the negotiations, he said.

E. J. Eagan, attorney for the board, said last night that he didn't see any reason why an immediate settlement could not be reached.

"I hope negotiations between the P-I and the Guild can be started at once," Eagan said.

Furniture Firm Swept by Fire

Fire starting from an explosion in a paint storeroom caused $25,000 damage to the plant of the Sound Furniture Manufacturing Company, 1815 N. 34th St., Saturday night in a spectacular "two-eleven" blaze which attracted a crowd of nearly 2,000 from the North End.

Firemen under the personal command of Fire Chief Claude W. Corning battled the stubborn flames in the one-story building for nearly an hour.

Lives of three firemen, fighting the blaze in the basement at the rear of the building, were endangered when the roof of the structure appeared ready to collapse. They were ordered out by Battalion Chief O. H. Ebbinghouse a moment before the walls fell.

Guild Recognition Was Involved in Pact

The now-repudiated agreement between the Seattle Post-Intelligencer and The Guild included direct recognition of the Guild, bargaining with its representatives, and arbitration, it was revealed yesterday when the American Federation of Labor executive council "washed its hands" of the Seattle Guild strike situation.

The agreement, negotiated by E. B. Fish, labor relations manager for the P-I, was to "interpretation" of the American Federation of Labor executive council president—with Dave Beck, Teamsters' Union head, being the actual which repudiated its own agreements.

The interpretation was to have been signed by Fish for the Post-Intelligencer and H. Richard Seller, local Guild president, for the Seattle Central Labor Council.

TEXT OF AGREEMENT

The repudiated agreement read:

"Preliminary to, and as a condition of acceptance of the recommendations of the executive council of the American Federation of Labor for authority to settle the dispute between the striking editorial employes of the Seattle Post-Intelligencer and the management of said paper, the following interpretation of the executive council proposals are agreed to:

1—It is agreed and understood that the following men, namely: Cliffe Erickson, H. Richard Seller, John Wrose, Leo Pambo, Jack Hesse and Forrest Williams, who constitute the executive committee of the Seattle Chapter of the American Newspaper Guild, shall be the official negotiating committee appointed by the Seattle Central Labor Council in all conferences with the Post-Intelligencer for the purpose of reaching an agreement between the management and its reinstated employes.

AN ARBITRATION SUBJECT

2—That in the instance of the national labor relations board or the courts ruling that they have no jurisdiction in the cases of Frank Lynch and Everhardt Armstrong or in the instance of the Wagner Labor Relations Act being ruled unconstitutional, these cases shall be a subject matter of arbitration in accordance with the machinery recommended by Dave Beck and concurred in by American Federation of Labor executive council.

3—It is further agreed that there will be no objection to the employment of non-union persons who may have worked for the P-I previously, provided any of them desire to continue to work after the matter has been presented to the Guild.

SELLER NOT SURPRISED AT REPUDIATION

Trickery Feared in All P-I Dealings, Says Guild President

The Post-Intelligencer's action in repudiating a agreement they had already entered into with the Guild was characterized last night by H. Richard Seller, local Guild president, as "no more than could be expected."

"They've done everything possible to break the Seattle strike and haven't made one honest attempt to settle it. We have always feared trickery on their part, and the fact that the latest trickery wasn't successful is only starting thing," Seller declared.

"We were pleased with the agreement," he continued, "and naturally something that pleased us was bound to displease the P-I. The agreement didn't contain everything we said contained sufficient to spell victory for the Guild."

Under the repudiated agreement, strikers would have returned to work "without discrimination or prejudice" while a Guild committee negotiated with the management over hours, wages and working conditions for a period of forty days, Seller pointed out.

POINTED TO RECOGNITION

"The committee was to have been the executive committee of the Guild, and as such meant direct recognition of the union," Seller pointed out.

Should the committee fail to reach an agreement with the management within forty days, the dispute was to be submitted to arbitration.

Dave Beck, Seattle teaming head, was selected by the Post-Intelligencer, under the agreement, to recommend the arbitration procedure. His recommendations were to have been acted upon by the A. F. of L. executive council yesterday—but the Post-Intelligencer's repudiation nullified action by them unnecessary.

RIGHT TO JOIN GUILD

Their cases were left with the National Labor Relations Board, which will decide whether or not they should be reinstated. However, should the board or the courts decide that the board had no jurisdiction or the Wagner act was unconstitutional, their cases would be referred back to Seattle for arbitration.

"This means but one thing," Seller declared, "and that is eventual reinstatement of the two men. Only legal technicalities could prevent it. If the courts, but under the agreement they haven't the protection of such technicalities."

The P-I, further agreed, under the repudiated plan, that any employe of the newspaper had a right to join the Guild if he so desired.

Other points of the agreement simply "made certain," Seller said, that all strikers sent back to work when the paper reopened.

(Continued on Page 2, Col. 6)

Publisher's Aid Calls Off Previous Offer

Harvey J. Kelly Talked for Hour to Tampa Group; Claims Hearst Negotiator Exceeded Power

TAMPA, Fla., Nov. 15.—(GWS)—The American Federation of Labor executive council tonight "washed its hands" of the Seattle Post-Intelligencer strike after the Hearst management announced repudiation of a strike-settlement agreement.

The agreement was entered into in Seattle last Wednesday and awaited action of the executive council simply as a gesture of confirmation.

However, when the confirmation was sought of the council today, Harvey J. Kelly, Hearst labor relations head, repudiated the agreement, declaring that the Seattle negotiator who completed the settlement for the Post-Intelligencer exceeded his authority.

Council Decides to Step Out of Seattle Situation

Hearing Kelly for more than an hour, the executive council finally declared it would step out of the Seattle strike picture, leaving the entire matter to negotiations between the Guild and the Hearst management.

The announcement was interpreted by union leaders here as making unnecessary any acceptance or rejection by the Seattle Central Labor Council of the A. F. of L. executive council's former proposal of settlement, which was accepted by the Post-Intelligencer.

The agreement, repudiated also by Kelly, was an "interpretation" of the council's proposal—and the repudiation was thought likely to be held by the council to be a refusal to meet the terms of their original offer.

During the hour in which Kelly talked to the executive council, he was interrupted repeatedly by William Green, president, and other council members, with questions, asking an explanation of the repudiation.

Apparently satisfied that Kelly was unable to explain the Hearst management's conduct in repudiating both the attle negotiations and their negotiator, the council took action "washing its hands" of the whole matter.

E. B. Fish, Seattle labor relations man for the Post-Intelligencer, entered into the agreement which interpreted the council's settlement offer last Wednesday. The agreement was to be kept secret until the executive council confirmed recommendations for arbitration—agreed to in the proposal.

Dave Beck Reveals Interpretation Agreement

Details of the "interpretation agreement" were revealed to the council by Dave Beck of Seattle, international vice president of the Teamster's Union, who declared that Fish had committed himself to the interpretation agreement in his presence.

At the conclusion of the session when the council returned to further consider the Seattle strike, Kelly went into session with Beck and Jonathan Eddy, executive secretary of the American Newspaper Guild, and attempted to make modifications in the agreement which he had repudiated.

The executive council refused to hear his proposed modifications.

Beck told Kelly firmly that the Post-Intelligencer now would have to deal directly and honestly with the Guild which had the united support of labor behind it.

Eddy declared that the Post-Intelligencer would now have to keep its original agreement or else submit all issues to arbitration with the Guild without any reservation.

History of Events Leading to P-I's Latest Piece of Trickery

Here's a brief history of the events leading up to the Post-Intelligencer's latest piece of trickery:

OCTOBER 24—A. F. of L. executive council submits proposal for strike-settlement.

OCTOBER 28—Post-Intelligencer agrees to accept proposal.

NOVEMBER 3—Guild accepts proposal for Tampa, Fla., to work out arbitration machinery to cover certain cases.

NOVEMBER 9—Post-Intelligencer repudiates agreement.

SUSPECT HELD OVER HIT-RUN AUTO MISHAP

Arrested by a state patrol officer after he had hit a parked car on the South End, Melvin E. Soley, thirty - seven - year - old motorist, was held by police yesterday on the hit - and - run motorist charge in connection with the injury of Sydney M. Higgins, fifty-eight-year-old woman, last night as she was crossing at Wallingford and Burton Sts.

Higgins was in critical condition last night in Seattle General Hospital. Physicians said he was suffering from rib fractures, head and bruises. His skull appeared to have been fractured when he was knocked down.

SIXTY KILLED AS 'FASCISTS' BOMB MADRID

MADRID, Nov. 15.—(GWS)—Sixty persons were killed today as the rebel Fascist army launched a new attack on the Spanish capital, aiming bombs in the streets, but suffering numerous reverses.

Two or three rebel planes which stormed the city were shot down.

A railroad station was bombed from the air and firemen "were searching for bodies within the ruins.

Perhaps the most dramatic event of the day was the blowing up of one of the huge bridges crossing the Manzanares River, which faces the capital. The government forces have mined all bridges crossing this river as a defense measure. Capture of several rebel tanks was reported by the government.

CHARGE CHANGED

...

MAN STRUCK BY AUTO, DIES

Struck down by an auto at Dearborn St. and Maynard Ave. Saturday night, Mike Danich, fifty-nine, died from his injuries at King County Hospital yesterday afternoon.

Danich was struck by an auto driven by Walter Smith, forty-four, 8437 64th Ave. Danich told police he tried to cross the street and was overcome by a dizzy spell and fell into the street. A few moments later a slide of coal rain came covering all of his body except his head.

Neil was married a little over a year ago. He is survived by his wife, Ethel, and a baby. The body was taken to the Fisher Undertaking Company at Issaquah.

Heart Stroke Takes Victim After Party

Stricken with a heart attack as he got into his automobile on his way home from a party, Walter Seeley of the Claremont Hotel fell dead early yesterday at N. 36th St. and Woodlawn Ave.

With him at the time were his wife, Ethel, and a friend, H. B. Woosley 346 N. 101st St.

TEACHERS AID SPAIN

NEW YORK, Nov. 15.—(GWS)—Teachers' Union, Local 5, has announced the collection of $2,000 for the purchase of food, clothing and medicine for the Spanish Loyalists.

Issaquah Miner Killed in Slide

Crushed beneath a slide of coal Howard Siel, twenty-five-year-old mine worker, was killed instantly yesterday in the Harris Mine located several miles west of Issaquah on the Sunset Highway.

According to fellow workers, Siel was working beside a coal chute and was overcome by a dizzy spell and fell into the chute. A few moments later a slide of coal came down covering all of his body except his head.

Siel was married a little over a year ago. He is survived by his wife, Ethel, and a baby. The body was taken to the Fisher Undertaking Company at Issaquah.

Late Flashes

JEWELRY STOLEN

Throwing a brick, wrapped in paper, through the window of the Peoples Jewelry Store, 711 1st Ave., a burglar dazzled the display window of $100 in rings and watches. Louis Pearl, proprietor, reported to police yesterday. Pearl said he found the brick in the store. He said approximately ninety rings were stolen.

THUG ATTACKS MAN

Attacked by a thug when he stepped from his automobile at 2nd Ave. and Pike St. S. R. L. Lafer, 1717 12th Ave., told police yesterday that the robber stole $25 from him.

Lafer said the assailant struck him several times.

P-I STRIKE SETTLED

WEATHER FORECAST FOR SEATTLE AND VICINITY—Fair today and tomorrow, probably with morning fog; little change in temperature; gentle north to east winds.

The Guild Daily

Vol. 1, No. 90 — PRICE 5 CENTS

THURSDAY, NOVEMBER 26, 1936

Guild Wins Recognition, Pay Increase, 5-Day Week; Plant to Reopen Monday

Grocer Shoots Man in Quarrel

Charity Football Game to be Today

Seattle's Thanksgiving Day will be well garnished with football. Two great gridiron classics are the program for today and each of each a caliber that houses are planning their Turkey dinners late—it'll be just impossible to keep dad and the kids away from either the Civic Stadium or the Husky Bowl.

It won today in the Civic Stadium the Seattle Parent-Teacher Association presents the annual high school charity football match.

At 1:30 p.m. the University of Washington Huskies make their bid for Rose Bowl honors, tackling the Washington State Cougars in the traditional championship contest which a year will probably see the winning over the Rose Bowl job an added plum. Washington was established favorite last night, odds of 2 to 1.

A sellout crowd is almost assured—both gridiron contests. Capacity of both houses will exceed the Cougars and the T. A. Charity event is expected draw a total crowd of 15,000 into Civic Stadium. Special bleachers have been added to the east side of the Civic Field to accommodate the capacity crowd. The schedule for the high school state—

Ballard vs. Cleveland.
Lincoln vs. West Seattle.
Broadway vs. Roosevelt.
Garfield vs. Queen Anne.
(For details see sports page.)

STORE OWNER JAILED; VICTIM BADLY INJURED

Pistol Drawn Following Argument Over 75-Cent Debt

By Jack Jarvis

"Why don't you shoot!"

Even as he defied Bruno Bertucci, twenty-six-year-old grocer, to shoot him, a man technically identified as Harry Wallace, speakeasy employe, fell with a bullet in his abdomen after an argument in Bertucci's grocery store at 1421 6th Ave. yesterday afternoon.

Wallace was in King County Hospital in critical condition last night, and Bertucci was held in the city jail without charge.

The man believed to be Wallace came into Bertucci's store early in the afternoon, Bertucci told police.

SCHWELLENBACH SEES HOPE IN PEACE PARLEY

SPOKANE, Nov. 25.—(G.W.S.) —The Pan-American peace conference in Buenos Aires is successful; it will do more to insure the peace and prosperity of the Union States than any other event since the World War, —Senator Lewis Schwellenbach told the League of Women Voters here today.

The senator declared that the real cause of war is the necessity of protecting the trade outlets for surplus American goods. If American producers could help to build up South America as an outlet for surplus commodities, we need have no fear at a general European war, Schwellenbach said.

DRINKING ALLEGED

"We had a bottle or and had been drinking quite a bit, I think," said Bertucci. "We wanted 75 cents I owed him, but I didn't have anything but a $5 bill and he said we'd come back later."

Wallace went back to the store shortly before noon, Bertucci said, and after arguing for a while, went to sleep in a room in the back of the store. Bertucci told him to get out.

Seattle Churches To Offer Thanks

Prayers of Thanksgiving will be offered today in all of the city's churches. A spirit of unity will mark the occasion with joint services being held in the various sections of the city.

Twelve Capitol Hill churches will hold services at 10:30 o'clock in Pilgrim Congregational Church, Broadway N. and E. Republican St. The Rev. Robert T. McFarlane, pastor of Westminster Presbyterian Church will preach on "The Goodness of Gratitude." The Rev. Frank Abbott, pastor of the North Broadway M. E. Church. The Rev. A. G. Lynch of the First Methodist Church and the Rev. M. E. Sawhill from the United Presbyterian Church will join in conducting the services.

PLAN JOINT DEVOTIONS

Joint devotions for the Madrona Presbyterian, Mount Baker Presbyterian and the Grace Methodist Churches will be held at the Grace Church, 36th Ave. S. and King St.

First Presbyterian, First Methodist Episcopal and First Baptist, will hold united services at 10:30 o'clock in Plymouth Church, 6th and University St. The Rev. Mark A. Matthews will preach the sermon. The Rev. Elmer Fridell, John B. Slater and L. Wendell Fifield also will participate. Music will be provided by the Plymouth vested choir, directed by A. Clark Bibbid.

University District churches will hold joint services at 10:30 o'clock in the University Christian Church, 15th Ave. N. E. and E. 50th St.

RAINIER CHURCHES MEET

Episcopal churches in Rainier Valley will hold a joint service at All Saints' Church, South St. & 46th Ave. S. Perry Sinfield, assistant lay reader, will preach the sermon and Reverend David Brown, lay-reader in charge, will conduct the ritual.

Thirteen Jewish organizations will hold union services throughout this city will hold special masses at Temple de Hirsch, 15th Ave. and E. Marion.

Services will be held at 11 o'clock in all churches of First Scientist and Christian Science Societies.

Guild Gives Thanks!

It's a Grand Thanksgiving Day! And the Guild is Thankful for—

The agreement which was signed last night with the Post-Intelligencer—the first agreement ever signed by a Hearst Newspaper and the Guild!

But—more than that—

The Guild is thankful for the support of the labor movement of the Northwest—the labor movement of the nation, for that matter, and the support of hundreds of thousands of local citizens—who actually WON the Guild Strike!

Without this support, the Guild might have achieved some measure of victory, but never would the editorial union have been granted full recognition, the five-day,

forty- hour week and substantial pay increases.

And on this Thanksgiving Day, the strike committee of the Seattle Newspaper Guild—offers its Thanks to you and you and you—

Armstrong, Lynch State Positions

Everhardt Armstrong and Frank "Slim" Lynch, the two veteran editorial employes of the Post-Intelligencer whose dismissals led to the strike that has kept the newspaper closed since August 13, gave the Guild Daily the following statement outlining their position regarding the settlement agreed upon last night:

More than three months ago our fellow Guildsmen on the Post-Intelligencer staff called a strike in protest against the management's arbitrary and illegal action in dismissing us for the part we played in organizing the Seattle branch of the American Newspaper Guild. They demanded our reinstatement. But both before and during the strike we have repeatedly confronted first more important than the question of our reinstatement—a question now

pending before the National Labor Relations Board—was the vital issue of RECOGNITION of the new union.

Now RECOGNITION is an accomplished fact and the staff is going back to work, with the best schedule of wages, hours and working conditions that any group of newspaper men in the Pacific Northwest ever had. The Guild's guaranteeing has not been easy. It has involved many hardships. But thanks to the determination of the strikers and the loyal support given them by organized labor and friends of labor throughout the United States, we have—

Text of P.-I. Guild Peace Agreement

Following is the text of the agreement concluded yesterday between the Seattle Newspaper Guild and the Post-Intelligencer.

As a result of negotiations between me and a committee of the Seattle Newspaper Guild for the purpose of ending the strike against the Post-Intelligencer the following formula was agreed to:

1—It is understood and agreed that all striking employes shall be returned to work without discrimination or prejudice and without reduction of salaries upon resumption of publication by the Seattle Post-Intelligencer, publication to be resumed within ninety-six hours after settlement is reached and the Post-Intelligencer is removed from the "unfair" list of the Seattle Central Labor Council.

2—It is agreed that the Guild will see to it that the Seattle Central Labor Council removes the Post-Intelligencer from the "unfair" list, or any similar list, forthwith and that its representatives on the Seattle Central Labor Council and its agents and others will do whatever may be done to have no difficulties with the Post-Intelligencer.

3—It is agreed that the provision for reinstatement of all striking employes shall apply to the following persons (list attached).

4—The cases of Frank Lynch and Philip K. Armstrong will continue to rest in the hands of the National Labor Relations Board.

5—The Post-Intelligencer here with outlines its editorial policy in settlement of all disputes concerning hours, wages and conditions of service. This is not a contract but it is the policy in operation on the paper which will be continued for one year from date and so long thereafter as economic conditions justify.

For the purpose of this statement editorial department employes shall be classified as those actually engaged in editorial work, to wit: Newspaper men including all directly charged with preparing, writing and editing of editorial news and feature material, photographers, artists and chief librarians, editorial writers, editors including copy desk, city and news desk, copy readers, rewrite men, reporters, sports-writers, photographers, make-up men, picture editors, columnists, financial writers, library, clerks, cable clerks, messengers and bona-commute employes.

No editorial department employe shall work more than forty hours per week. He shall have been put to work, the said forty hours to fall within this consecutive days. This guarantee shall become effective on or before March 1, 1937. In the meantime no editorial department employe shall work more than forty-eight hours per week, the said forty hours to fall within six consecutive days. This shall not interfere with the performance of any necessary overtime. Any employe required to work in excess of the hours set forth above shall be compensated for the overtime at the ordinary rate. This guarantee shall apply to the part-time and probationary employes who shall become either temporary or permanent employes after the expiration of six months probationary period.

Each hour so granted with full pay, provided, however, that the

(Continued on Page 2, Col. 2)

Agreement Signed by Publisher and President of Newsmen's Union; Paper Taken From Unfair List

The fifteen-week-old strike of the Seattle Newspaper Guild is over!

In an agreement signed by the Seattle Post-Intelligencer and the Guild at 9:30 o'clock last night, the Seattle Guild was awarded complete and full recognition of its organization.

The agreement provided for no discrimination against editorial employes and declared that "no editorial department employe will be discharged because of membership in the Guild."

Under terms of the agreement the Post-Intelligencer will resume publication Monday with all strikers returning to work.

The agreement provided wage minimums—granting increases of from $2.50 to $7.50 per week for all but four strikers, and gave to Guild members the five-day, forty-hour week—long sought by editorial employes.

Armstrong and Lynch Approve Agreement

The settlement received the full approval of Frank "Slim" Lynch and Everhardt Armstrong, the two victims of discrimination who have become nationally known for the sacrifices they made in building the Seattle Guild.

In accordance with many statements made to the Guild martyrs, they waived all claims to considerations to which the management was committed in previous agreements, subsequently repudiated in order to win direct recognition for the union.

P.-I. Removed From Council Unfair List

Following the signing of the agreement, the executive board of the Seattle Central Labor Council removed the Post-Intelligencer from its unfair list at the request of the Guild. In this connection the Guild demanded and was given assurance that the interests of other printing crafts who have or have not had differences with the Post-Intelligencer will be assured of adjustment through an understanding between the Central Council and E. F. Fish, labor relations counsel for the paper.

Only two votes were cast against the proposal when the settlement was submitted to the strikers for ratification. Although they were not enthusiastic about the schedule of wage minimums, they expressed the opinion these were not a primary issue in the controversy and that recognition and protection against discrimination were the important considerations.

The strikers praised the members and officers of the printing crafts, who suffered without complaint while their junior associates in the labor movement won the victory which the former had to win years ago.

P.-I. TAKEN OFF 'UNFAIR' LIST

Within one hour after the Associated Newspaper Guild had settled, its Newspaper Guild had settled all the differences with the Hearst Post-Intelligencer last night, the executive board of the Seattle Central Labor Council removed the P.-I. from its unfair list.

Since the labor council did not travel last night in its regular meeting because of the holiday, officers of the council were contacted immediately and notified that the Guild had settled to its satisfaction.

TYPOGRAPHICAL HEAD SATISFIED

Characterizing the settlement of the Post-Intelligencer strike as a victory not only for the American Newspaper Guild but for organized labor all over the United States, J. M. Lineman, president of Typographical Union, Local 202, last night expressed satisfaction with the settlement reached.

"I am satisfied with the Guild settlement," Lineman said, "with its full recognition of the Guild, and I consider it not only a victory for organized labor in the Northwest but all over the United States.

"I consider the hardships members of the Typographical Union have undergone during the strike will be well repaid by the recognition given the Guild."

Both Hearst, C. W. Dogie, James S. Duncan and J. H. Oulvie, who were contracted, called members of the executive board of the council. When the five members contacted had not reached at their homes, but enthusiastically approved the action taken.

Members of the board who concurred were Basil Grey, Thomas Shields, H. N. Findorsey, George Johnson and William Stephenson.

Publisher Issues Statement

The following statement was issued tonight by Charles R. Lindeman, associate publisher of the Post-Intelligencer:

"The strike on the Post-Intelligencer has been settled. The terms rest upon a basis incorporated in the craft of the recommendations of the executive council of the American Federation of Labor."

(Continued on Page 2, Col. 2)

Attention, Guild Subscribers!

The Guild Daily will be published as usual Friday morning!

Lineups for Today's Game

WASHINGTON STATE

Right Halfback	Left Halfback
ZUGER, NO. 36	LITTLEFIELD, NO. 45

| | Quarterback | |
| | GODDARD, NO. 28 | |

Right End	Right Tackle	Right Guard	Center	Left Guard	Left Tackle	Left End
KLUMB NO. 22	BELL NO. 25	DOUGHERTY NO. 66	SMITH NO. 72	CAMPBELL NO. 52	SCHEYER NO. 37	TERRY NO. 40

vs.

WASHINGTON

Left End	Left Tackle	Left Guard	Center	Right Guard	Right Tackle	Right End
MARKOV NO. 6	STARCEVICH NO. 4	WIATRAK NO. 13	SLIVINSKI NO. 14	BOYD NO. 36	PETERS NO. 9	

| | Left Halfback | | Right Halfback | |
| | WASKOWITZ, NO. 15 | | CAIN, NO. 62 | |

| | | Quarterback | | |
| | | LOGG, NO. 14 | | |

| | Left Halfback | |
| | NOWOGROSKI, NO. 17 | |

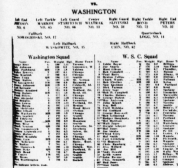

Washington Squad						
Name	Pos.	Weight	Age	Home Town

W. S. C. Squad						
Name	Pos.	Weight	Age	Home Town

Guildsmen Join in Labor Parade

PUBLISHERS ARE ORGANIZED Why Not Their Employees?

"HEARST AINT NO LILY WHY GUILD HIM? —Secret Six

NEWSPAPER GUILD News Endorses THE NATION WHY So Does the Guild Pct. Sec "SOS" Read the Guild Daily

Guildsmen went parading yesterday with 25,000 fellow unionists—men and women—of the Seattle labor movement. Above is a view of a group of Guildsmen lining up for the march. They had a sound truck, and everything, including many banners which, held aloft, epitomized the struggle against Hearst.

"Publishers are organized—Why not their employes?" read one sign. Another banner wanted to know: "Why is the Secret Six so Secret?" Seattle's youngest union, as judged by the applause, was one of the most popular in the line of march.

The Post-Intelligencer city room (taken in 1934)

Here's a 'Striking' Picture

IN NEW HEADQUARTERS—Striking editorial employes of the Post-Intelligencer are shown at work in a corner of their spacious new headquarters at 609½ Union Street.

Dave Beck, Teamster leader

Mayor John F. Dore

*Charles Lindeman,
P-I negotiator*

Joseph Corbett,
telegraph editor and Guildsman

Emerson Daggett,
Voice ot Action editor

John Boettiger and Anna Roosevelt Boettiger

Everhardt Armstrong, Richard Seller and Frank Lynch

Everhardt Armstrong

Frank (Slim) Lynch

Governor Martin Greets Guild Supporters

WHEN GUILD TOOK SPOTLIGHT—Gov. Clarence D. Martin shown smiling up into the face of Senator Mary Farquarson yesterday as she stood atop a mahogany table in his executive offices as leader of more than 150 Seattle club women who staged a second "march" on the capitol to surprise a half-hundred Pro-America women who had planned another "march" in protest against union labor. So surprised were the anti-labor delegation by the appearance of the true club women, they heckled the governor.—(Picture by Guild Daily Staff Photographer

He's on Strike, But They Wed

HONEYMOON DAYS started yesterday afternoon for Forrest Williams, striking newspaper man, and his bride, shown above, as they departed on a trip to Spokane and Portland following the Newspaper Guild's first "strike wedding" here. Happy? The picture gives the answer, proving that strikes can't dim young love.

Morgan Hull, Guild organizer

Richard Seller

RST BEHIND SKIRTS—Reversing ordinary procedure, women are shown here as they picketed the offices of eamsters' Union yesterday afternoon over the closing of the Post-Intelligencer. Earlier in the day they threw a short-lived picket line around the Labor Temple.—(Photo by Art French, Guild Daily Staff Photographer.)

THREE MEN IN A QUANDARY

Heffernan Building (Sixth and Pine), P-I plant at time of strike (taken 1921)

Raymond D. Holmes, P-I librarian and Guildsman

both the industrial and craft unions to picket together. It was equally unexpected that the Printing Trades Council, while claiming the members would report for work if they could, was willing to go along with the strike. The Guild counted heavily on the printing trades' support and paid from local funds to send Jean Litonius, president of the Seattle Typographical Union, to a negotiating conference in Washington to represent the Seattle Guild interest. [59]

Other factors also were working in the Guild's favor. The National Labor Relations Board provided an appeal for Lynch and Armstrong and forced Hearst to prove his right to fire these employees. No one knew how the hearings might end, but the fact that Hearst had to tell his side of the story was important. He did not submit to the Board's requests easily, and as late as the opening day of the hearings, September 10, 1936, his attorney denied the Board had any jurisdiction in the case. [60] Hearst officials contended that the *Post-Intelligencer* and the work done by Armstrong and Lynch was primarily within the State of Washington and therefore did not fall under interstate commerce. Indeed, contended the Hearst attorney, this was clearly a case of "freedom of the press and of speech." [61]

The Guild, on the other hand, cooperated with the Board to the fullest on the basis that the union, Lynch, and Armstrong had nothing to lose. In fact, once the hearings started, it appeared impossible that the Guild and its discharged employees could lose. Trial examiner for the Board was Edwin S. Smith, a short, stocky, former newspaperman whose liberal ideas had brought him into the Roosevelt administration. He previously had sat on the Jennings case in San Francisco. Accompanying him was Malcolm Ross, director of publications for the National Labor Relations Board. The tall, lean Ross also had been a former newspaper reporter before joining the labor agency. [62]

The hearings continued until September 30, when Smith left Seattle for California en route to Washington, D.C. The hearing rooms in the Federal Building were packed as Guild and Hearst witnesses paraded before the examiner. For Hearst, there were Tanner, the publisher, and Lindeman, the associate publisher, making a favorable impression and offering a rather tolerant attitude toward the Guild. There also were Oliver Morris, Marion Stixrood, Helen Wadleigh, Douglass Welch, Hunt, Fred Niendorff, Paul Stoeffel, Edith

White, Ray Colvin, Arthur Dunning, and many more. All told of the fine working conditions on the *Post-Intelligencer*, the complete lack of intimidation on the part of Hearst management as far as Guild membership was concerned, and many tried to disclose the violence on the picket line during the opening day. Smith accepted only Lindeman's testimony.

The cast which the Guild presented was less impressive as far as position on the paper was concerned, but the story which each told was more likely to win the sympathy and support of readers of the news reports of the hearing in the *Seattle Times*, *Star*, and *Guild Daily*. Lynch and Armstrong, Seller, Holmes, Erickson, Fritzi Swanstrom, Williams, and others — all told of the courage it took to belong to the Guild and of the intimidation they suffered once their membership was known. They played the role of the underdogs well. They, as they told Smith, were the persecuted, and Hearst and his management staff were the persecutors. [63]

Evidence was presented to prove the *Post-Intelligencer* was engaged in interstate commerce after it had been ascertained that Hearst was really the owner of the paper. Then there was the testimony concerning the firing of Lynch and Lynch's competence as a manager — and not even Lynch bothered to deny that he had not been much of a manager. (There were threats that the *Post-Intelligencer* management might reveal the sex peccadillos of one of the Guildsmen, a threat made several days before the hearings opened. Although the threat shook the Guildsmen considerably, they were assured by the woman that they needn't worry about her reputation. Defeating Hearst was far more important.)[64]

Rumors circulated that Dave Beck might be called to testify, and the self-confident labor leader did appear at the hearings one morning in response to a Board subpoena. The *Post-Intelligencer* management was anxious to question him about his connection with the strike, but somehow the testimony never was given. The hearings ended in Seattle on September 29, and Edward G. Woods, attorney for Hearst, announced that he would appeal if the NLRB ordered Lynch and Armstrong reinstated. [65]

Guildsmen felt that Hearst had gained no ground from the hearings. Some believed that Smith had allowed the Guild to use the hearings as a publicity forum for their cause against Hearst, and Ross, in his written reports, noted that he found a great deal of support in Seattle for the strike.[66]

No decision on the matter was expected before the November elections, and no one was surprised when the case was reopened and further testimony was taken in Washington, D.C. Somehow the NLRB decision had little to do with the strike, and most Guildsmen realized that a settlement probably would come before the NLRB had reached its decision concerning Lynch and Armstrong. Seattleites were left to determine for themselves whether these were two mistreated working men, or whether Lynch was an incompetent and Armstrong a radical hothead. There was evidence to support any conclusion.

In addition to the NLRB hearings, which created a generally favorable climate for the Guild and the strike, the Guild experienced another stroke of fortune. Since the international presidents of the printing-trades unions were unhappy because their local chapels and chapters refused to cross the picket lines, pressure was brought on William F. Green, president of the American Federation of Labor, to investigate the situation in Seattle and to act on the basis of this report. Sent to Seattle to make the report was Rowland Watson, of the AFL, who arrived August 25 and made his report on September 5. The report cheered the Guildsmen and aroused Harvey Kelly, the Hearst negotiator. Watson, who a year later admitted to the Washington State AFL convention that he had white-washed the Guild in the report,[67] agreed that Lynch and Armstrong had been discharged for union activities and that pleas from such groups as the State Federation of Labor, the Central Labor Council, and the National Labor Relations Board all had been unheeded. In fact, the *Post-Intelligencer* had refused to appear before the Labor Council and instead sent a discourteous letter. Watson did admit that the printers had protested the unfair vote because of their contract obligations, but no protests had been made after the vote to place Hearst on the unfair list was taken in the CLC. Further, he found that Hearst had been guilty of using hired guards known as "gunmen" prior to the strike.[68] Despite all this, Watson found the *Post-Intelligencer* management unwilling to make any effort to settle the strike except on its own terms. Further, he admitted that labor within the city of Seattle was upset by the criticism which it had experienced because of the strike. He particularly noted the criticism against Beck.[69]

With such a report, Green was hardly in a position to order the printing trades through the picket line. The fear that the Guild might be forced into settlement by the printing trades faded for a time.

In order to rally support for the Guild in Seattle, a citizens' committee was organized to help the public obtain an objective account of the strike. The group, organized at Howard Costigan's (secretary of the Washington Commonwealth Federation) suggestion, claimed to be unbiased, desiring only to bring a calm, rational approach. However, most of its work was decidedly pro-Guild. The committee, organized during the early days of the strike, first was headed by N. P. Atkinson, a state senator and an active liberal. Atkinson conceived the role of the committee as one of support for the Guild and spent his few days in office lining up telephone committees to solicit strike funds and other support.[70] The remainder of the committee thought he had misconstrued its purpose and elected in his place Marcus Rohlfs, a Seattle attorney.[71] Members of the committee in general were the liberal element of the community, including ministers, a rabbi, university professors, and the president of the American Civil Liberties Union. Included were Herman Horowitz, proprietor of the Washington Printing Company; Fred Lind, an attorney; Ward Bowman, educational director at Plymouth Congregational Church; and Mrs. Elizabeth Hanson, chairman of the Women's Radio Club. University professors who were members of the committee included Joseph Harrison, Edward Cox, Angelo Pellegrini, Melvin Rader, and Ralph Gundlach. Also active were Warren G. Magnuson, prosecuting attorney; Lady Willie Forbus, an attorney; and Carroll Carter, county clerk.

It was a prominent group of Seattle citizens, not from the business community, but from the professional, religious, political, and educational circles of the community. Seattle at the time had a generally liberal climate. Citizens little feared being associated with left-wing activities, and there was little inclination to associate every liberal movement with communism.

Differences of opinion existed as to just what the committee should do, but eventually, under the chairmanship of Rohlfs, a decision was made to put all the efforts for the time being on the *Post-Intelligencer* strike and not attempt to deal with the threatening longshore situation. But, at the same time, the committee was not to consider itself as formed just to deal with the strike against Hearst. [72]

Probably the outstanding contribution of the committee was a pamphlet, *The Truth About the Post-Intelligencer Strike*, which was produced at the committee's expense and sold for a nickel to raise funds. The booklet was subtitled, "The story of William Randolph Hearst's effort to crush the American Newspaper Guild in Seattle by dismissals and economic terrorism." The tone of the pamphlet strongly supported the Guild and hardly seemed to fit the objective goal which the committee contended it wished to achieve. It read:

In a dramatic and stirring way, the struggle between the world's richest publisher and a plucky group of news writers has revealed the sharply-drawn line that now divides reactionary and progressive thought in the United States. The fundamental issue involved is simple. The strikers, who left their jobs in protest against the dismissal of two active members of the *Post-Intelligencer* unit of the Guild, are fighting grimly for recognition of their lawful right to form a union. Hearst, with millions of dollars and a vast network of newspapers, wire services and radio stations at his command, doggedly contests the right; and since the first day of the strike, a barrage of newspaper editorials — and radio broadcasts financed by the *Post-Intelligencer* management — has served to keep the public mind confused regarding the motives behind the Guild unit's action and the unanimous support the new union has received from organized labor.

The pamphlet then continued for twenty pages to show that the Guild's cause was right and just, that Dave Beck was unjustly blamed for his role in the strike, and concluded: "Continued public support of the Guild is the only guarantee that justice will be done." [73]

Outside of the *Guild Daily*, this was the only publication which attempted to bring understanding of the Guild's positions to Seattle citizens. It was admittedly pro-Guild, and much of the writing for the publication was handled by Ray Holmes, a Guild member and librarian of the *Post-Intelligencer*. Much of the investigation for the publication was done by Selden Menefee, from the Sociology Department of the University of Washington, and Irving

Clark, American Civil Liberties Union president, and Rohlfs handled the final preparation. [74] Despite its good intentions, it is doubtful if the Citizens' Committee contributed greatly to the strike. That it made any contribution amazed Hull, who at one time was eager to dump the entire committee into Puget Sound. [75]

Although the strike, from its very beginning, had something of the feeling of a victory celebration to the Guildsmen, it was not without its long hours of work and its days of despair as to the outcome. Accompanying it always were the uncertainties and tensions of the situation. In addition to the strains caused by the fight against Hearst, personal animosities plagued the Guild from the strike's beginning. Most bothersome of the personal feelings were the anti-Hull sentiments held by Charles Daggett, city editor of the *Seattle Star* and first president of the Seattle Chapter. Hull and Daggett had known each other before the two arrived in Seattle, and Daggett made little effort to mask his dislike for the union organizer. Daggett may have been responsible for the anti-Hull feelings which developed in the Seattle chapter, particularly at the time of its organization and then again during the first weeks of the strike. Seller and Erickson felt strongly against Hull, and both expressed their views to the national office. [76] Both had made little effort to hide their feelings, and both had requested that the national office not return Hull to the Seattle scene. The two believed that Hull was a greater handicap than an asset in handling the strike, a conclusion not borne out by the facts of the case. Erickson, inclined to be a bit defensive and irritable, felt that Hull was guilty of withholding information from the Seattle chapter with regard to negotiations. Both Seller and Erickson felt that Jonathan Eddy would have handled the situation much better and that the Guild would have been freed from the taint of communistic leanings which Hull lent to the organization.

However, by the end of September most of these feelings appear to have been forgotten. An eight-page memo from Daggett to Hull gave the city editor a chance to air his feelings about Hull, Eddy, the strike, the Guild, the *Star* management, and the world in general. At about this time also, Seller reportedly told French and Lynch that he had raised "hell" about Hull's coming to the strike scene, but the executive board would "raise even more hell" were Hull to leave. Hull didn't quite know what to make of the remark, but he concluded: "Discounting the alcohol which contributed to the conviviality of the moment, I think there was at least some truth in the statement. . . ." [77]

FOOTNOTES CHAPTER VI
BALLAD OF THE RED MILL

1. Quoted in Dave Beck and Dorothy Beck v. Hearst Publications, Inc. and Seattle Broadcasting Co., King County (Washington) Superior Court, No. 296157.
2. Interviews with Mr. and Mrs. Floyd Larkin, May, 1959; Mr. and Mrs. Terry Pettus, October, 1959; and Frank Lynch, May, 1959.
3. Richard Seller interview, May, 1959.
4. Pettus interview, October, 1959, and interview with Mr. and Mrs. Claude Smith, August, 1960.
5. Lynch interview, May, 1959, and Harvey J. Kelly interview, April, 1959.
6. Pettus interview, October, 1959.
7. Pettus interview, October, 1959; Smith interview, August, 1960; and Larkin interviews, May, 1959, and July, 1960.
8. Complete files of the *Guild Daily* are in the University of Washington Library and in the School of Communications at the University of Washington.
9. Report of Investigator A.K. #4 to Federal Bureau of Investigation, August 17, 1936, Folder 227, Peyser Papers (MSS in Manuscript Division, University of Washington Library). Referred to hereafter as Peyser Papers.
10. *Ibid.*
11. Report of Investigator A. K. #4, September 3, 1936, Folder 227, Peyser Papers.
12. National Association of Manufacturers, *Labor Relations Bulletin*, July 30, 1936, p. 278. The formula listed these keys to successful strike breaking: "Label union leaders as agitators to discredit them with the public and their members, disseminate propaganda to stress the arbitrary demands of the strikers, align influential members of the community into a cohesive group opposed to the strike, form a large armed police force to intimidate the strikers, secretly organize a puppet association of 'loyal employees' to demoralize the strikers

and use publicity to suggest that the strikers interfere with the right to work."

13. Stephen Chadwick to T. D. Carlson, September 9, 1936, Chadwick Papers (MSS in Manuscript Division, University of Washington Library).
14. Seattle Chamber of Commerce Board of Trustees minutes, September 15 and 22, 1936.
15. For a detailed description of the campaign of 1936, see Arthur M. Schlesinger, Jr., *The Politics of Upheaval* (Boston: Houghton Mifflin Co., 1960).
16. *Seattle Times*, June 6, 1935, and November 1, 1936; also, see W. Cameron Meyers, "The Chicago Newspaper Hoax in the '36 Election Campaign," *Journalism Quarterly*, Summer, 1960, pp. 356-364. The article discussed a *Chicago Tribune* assertion that Russia's Communist Party had ordered United States Communists to support Roosevelt.
17. For a study of Dave Beck's anti-Communist views, see John Dailey, "Labor Omnia Vincit" (unpublished research paper, School of Communications, University of Washington, 1959).
18. Schlesinger, pp. 538-539.
19. *Seattle Times*, August 24, 1936.
20. John F. Dore, Jr., interview, April, 1959.
21. For accounts of the election, see the *Seattle Times* and *Seattle Star*, July-November, 1932.
22. Washington State Federation of Labor, *Proceedings of the Thirty-fifth Annual Convention*, Vancouver, Washington, July 13-16, 1936 (Seattle: The Trade Printery, 1936), pp. 5-8.
23. Larkin interview, May, 1959.
24. *New York Times*, August 26, 1936.
25. For an account of the state election in 1936, see Alice J. Kling, "A Political Press; Policies of the Washington Commonwealth Federation" (unpublished Master's thesis in Communications, University of Washington, 1966).
26. *Ibid.*
27. Lester Hunt interview, April 20, 1960.
28. Instruction issued to solicitors on September 11, 1936. Copy in Newspaper Guild Collection, Archives of Labor History and Urban Affairs, Wayne State University, Detroit. Hereafter referred to as Newspaper Guild Collection.

29. *Seattle Times*, September 6 and 16, 1936.
30. *Guild Daily*, September 16, 1936.
31. Morgan Hull to Jonathan Eddy, September 20, 1936, Newspaper Guild Collection; Larkin interviews, April, 1959, and July, 1960.
32. *Ibid.*
33. *Seattle Times*, August 26, 1936.
34. *Ibid.*
35. *Seattle Times*, *Seattle Star*, and *Guild Daily*, August 26, 1936.
36. *Seattle Times*, August 26, 1936.
37. *Seattle Times*, August 30 and September 2, 5, and 6, 1936.
38. Kirk Hillman interview, April, 1959. Records of the League were destroyed after the death of Robert Bronson. Hillman recalled that Mrs. Bronson dumped all the records into Lake Washington for fear that someone might "want to get back" at her and her children.
39. Marcus Rohlfs interview, April, 1959.
40. Report of Ballard meeting by Investigator A. K. #4, September 3, 1936, Folder 227, Peyser Papers.
41. Cliffe Erickson to Eddy, October 12, 1936, Newspaper Guild Collection; *Seattle Times*, October 12, 1936.
42. *Seattle Times* and *Seattle Star*, October 13, 1936.
43. *Seattle Times*, October 14, 1936, and Mrs. Mary Farquharson interview, May, 1969.
44. Erickson to Clyde Beals, October 12, 1936, Newspaper Guild Collection; *Seattle Times*, October 14, 1936.
45. *Ibid.*
46. *Seattle Times* and *Seattle Star*, October 14, 1936.
47. *Seattle Times*, October 14, 1936.
48. *Seattle Times*, October 24-25, 1936; *Guild Daily*, October 25, 1936.
49. *Seattle Times*, November 1, 1936.
50. *Seattle Times*, October 27, 1936.
51. *Ibid.*
52. *Seattle Times*, see November, 1936, issues.
53. Hull to Guild Headquarters, November 1, 1936, Newspaper Guild Collection.
54. See John Gustaf Westergreen, "Editorial Reactions of Eight Daily Newspapers Concerning the 1936 *P-I* Strike," (unpublished research paper, School of Communications, University of Washington, 1959); see

Bellingham (Washington) *Herald*, August 26 and 30, and September 9 and 12, 1936.

55. Westergreen, p. 5.
56. *Seattle Times*, August 23, 1936.
57. *Seattle Times*, October 2 and 10, 1936.
58. Erickson to Eddy, September 27, 1936, Newspaper Guild Collection.
59. Erickson to Eddy, October 14, 1936, Newspaper Guild Collection.
60. *Seattle Times*, September 10, 1936.
61. *Ibid.*
62. *Seattle Times*, September 9, 1936; Malcolm Ross, *Death of a Yale Man* (New York: Farrar & Rinehart, Inc., 1939).
63. National Labor Relations Board, "Transcript of Hearings in Case C-136" (Seattle hearings), p. 30 ff.
64. Morgan to Eddy, September 12, 1936, Newspaper Guild Collection.
65. *Seattle Times*, September 29, 1936.
66. Ross, pp. 261-263.
67. Washington State Federation of Labor, *Proceedings of the Thirty-sixth Annual Convention*, Bellingham, Washington, July 12-15, 1937 (Seattle: The Trade Printery, 1937), p. 88.
68. For proof, see Report of A. K. #4, August 17, 1936, in Folder 227, Peyser Papers.
69. John Addison Wolfard, "The History and Significance of the American Newspaper Guild Strike Against the Post-Intelligencer" (unpublished Master's thesis in History, University of Washington, 1937), p. 44.
70. Rohlfs interview, April, 1959.
71. *Ibid.* A report on any possible connection between Rohlfs and the Communist Party was made by Investigator A. K. #4, September 18, 1936, Folder 227, Peyser Papers.
72. Rohlfs interview, April, 1959.
73. *Ibid.*
74. *Ibid.*
75. Hull to Eddy, September 30, 1936, Newspaper Guild Collection.
76. Hull to Eddy, September 24, 1936, Newspaper Guild Collection.
77. *Ibid.*

CHAPTER VII

THE COUNTING HOUSE

The American Newspaper Guild's strike against Hearst carried largely on enthusiasm, but fervor counted for little in at least one phase. This was the area of finances. From the beginning, the strike rested on a shaky monetary base, for the Seattle Chapter of the Guild showed a nearly empty treasury. National headquarters was equally desperate, for funds to finance the *Wisconsin News* strike had taken what money the Guild could accumulate.

Finances from the national office had not been promised to Seattle and were not forthcoming during the early weeks. Yet funds were needed to run a strike — to pay the strike benefits, meager as they were, to finance the *Guild Daily*, to keep the picket line going, and to keep supplies in the strike kitchen. Morgan Hull, Guild organizer who represented the national office in Seattle during the strike, estimated the cost of the strike at $1,500 a week, and after the first weeks of the strike, union contributions failed to approach this amount.[1]

Strikes during the 1930s were supported largely by donations from unions throughout the country, and when Guildsman Forrest Williams made his regular appeals for funds for the Milwaukee strike, he had a glimpse of the desperate need for money which developed once the Seattle strike was under way. Labor responded well during the opening days of the *Post-Intelligencer* strike against Hearst. Contributions arrived at the strike office before the strike was a day old. The Maritime Federation, the Teamsters Union, and the Meat Cutters Union #81 sent the largest contributions, but the rest of the list read like a roll call of organized labor in Seattle. Included were the crew and officers of the SS *James Griffiths*, the taxicab drivers, the postal clerks, the meat packers, Workers Alliance, International Workers Order, Postal Workers Union #12, the "Sailors," the plywood and veneer workers, the crew of the SS *Diamond Cement*, the boilermakers, the marine firemen, the flour and cereal workers, the hoist and shovel engineers, the blacksmiths, the drop forgers and helpers, the electric railway employees, the street pavers, sewer, main, and tunnel workers, and on and on. The amounts were small in many cases, with only the Meat Cutters Union #81 donating as much as $100. The Teamsters gave $75, but by the end of September these contributions were withheld as Dave Beck planned his strategy for maintaining control over the strike.[2]

By the end of the first week of the strike, contributions arrived from unions throughout the State of Washington, with the printing and typographical unions being especially prominent on the list. The first of the contributions, $15, came from the Olympia Typographical Union, and the largest contributions came from the Central Labor Council in Tacoma and the Lumber and Sawmill Workers, #3646 of Lyman. Both groups donated $50. Other donations ranged as low as $1, but the small and numerous donations provided the backbone of the strike's finances.[3]

Most money sent by the unions came from within the State of Washington, although a trickle of out-of-state checks began to flow into the Red Mill after the first two weeks of the strike. The Sailors Union in Portland sent the first contribution, $10. Not until September 5 were the next national funds received — a $5 check from the Stockton Musicians' Association in California. However, the amounts were small, and it was an exceptional day which brought as much as $50 in national funds to the treasury, and it was not until October 10 that such a total was reached.[4]

Part of the financial problems of the Guild stemmed from the lack of organization which characterized the treasury operation from the beginning of the strike. Cliffe Erickson, one of the most enthusiastic supporters of the strike, was named treasurer, not on the basis of financial ability but because of his enthusiasm and willingness to accept a Guild office during the days when Guild offices required more courage than ability.[5]

During the early days of the strike, the Guild counted on support from the local unions to carry it through. Many Guildsmen took seriously the stories that the Seattle unions were ready to underwrite the strike once it was under way. However, a successful strike would need something more than this. During the early weeks, Erickson directed the circulation of requests to all forty-eight states, asking state federations to send complete lists of every union in each state. Only two of the states complied — Oregon and probably the least labor organized state of the union, South Dakota. Missouri union headquarters claimed a federal regulation prohibited the dissemination of such lists, but offered to solicit their own unions if the Guild would furnish the letters and material. [6]

By the end of September, despite contributions from the unions, the strike showed a deficit of something over $1,600. Desperate letters were leaving Seattle under Erickson's signature, pleading with the national office to send what funds were available. [7]

This financial picture bothered Guild representative Hull who otherwise felt the strike had been "an almost perfect chain of circumstances." Particularly alarming was the lack of support from Dave Beck, who seemed to be cutting off the Guild at the pocketbook. Beck's position was, Hull said,

". . . the teamsters are not going to support this strike by themselves; it is not going to be said that it is their strike," and "it is up to you fellows to see to it that expenses are assessed or pro-rated over the labor movement of the city and the state.".

In Beck's terms, it was up to Charles Doyle and Claude O'Reilly, Central Labor Council officials, to see that the funds were raised. The Guildsmen had talked to both Doyle and O'Reilly and received their commiseration and "voluble assurances," but nothing happened. Hull feared that the Guild's refusal to go back to work under almost any terms hurt the strike and upset the printers. Hull was certain the Teamsters were raising funds but that Beck was holding them back. Attempts were made to get the Metal Trades Council and the marine unions to pool their contributions so the amounts would seem greater and much attention would be given to these contributions in the Central Labor Council meetings. In late September Beck was out of town, and Hull hoped the Teamster leader would take matters into his hands when he returned. [8]

To dramatize the financial situation, members of the Guild appeared at the meeting of the Central Labor Council on Wednesday, October 1, and formally applied for a $1,000 loan from the Central Labor Council strike funds despite the loud and almost tearful objections from Doyle. At the same time the members from the metal trades and marine group, who were not able to pool their contributions, appeared and reported on the financial state of the Guild strike fund. [9]

By Thursday morning there was indication of a break in the dam which was holding back the Teamster fund. Dick Seller barely had gotten to Guild headquarters when he received a call from Beck to report immediately to the Teamster headquarters. Both Seller and Hull made the pilgrimage to the "potentate in the throne room," where "all the emissaries and functionaries" were gathered. Beck was disgusted with the nominal leaders of the labor movement for their failure to put into effect a money-raising plan which he had outlined for them. The upshot was that Beck ordered all checks held by the Teamsters to be forwarded immediately to the Guild headquarters, and he summoned all the more prominent figures in the labor movement to appear in his office at three that afternoon. 10

The executive committee of the Central Labor Council and prominent representatives of all the sectional groups in the council were seated in the Teamster boss's office at three o'clock. Shortly after they all gathered, Beck's secretary appeared in the door and began calling the roll, noting those who were absent. She then handed the list to Beck when he came into the room. "He brusquely called the meeting to order, told everyone to quit smoking and briefly defined the purpose of the meeting, namely, to spread the cost of financing the strike over the local labor movement." Without argument or comment, he snapped questions at Seller and Hull: How much in the hole were they? What contributions had been made? What local unions had contributed regularly? What did the Guild need per week? 11

No one questioned the $1,500 figure presented by the Guild officials, and Beck turned to the group: " 'We've got to pledge local unions to produce that amount every week for a thirty-nine-day period and longer if necessary.' "

He announced that the seven Teamster unions which were established — two were just getting under way — would give $285 a week. Without ceremony, he then assigned tasks to the entire group in such a way that they could contact every union in the city within the next few days. " 'Be back here next Tuesday at the same hour and we'll expect to have every union on the line by that time. The meeting is adjourned.' " With this Beck left the room. None of the labor officials demurred, and all seemed eager to comply. It was an incredible meeting to Hull and Seller — even a bit appalling.

After the Central Labor Council leaders had left, Beck took the Guild men into his office and questioned them about advertising and circulation of the *Daily*. Beck assured them he could handle this situation also. He had about 400 in his precinct organization, and the entire city could be solicited within thirty days. Beck also turned over $800 in checks which he had been holding.[12]

The meetings with Beck were important. For one thing, he still was willing to support the strike and gave $800 to prove it. Also, Beck had taken on the financial organization of the Seattle labor unions, and Beck had a way of getting things done. Perhaps this meant that the money problems which had plagued the strikers now would diminish.

The next day Beck again called for Hull and Seller, this time to discuss the possibility of raising $5,000 to put the *Guild Daily* on an eight-page basis for thirty days. Mayor Dore also had talked of such a plan, but nothing ever came of this.[13]

If the Guildsmen had hoped that this would solve their financial problems, they were disappointed. Within a few days the strike leadership was not only tired and discouraged, but disillusioned as well. Where was all this support that everyone had talked about? The national Guild office was as quiet as any of the rest. No one in New York seemed to realize that this strike in Seattle was much bigger than anything the Guild had been involved in before. Just a few dollars were no help at all. The situation demanded hundreds of dollars. Erickson was tired of having to beg for money constantly. As he pictured it, he and his fellow Guild member Fritzi Swanstrom were keeping the entire strike going by constantly begging for more credit.[14]

As of October 14, Erickson saw the strong possibility that the *Guild Daily* might have to fold despite the fact that just two weeks before both Beck and John Dore were talking about pouring $5,000 into the newspaper. The Anchor Press, printers for the *Daily*, held a bill for $607. Pigott Printing, where the composition was done, was owed $270. The business office of the Pigott firm was riding Erickson for payment of the bill, and Erickson was annoyed. In addition, unless the telephone bill of $315 was paid, the company was threatening to shut off service. What was the Seattle Guild to do? There was talk, because of some personal friendships, of being able to borrow from the Fishermen's Union. Somehow, it seemed to Erickson, if Jonathan Eddy could make himself a committee of one and return to Seattle, perhaps all these matters could be worked out. Erickson never was part of the Morgan Hull fan club. [15]

The Guild had sent sheets of "Unionism or Hearst" stamps to unions around the country and by mid-October, returns were coming in, and for the time being the heat was off financially. Now it was the national office's turn to complain. Erickson was failing to provide any accounting of the funds received, and this was bad as far as soliciting funds was concerned. Hull received numerous requests to get Erickson to comply with the auditing requirements. Erickson seemed to be becoming more of a problem than an asset, both to national and local Guildsmen. Not only were his books in a mess, but he seemed to go out of his way to annoy others in the Guild. [16] When the debt finally was down around $900 and funds appeared to be coming in better, primarily because of the stamps, Erickson on his own initiative raised the strike benefits for single men from $10 to $12.50, and no one discovered this for ten days. [17] However, the chapter immediately voted to hold to the lower figure, with only Erickson supporting the raise. Another annoyance was Erickson's hiring of a bookkeeper to help with the audit, again without anyone's sanction. The chapter lowered her salary from $22.50 a week to $18 and notified her that she would be needed for only a couple of weeks. But then, even Hull admitted that "somebody has to put some system in that office." [18]

By the first part of November the income from the stamps had dropped from a high of $300 daily to around $50 and contributions from the Central Labor Council from about $350 to $50 a week. This was about the extent of the regular finances, but the national office during the closing weeks of the strike was sending around $200 each week to help meet the Saturday payroll. [19]

By this time negotiations which were to lead to the final settlement were under way, and even Erickson no longer was vitally concerned about the finances. All Guildsmen realized they would end the strike owing money, but somehow the victory seemed worth the price. The flow of funds slowed appreciably as the negotiations moved toward conclusion, and a debt of nearly $3,000 still hung over the head of the Guild as the final settlement was made.

Although many felt Dave Beck and his Teamsters played the key role in supporting the strike, such was not the case.

The Teamsters did make a solid contribution to the strike, but in total it was something under $1,000. Some of this came early in the strike ($75), and the remainder came early in October when Beck surrendered the checks he had been withholding to Seller and Hull. Teamsters in other parts of the state contributed around $100. [20]

Total cost of the strike was $31,608.61, and by the time the audit was completed, all but $2,937.60 had been paid. By far the biggest share of the financial backing for the strike came from contributions, primarily from labor unions, but also from individuals. Although much support from the national office came after the strike settlement had been worked out, the funds furnished by the Guild headquarters were the largest provided from any one source. These amounted to $5,035.50, a sum much larger than most strikers believed the national office had contributed. The second largest contributor was the Seattle Central Labor Council, which pooled the donations of many Seattle unions and contributed $3,099.55 to the strike against Hearst. [21]

Probably the contribution which represented the greatest personal sacrifice on the part of the givers was the $417.20 furnished by the Guild chapter in Tacoma, the chapter which had spawned the birth of the Seattle chapter. The Tacoma group was small, but primarily due to the exhortations of Terry Pettus, funds were contributed regularly to the cause of the "brothers and sisters" in Seattle. The only other Guild chapter making a major contribution was that in Washington, D.C., which gave $526. [22]

Most other contributions were small and came from such diverse sources as "college kids" who contributed $5, a grade school in Kirkland which gave $3, and unidentified "friends" who gave $.15. Radio Speaker John Stevenson, candidate for the Democratic nomination for governor, gave $100, and Irving Clark, Sr., active in the liberal movement in Seattle, gave $50. For the most part, however, the contribution was like a roll call of unions stretching across the nation, representing every state and every type of union.

Other major sources of income included the sale across the country of the Hearst stamps, which contributed $2,604.94. Circulation receipts from the *Guild Daily* totaled $4,217.86, and another $2,608.03 came through the sale of advertising. The remainder of the total came from Guild dues, miscellaneous receipts, and $1,372.68 credited as a discrepancy — an amount not traceable to any source but believed to have come from early contributions when careful records were not kept.

The biggest expenditure faced by the Guild during the strike was the payment of strike benefits and the rental fees on printing equipment used in producing the *Guild Daily*. These outlays accounted for $21,066.71. The remainder went for such strike activities as publicity, $2,662.24; telephone and telegraph, $1,024.50; food for strikers and pickets, $2,155.26; and transportation expenses, $942.86. Also included in the Guild expenditures were $232.65 for the funeral expenses of Everhardt Armstrong, who died before he had been reinstated on the *Post-Intelligencer*. [23]

The audit, made in the spring of 1937, showed much was wrong with the accounting system which had been used by the Guild during the strike, but it also found there was no dishonesty in handling the funds and that the poor records were the product of conditions in the Guild headquarters. These were described as being "extremely crowded, pressure on all sides was unbearable, funds were lacking, opposition was violent, the strikers were hardly even recruits." The auditor, F. L. Kerzie, realized that parts of the audit just couldn't be explained because of the manner in which the records were kept, but these generally were insignificant, and he advised that "all further disquisition would be a waste of valuable time. Let there be said — FINIS."

But even the auditor had been caught in the spirit of the strike and added a brief note to place the deficit in a light shedding honor rather than discredit on the union. He contended that in fairness to the officials it must be remembered that a weak, newly-born union was overnight thrown into one of the wildest and most savagely antagonizing strikes in the history of this nation. "Not that the officials have not done better should be charged to them, but the fact that they have done so well should be recorded in American social history." [24]

FOOTNOTES CHAPTER VII
THE COUNTING HOUSE

1. Morgan Hull to Jonathan Eddy, October 2, 1936, Newspaper Guild Collection, Archives of Labor History and Urban Affairs, Wayne State University, Detroit. Hereafter referred to as Newspaper Guild Collection.
2. Audit, American Newspaper Guild Strike against the *Seattle Post-Intelligencer*, submitted on July 22, 1937, by F. L. Kerzie and Company, Certified Public Accountants, Seattle, Washington. The audit is part of the Guild file (MSS in Manuscript Division, University of Washington Library).
3. *Ibid.*
4. *Ibid.*
5. For criticism of Cliffe Erickson's management of the strike funds, see letters from Hull and Richard Seller to Eddy and Victor Pasche for the months of October and November, 1936, Newspaper Guild Collection.
6. Erickson to Pasche, November 5, 1936, Newspaper Guild Collection.
7. Erickson to Eddy, September 27, 1936, Newspaper Guild Collection.
8. Hull to Eddy, September 30, 1936, Newspaper Guild Collection.
9. Hull to Eddy, October 2, 1936, Newspaper Guild Collection.
10. *Ibid.*
11. *Ibid.*
12. *Ibid.* See also Audit for the flow of funds during this period.
13. *Ibid.*
14. Erickson to Eddy, October 13, 1936, Newspaper Guild Collection.
15. *Ibid.*
16. Interview with Mr. and Mrs. Terry Pettus, October, 1959; Erickson and Hull correspondence to national Guild officials during October and November, 1936, Newspaper Guild Collection.
17. Audit.
18. Hull to Eddy, November 1, 1936, Newspaper Guild Collection.

19. Erickson to Pasche, November 5, 1936, Newspaper Guild Collection.
20. Audit.
21. *Ibid.*
22. *Ibid.*
23. *Ibid.*
24. *Ibid.*

CHAPTER VIII

VICTORY THROUGH DIVISION

The Guild struck the *Seattle Post-Intelligencer* over the firing of two Guild members. The dismissals and the strike had locked the union and the huge publishing organization in combat over the crucial issue of union recognition. At least, the issue was crucial to Hearst, who recognized that giving a foothold to white-collar unions would accelerate the disintegration of his financial empire.[1] While the Guild generally saw recognition as its goal, lesser prizes often beckoned. By immediately turning the two dismissal cases over to the government for adjudication, the Guild had left itself vulnerable to pressures to settle on terms less than recognition. Without the issue of the dismissals to support its case, the union had little reason to expect that Hearst, who never had bowed to the Guild in any city, would recognize the Guild in Seattle. To the Guildsmen's surprise, however, their sometimes faltering efforts led to exactly that result. On November 25, 1936, a Hearst newspaper granted the Newspaper Guild formal recognition.

The strike accord, however, signified events of far greater importance than those that had unfolded in Seattle. If there was a central theme to labor history in the mid-1930s, it was the struggle of unions to win recognition throughout American industry. The division within the American Federation of Labor, the sitdown strikes in the auto industry, and the formation of the American Newspaper Guild all were elements of the development of collective bargaining in the depression decade, and the *Post-Intelligencer* strike must be seen in the broader context of national issues.

The National Labor Relations Act (Wagner Act), passed in 1935, promised effective protection for labor's right to organize and to be recognized by employers for the purpose of negotiating working conditions.[2] Enactment did not, however, assure compliance. In fact, the Act was bitterly opposed by a large share of the country's employers, especially by industrial associations such as the National Association of Manufacturers, the United States Chamber of Commerce, and the American Newspaper Publishers' Association.[3] From industry's viewpoint in 1935, there was good reason to expect that the revolutionary legislation never would be effectively enforced. First, it was clear that a repudiation of Roosevelt in the 1936 election would hamper union expansion and possibly lead to restrictive legislative amendments to the Wagner Act. Second, the conservatism of the Supreme Court augured well for a decision that would invalidate the Act. American business thus turned its efforts to framing legal arguments against the Act's constitutionality. The Court did, of course, uphold the Act, but from its enactment July 5, 1935, to April 12, 1937, [4] the promised government protection for union organization could not be fulfilled against the resistance of industry. And it was not until November 3, 1936, that business finally was convinced of the immense popularity of Franklin Roosevelt.

Settlement of the *Post-Intelligencer* strike also was complicated by the division within organized labor. At a time when the government was attempting to protect union organizing activity, the labor movement was badly split over the way to exploit the new era of government protection. During the strike the Guild, a member of the AFL, was shackled by the federation's reactionary interference with Guild objectives. To a large extent, the final victory in the Guild strike was won against other elements of organized labor.

The first settlement attempts came early, as political figures responded to the drama of the strike with headline-catching efforts to end it. The efforts failed, largely because the would-be mediators did not recognize the aims of the strikers or the labor movement that supported them.

On August 17, the fifth day of the strike, Mayor Johnny Dore met with Guildsmen at City Hall. Word had spread among the city's labor leaders that day that Dore, who shivered when Dave Beck felt a draft, wanted the strike stopped. The adverse publicity worried the Teamster official, so Dore was expected to be ready to call out his police to enforce the plant reopening. The union men went to the meeting, ready for Dore.

Union official after union official assured Dore that the labor cause was helped, not hindered, by the strike. And if this assurance were not enough, the printers added that they surely would consider the *Post-Intelligencer* unsafe under the terms of their contracts if police were required to reopen it.[5] Dore wavered. Then the Guild's West Coast organizer,

Morgan Hull, showing his persistently uncanny ability to manipulate events to the Guild's advantage, suggested that the mayor lend his prestige to settlement of the strike. The Guild, Hull said, would agree to the decision of any arbitration committee appointed by the mayor. Dore agreed to publicly propose the plan, although everyone in the room knew that the *Post-Intelligencer* had vowed it never would compromise on its refusal to recognize the Guild, and it was too soon to expect any change in that position. [6] Arbitration, by whatever group, would have implied recognition, since the Guild would have to be one of the parties to the dispute. The newspaper, of course, rejected the mayor's offer. [7] It isn't likely that Dore really expected his plan to be accepted; rather, he probably relished the discomfort it caused the *Post-Intelligencer*. When the newspaper answered the offer with more attacks on Dore's alliance with Beck, the mayor denounced the paper with characteristic bombast, then stamped to a mass rally a week later and declared, "I don't care now if the *P-I* never publishes and I think it would be a good thing for the town if it didn't." [8] Needless to say, similar early efforts at ending the strike by Governor Clarence Martin and County Commissioner John Stevenson, both Democrats, met with no success. [9]

Since the *Post-Intelligencer* had threatened to quit Seattle, it was in the interest of the community's businessmen to end the strike before such drastic action took place. In the 1930s, the threat to move out of a city typically was a bluff, but Seattle's business leaders hardly could concede that.

In September, Seattle businessmen tried to use a committee of the Seattle Central Labor Council to bring about Guild surrender. The ploy should have been expected. In the settlement of the *Wisconsin News* strike on September 2, negotiations were conducted not by the Guild, but by the Wisconsin State Federation of Labor and the Milwaukee Federated Trades Council. [10] Hearst's trumpeting through radio broadcasts of his refusal to accord recognition clearly indicated the same tactic would be employed again, which irritated the Guild.

The effort by the business leaders led to one of the few bargaining sessions in the early days of the strike. The attempt began with the business group telling the labor committee that the associate publisher, Charles Lindeman, was dead serious in his threat to close the newspaper permanently unless the strike ended quickly. The word was relayed to the Guild, which stood its ground, arguing that the paper was bluffing. The labor committee went back to the businessmen, who made an appointment to meet again with Lindeman at ten a.m. on Friday, September 4. The false scent of a settlement prompted the postponement of the National Labor Relations Board hearing. 11

The businessmen didn't get to the *Post-Intelligencer* Friday morning, however. Instead, the paper called for a meeting with its "striking employees," and at noon Dick Seller, Walter Rue, and Art French walked into the labor board offices for their first negotiating session. They talked three separate days with Lindeman and Edward G. Woods, representing the newspaper, and Charles Hope and Robert Watts, labor board officials. The Guild wanted concessions on recognition of the union, on reinstatement of Lynch and Armstrong, and on working conditions. The company did not move in any of the three areas. 12

On the second day, the company offered an "office policy" that, in effect, continued the practices at the time the strike began. The *Post-Intelligencer* offered to pay the "highest possible wage consistent with economic conditions and the operation of the property." Other terms were not as favorable as those stated in the Milwaukee bulletin-board agreement. The offer provided for a six-day, forty-hour week, a minimum of $30 a week for two years of experience, "equivalent time off or pro-rate pay" for overtime, sick leave with full pay, two weeks' vacation after a year, and a week of severance pay for each year of service up to three years. 13 French read the statement with a guffaw, tossed it on the table, and asked Lindeman if the *P-I* had any intention of getting down to business. 14

After lunch, the Guild committee put together its own "office policy." Its salary scales were graduated up to $40 a week after three years' experience with different scales for the employees of the newspaper's several departments. It provided for time and a half or compensatory time off for overtime, five weeks of severance pay, and vacation and sick leave similar to company policy. 15

At this point, Hull urged the Guild committee to press for the five-day, forty-hour week over other demands. In turn, he urged Jonathan Eddy in New York to guide the negotiating committees on the *San Francisco Call Bulletin* and the *Oakland Post-Enquirer*, both Hearst newspapers, to seek the five-day week. He believed that the Seattle strike had made the California managements uneasy and that an impending maritime strike would weaken their opposition to the demand. And, any progress on the issue in California would aid the Seattle strikers. 16

During the talks, the company's only concession had been to agree to consider a "stipulation" to be entered in the NLRB records in place of a signed agreement, as long as it did not recognize the Guild in any way. The Guild's proposed "office policy," however, was out of the question. The terms would not be "one iota better," Lindeman said, than conditions before the strike. Seller shouted that the *Post-Intelligencer* obviously did not want to settle the strike, wanted to postpone the labor board hearing, and wanted an unconditional surrender from its strikers. The three Guildsmen had put their heads in a noose by the weak terms they had proposed, he said, asking for movement by the newspaper "on at least one point." There would be no movement, said Woods. "I want you to know that the Hearst organization doesn't intend to recognize the Guild today, tomorrow or a year or two or three years from now, no matter what percentage of membership you have on our staff." The Guild told the NLRB to proceed with its hearing. 17

The early settlement attempts can be viewed most usefully as events that froze the parties in initial stances. Since no bargaining preceded the strike, no basis for maneuver had been established for either side. Recognition of the Guild and reinstatement of Lynch and Armstrong, of course, were issues before the strike, but progress toward settlement was not to be achieved by any simple direct movement toward these two goals. The process of negotiation, however, needed a starting point, and the early well-meaning efforts of politicians, labor leaders, and businessmen served that purpose.

In the sessions in the NLRB office, it was evident that the *Post-Intelligencer* intended to hold hard and fast to its position of non-recognition until it was moved by something with greater impact than the Guild itself could muster. Those meetings show dramatically that Guild members were perilously unsure of the Guild and its bargaining goals. Guildsmen had little hope of being recognized by Hearst; the

Milwaukee settlement, if nothing else, showed them this. So, for the moment, their eyes were on a simple change in working conditions, the five-day week. It was to be only a short time, though, before recognition again became the burning issue of the strike.

The American Federation of Labor made several attempts to intervene in the strike, but the Guild, already sympathetic with the progressive movement of John L. Lewis, viewed most of them as meddlesome. If the national federation had been a monolithic power in the labor movement, it probably could have dictated the settlement terms to suit its own desires. But the dominance of the AFL was badly threatened by the efforts of the CIO insurgents at the national level. In the Pacific Northwest, the break in labor's front was even wider. The federation could not command the support of the printing-trades unions in the region. Moreover, the support given the strike at its beginning by both the State Federation of Labor and the Seattle Central Labor Council worked against either of those bodies effectively carrying out AFL settlement mandates. The Guild, for its part, interpreted the settlement attempts of the AFL as damaging to Guild interests, and, with the apparent encouragement of Lewis, resisted their implementation.

The Guild did not formally affiliate with the AFL until July 22, 1936, only a few days before the strike. The event was marked by a $2,000 loan to the Guild by the federation, although at the same time John L. Lewis loaned $4,000 to the Guild and his good friend Heywood Broun. [18] On September 14, the Guild was admitted to the Northwest Printing Trades Federation, and Richard Seller was elected a vice president. [19] With the Guild thus tied to the AFL on both the regional and national levels, AFL President William Green asked Rowland Watson, a vice president of the Washington State Federation of Labor, to investigate the strike.

A year later, at the state federation convention in Olympia, Watson discussed his report to Green:

You all remember when we had the *Post-Intelligencer* strike, started by the American Newspaper Guild? You know what a fight we put up. You know that I wrote

116

the report backing up the Seattle Central Labor Council. I even go so far as to convict the *Post-Intelligencer* without ever giving them a hearing in my report. [20]

Watson arrived in Seattle August 24, hastily reviewed the situation, and sent off his conclusions to Green. The report backed the strikers to the letter. The *Post-Intelligencer* had fired two men for their Guild membership. Furthermore, Seattle labor was solidly behind the strike. The only violence was the deserved beating of the guard, Harold Hiatt. Beck, a great labor leader, had been shamefully embarrassed by the unjust charges against him. [21]

Harvey Kelly, a Hearst labor relations official, raged at the published Watson report. "Mr. Watson either did not confine himself to the facts or was not sufficiently interested to ascertain what the facts were." [22] However, since the strike had been "legal and orderly," Green decided for the moment that the AFL could not interfere. [23]

But, while local negotiations struggled along, pressure to end the strike built up in the AFL's international headquarters. Four international presidents of printing trades unions involved in the strike tried to persuade AFL President Green that the newspaper's closure violated the unions' contract agreements. Charles Howard, international president of the Typographical Union, wired the Seattle local that the strike was illegal and that ITU members "must ignore" it. Protests also were made by George L. Berry of the Pressman's Union, Monroe Roberts of the Mailers Trade District Union, and Edward J. Volz, president of the International Photo-Engravers Union. [24]

Seattle printers were not inclined to heed the advice of their international officers. Past disputes, including a bitter 1924 ITU strike, continued to rankle. For the mailers, too, it was a chance to regain rights lost in the 1924 dispute. "We knew something about Hearst from that one," a mailing-room employee later recalled. [25]

Then, completely disregarding his earlier decision, the views of the Guild, and the significance of the coming national election, Green yielded to the printing-trades chieftains in mid-October and called all the strike parties to a meeting of the AFL Executive Council in Washington, D.C. In addition to the international officials of the unions, Hearst and Seattle Labor Council representatives were summoned by Green. Hull, along with Jean Litonius, ITU; Claude O'Reilly, Labor Council president and a Teamster; and Bert Swain, Teamsters Union, made up the Seattle delegation. [26]

The meeting was ill-timed, to say the least. The Seattle ITU local had sidetracked its own dissident typographers. [27] Beck, for the moment, was supporting the strike with cash; [28] and the Guild had just rejected another management proposal with only two dissident votes. [29] The Guild was more confident than at any time since the strike began and saw no value in flying back to Washington, where the labor chiefs could rant, rave, and possibly force the Guild into a bad settlement.

In the matter of the national election, more than any other, Green revealed himself as an enemy of the Guild aims. Beck clearly was a more astute tactician than Green. On October 20, Beck wired Green and Tobin, international president of the Teamsters, that no settlement should be attempted before the election, other than one which recognized the Guild. [30] Hearst, of course, gambled on the outcome of the vote. Until November 3, he was content to let strike matters drift, if they could not be turned to his advantage. The publisher had been influential in promoting the candidacy of Alfred M. Landon, the Republican governor of Kansas, [31] and Hearst shared a longing with many of the nation's industrialists to see the end of the New Deal and a reversal of the tide of unionism it seemingly had allowed to sweep over factories, offices, and newspaper plants.

Hearst set in motion the machinery of the press blitz for Landon, ordered his papers to print frequent and large pictures of the candidate, and then sailed off to Europe to wait for the outcome. [32] In addition to Landon, whose ideology Hearst felt was safer than that of Roosevelt, the GOP ticket included Col. Frank Knox, who had directed the operations of the Hearst system for four years before he became publisher of the *Chicago Daily News*.

The stage thus was set for a climactic scene in the national drama. Without waiting for it to unfold, the nation's key labor leaders met in Washington from October 15 to 20 to argue the case for continuing, or ending, the Seattle newspaper strike.

Clearly, the AFL Executive Council was determined to settle the strike. "The heat must have been terrific," wrote Erickson, after hearing Hull's report of the meeting. 33 The international printing-trades presidents were joined in pressing for a settlement by Kelly, the Hearst labor-relations official, who argued that a 1909 resolution of the Seattle Labor Council barred placing a firm on the unfair list if the firm had contractual obligation with AFL affiliates. His efforts failed. His research into labor council archives was answered by the Executive Council decision that the 1909 resolution never had been acted upon officially by the Seattle Council, and that the strike was legal. 34 Even so, the national board pressed for a settlement. It wrote a settlement proposal, which it dispatched to the Seattle Central Labor Council with a polite, but firm, request for its acceptance. The strike, said the letter from President Green to Claude O'Reilly, Central Labor Council president, "has caused and is causing great human distress and community dissension. . . ." 35

The AFL proposal was no solution. Under its terms, the paper would be removed from the Labor Council's unfair list, publication would resume, and employees would return to work without prejudice. Disputes about working conditions would be referred to a Labor Council committee which would work them out with the *Post-Intelligencer*, using Green's assistance. If an issue became really knotty, Green and the paper would work it out. The proposal seemed to indicate that the AFL was no more interested than the Hearst organization in seeing the maverick Guild gain recognition. It would have bound the newspapers to meet "with any employee or the representatives of its employees in any department to consider hours, wages and working conditions," but it already had been demonstrated that the company could meet with its employees, quickly dismiss the meeting, and consider its bargaining obligation to be met. Moreover, the proposal praised the newspaper's record in collective bargaining, even though the basis for broad labor support of the Guild strike was an accumulation of bargaining grievances against Hearst's Seattle newspaper. 36

The proposal was mailed October 24 to Seattle, but it must have been evident to Green that it would not be accepted. Even during the Washington meetings, labor locals in the

Northwest, at the urging of the Seattle Guild, sent wires to Green opposing a settlement.37 Dave Beck's message to Green and Tobin, urging that a settlement attempt be postponed until after the election, was echoed by a resolution of the Seattle Central Labor Council.38 It is probable, too, that the Seattle delegation to Washington indicated clearly its opposition to settlement efforts, if not in the caustic terms Hull used in a letter to Jonathan Eddy:

I repeat that I believe in spite of the implications and what it may do to us nationaly (sic), that we sell ourselves down the river if we once permit the precedent of allowing 15 fakers to act as slave brokers to Hearst — certainly we participate in a terrific blow to labor solidarity in the Northwest and that is a blow the executive council wants to deliver. 39

Thus, when the AFL proposal reached Seattle, it was tossed to a joint CLC-Guild committee, the same one that had been conducting the strike. 40 The committee decided not to meet until after the election. 41 Meanwhile, the Mailers Union told the newspaper that its workers would not go back to work, even if a settlement were reached, until differences with the paper were resolved. 42 Finally, executive boards of six mechanical unions in Seattle, in defiance of instructions from their internationals, voted unanimously to "go on record endorsing the very fair attitude of Seattle Chapter of the American Newspaper Guild in offering arbitration." 43

As Broun saw the situation, the "executive committee of the AFL had worked hand in glove with the Hearst management in an effort to compel acceptance of defeat in the Seattle strike." He credited this attempt at forcing settlement with being one of the key factors in bringing about the move of the Guild to the CIO the next summer. 44

With the Executive Council proposal neutralized, the Guild in its publicity again stressed the failure of the *Post-Intelligencer* to agree to arbitration, a theme first exploited by Mayor John Dore. Shippers on Pacific Coast waterfronts struck by Longshoremen were crying for arbitration, and the newspaper's distaste for it gave the Guild the benefit of favorable public opinion. The call for arbitration, of course, was a stalling tactic by the union. Had the newspaper agreed to arbitration, the Guild probably would have yielded because of the strong possibility that working conditions would be favorably altered by an arbitration decision. The Guild, however, did not expect Hearst to accept arbitration. Hearst, they reasoned, hoped for a better outcome — no interference at all with the way he ran his newspapers. Beck and the Guild recognized, however, that at least for a short time the Guild could rally Seattle unions around it by urging a position that was both fair, in the public mind, and repugnant to the *Post-Intelligencer*. [45] On October 29, the Guild offered to sign an agreement submitting all issues to arbitration. [46] Management made no move to accept the offer. Eddy suggested later that, in addition to its unwillingness to recognize the Guild, which would be implicit in acceptance of arbitration, the publishing company feared that arbitration by a Seattle agency probably would have brought higher minimum wages, more severance pay, and the five-day week. [47]

Beck had wisely reasoned that the election would provide the key to settlement of the strike. Indeed, it wasn't until the radio broadcasts and black headlines had proclaimed the thundering victory of the New Deal that the Hearst organization revealed any interest in relaxing its inflexible position. Prior to the election, Hearst officials seemed to be playing games with the Guild, refusing to make it clear to anyone what authority, if any, they possessed to deal with the strike. Their boss, plagued by a growing realization that his empire was in deep financial trouble, [48] avoided all contact with the principal parties to the strike until the election.

Hearst's graceful public response to the election marked a turn of events for the Seattle strike, as well as the nation. The publisher answered an election-night telegram from the *Guild Daily* in Seattle:

> In answer to your request let me say frankly that in my opinion Roosevelt's victory is absolutely stunning to those who opposed him and utterly astounding even to his supporters.

> It justifies very largely the comparison of Mr. Roosevelt to Andrew Jackson, who is the only man in American history who had an equally overwhelming popular appeal and popular victory.

If Andrew Jackson's policies were essentially democratic, why is it not reasonable to concede that Mr. Roosevelt's policies may be equally so — dictatorial in manner, but democratic in essence.

The election has shown one final thing conclusively, and that is that no alien theory is necessary to realize the popular ideal in this country.

All that is needed is a vigorous application of fundamental democracy and a free exercise of American rights and liberties. [49]

The *Guild Daily* answered Hearst with a call for arbitration, an application of the democratic principles manifest in Roosevelt's election. Hearst's reply was further evidence to Guildsmen that the Chief realized the weakening of his position. He had condemned the nature of the Seattle shutdown, with its violence and ultimate success in interfering with publication of his newspaper, but he professed ignorance of "all the details of the situation in Seattle," and endorsed his own officials.

As far as I personally am concerned, I am perfectly willing to go as far as is consistent with the maintenance of a free and untrammeled press and of the essential rights of a free citizen to bring about a mutually acceptable adjustment.

There was only one problem: since the matter was already in the hands of the AFL, "of which I understand you are members," that body's decision should be "particularly acceptable."[50] Eddy called the New York Guild office to "urge that amicable overtures be made at once through the international." Heywood Broun met Hearst on November 9, and in Eddy's words, performed "splendid diplomatic service." [51] Broun described Hearst as "highly friendly and amiable," and added, "he expressed the hope that he had always been friendly to newspapermen and he wanted newspapermen to be friendly to him." Hearst, though weakening, clung to the position that his only remaining chance lay with the shallow terms of the AFL proposal. On the labor side, Eddy pressed his feeling that the Guild had gained a great deal because of the election. In a report to the Guild's International Executive Board after the strike settlement, Eddy said:

It had been realized by those watching the situation most closely that no halfway settlement in Seattle would enable the Hearst paper to re-enter the field with any prospects of financial success. As in Milwaukee, it was necessary that the management be able to go before the public on terms of complete agreement with its editorial employees.

Indeed, in both sides there was a distinct tendency in negotiations to proceed on the same basis as prevailed prior to these developments. Some of our best friends could not see the justice of our going far beyond what we might have settled for earlier, and on the Hearst side there seemed to be among lower executives a failure to realize that a halfway settlement would not meet the situation even from the Hearst point of view because it would not afford a means by which a Hearst publication could hope to re-establish itself with the people of the Northwest.[52]

Eddy's remarks were perceptive, although he probably did not realize how fragile was the financial organization Hearst headed.

In fact, the Hearst lieutenants were frantically proposing solutions to a financial crisis Hearst evidently had allowed to develop rapidly early in 1936. John F. Neylan, the San Francisco attorney who was a close adviser to Hearst in the 1920s and 1930s, once reminded the Chief that at the beginning of 1936 "you were in the best condition you had been for many years."[53] By mid-1936, however, Hearst was being shown financial forecasts that predicated continued profit levels only on "continued fair weather of every kind," and that acknowledged the company was hostage to rapidly rising costs (including wage increases for mechanical, but not white-collar employees). No longer could the Bart Guilds and other "efficiency experts" of the Hearst organization squeeze the difference out of the operations of the newspapers. On August 30, 1936, Hearst was told:

For six years, most of our efforts have been devoted to a persistent drive for economy. The results of these six years' work have taken us to a point where we cannot count on any sums of worthwhile importance from further economies.[54]

By the summer of 1937, the country knew that the Hearst organization was in deep trouble. The Securities and Exchange Commission asked Hearst to withdraw an issue of debentures; it was painfully evident the company could not bear the extra debt. With the company near bankruptcy, Hearst yielded to his creditors and gave up personal financial control.[55]

For two weeks after the election, neither side gained strength. The Guild held to its demand for arbitration,[56] while Hearst awaited the national AFL convention in Tampa, Florida, beginning November 15, where he hoped the Guild would be compelled by convention action to accept the AFL Executive Council terms.

In Seattle, Dave Beck lost patience with the Guild. Beck had not liked being the villain of the strike, cast in that role by the *Seattle Times* and the *Post-Intelligencer*. And, although he supported the strike, he probably saw no benefit in a sharp split between the local unions and their international officers. Moreover, Beck was emerging as a powerful figure in the Teamsters and the AFL and was disturbed at the Guild's growing cockiness and friendship with the disruptive Lewis CIO element. When the election failed to produce a quick capitulation by the newspaper, Beck acted. Though he had urged arbitration before the election, he sought to swing the Guild toward the AFL settlement, or, at least, "an interpretation" of it.

His effort was foiled by the very arbitration demand the Guild had made at his urging. As long as the Guild held to that position, it was unlikely that the Executive Council would force it to accept the AFL proposal. To a New York officer of the Guild, Hull wrote:

I gathered . . . that it was felt in N.Y. that a more aggressive stand could be taken than one of arbitration on all issues. I grant that it may look that way after the election, etc. Nevertheless, I cannot too much emphasize the necessity locally of taking a very firm stand in that position. It is the only thing that is saving us from the wolves. Beck and the right wing now are getting very damned nasty to us privately and threatening us even while they constantly admit, inadvertently, that our arbitration stand puts them and keeps them right over the barrell (*sic*). [57]

Then on November 9, Hull explained again to the New York officers why arbitration had been demanded. It "was a necessary strategic move to counter the A.F. of L. treachery," he said. In reality, neither the Guild nor Seattle labor likes nor wants arbitration. However, in a showdown between the AFL proposal and arbitration, the Guild position "would be our salvation." If a better offer came from Hearst, it would be easy enough to move away from arbitration, he said; until then it provided a safe base for "a lot of hell-raising . . . to discredit these fakers" (the AFL Executive Council). [58]

Although the Central Labor Council had provided solid support for the Guild, it should not be forgotten that Beck controlled the Council and that the vote obviously reflected his sentiment at the time. Soon after the election, however, Beck cut off union contributions, amounting to $400 to $500 a week from the local unions. Then he approached E. B. Fish, trying to find a way out of the troublesome impasse.

The Fish involvement with the strike began in September, about a month after the strike started. He was the *Post-Intelligencer's* own labor negotiator, whose duties overlapped in some ill-defined way the negotiating efforts of Harvey Kelly, who represented the national Hearst interests. Predictably, the *Post-Intelligencer's* left hand began to do things its right hand, Kelly, knew nothing about.

Fish had been a member of the automobile dealers' negotiating team in a Teamster strike in the summer of 1936. At some point, perhaps during that strike, Beck won Fish to his side, and during the *Post-Intelligencer* strike, the two men worked more closely than most labor officials, and perhaps even the newspaper's executives knew. Hull, one of the few who saw the danger in Fish's appointment, viewed him as "dangerous and unscrupulous" because of his former association with the Washington Industrial Council. [59]

Fish told the Teamster leader that several international presidents were collaborating with the Hearst management and that Beck personally was in trouble with them because of the recalcitrance of the Guild. Beck asked for a letter from Fish, showing he had full authority to negotiate for the newspaper. [60]

Fish, Beck and the Guild worked out an agreement extremely favorable to the Guild, and the Guild accepted it, subject to approval of the AFL. Seemingly, Fish then lost control of the situation. The Guild approved the agreement at the same time Fish tried to renege on it. [61] The proposal made the executive committee of the Seattle Guild the official committee to negotiate with the *Post-Intelligencer* (recognition, at last); referred the cases of Lynch and Armstrong, in the event the Supreme Court should void the NLRA, to an arbitration board recommended by Beck and concurred in by the AFL Executive Council; assured reinstatement of all striking employees without discrimination; and established that

E. B. Fish, speaking for the *Seattle Post-Intelligencer*, accepts in its entirety the settlement as submitted by the executive council of the A. F. of L. having to do with arbitration which does not affront the executive council or President Green. [62]

The *Post-Intelligencer* management had no choice but to repudiate the agreement. Although the managers had expressed willingness to accept the AFL settlement terms, they had not counted on an "interpretation" that gave Dave Beck the authority to arbitrate differences between the Guild and the newspaper. Only a few weeks before, Beck had sued the *Post-Intelligencer* for $500,000 for libelous criticism. Now Fish, a *Post-Intelligencer* employee, had invited Beck to settle this strike in any way he saw fit. It may have been humiliating to repudiate one's own negotiator, but it was suicidal to let Fish and Beck carry out their scheme. Lindeman called Kelly, who was at the Benjamin Franklin Hotel, to warn him that Beck was bound for Tampa to obtain a resolution denouncing the Hearst organization. At first, the negotiator balked. He had not liked Lindeman's decision to let Fish negotiate a settlement. Now, he reflected, "Let them pull their own chestnuts out of the fire." Kelly reminded

Lindeman that he had a reservation to California that day. But a few minutes later, Lindeman was on the line again, and Kelly finally agreed to try to head off Beck in Tampa.[63]

Kelly flew to Chicago and managed to board the same Florida-bound plane as Beck had. At that point, Kelly probably was the person best able to deal with Beck. In fact, the two had been working informally to bring about a settlement for some time. Beck later recalled Kelly's flattering confidence that the Teamster was "the one person in Seattle that he could deal with in a confidential manner and be absolutely assured that if we did not agree that the results of our conference would remain with each other."[64]

On the plane, Beck told Kelly that the *Post-Intelligencer* had double-crossed the Seattle Central Labor Council. Kelly asked to see a copy of the Fish-Beck agreement, which Beck pulled out of his briefcase. "Hell, this is no agreement," Kelly said. It had not been signed by the *Post-Intelligencer.* By the time the four-engine airliner landed in Tampa, Kelly was certain of his position.[65] Jonathan Eddy, innocently perhaps, happened to be waiting when the two men left the airplane, and the three rode together to a Tampa hotel.[66]

In discussions, Kelly took the position that the Fish agreement wasn't valid, while Beck painted Kelly's stance as a repudiation of a firm agreement by the Hearst organization. Green let Kelly take the blame for the Hearst blunder in allowing Fish to represent himself as empowered to settle the strike. Kelly recalled later that he lost his Irish temper:

> There isn't a damn one of you international presidents who is sending out representatives who hasn't given them wires or letters showing management how they're privileged to strike, if he once sees fit, and yet he's got to call you back before he can effectuate that and you damn well know it.

Finally, the council heeded Kelly's plea that there be no resolutions attacking Hearst and that the Seattle executives and the Guild be permitted to continue to work toward a settlement.[67] "This seemed to be a victory for the Guild, inasmuch as it left the management at last with nobody with whom to do business except us," Eddy said later.[68]

Then, in Seattle, Lindeman asked the Guild to meet with him.[69] There seemed to be compelling reasons for the newspaper, at last, to negotiate. The election was over, advertising contracts for the holiday season were unsigned, and every ploy tried by management to block recognition of the Guild had failed. Moreover, word that the newspaper had repudiated its own negotiator, Fish, reached Seattle businessmen who began to complain to Lindeman.[70] Even so, it was not Lindeman, but Hearst, who at last decided to end the strike. Lindeman said in 1959 that he had negotiated for several weeks with no support or guidance from the Hearst officials. Then Hearst personally gave him the go-ahead, and the settlement was quickly reached.[71]

Suddenly, all the stalling devices were dropped. Morgan Hull no longer was so offensive to Lindeman that his presence prevented the two sides from talking. The exhausted, tense Guildsmen, sensing that settlement was close, began to bargain. At times the Guild weakened, and Hull called recesses to rally his men and plead for a more militant stand. He wanted the contract to include a $50 a week minimum after five years of experience and arbitration of the Lynch and Armstrong cases. A little more time, he believed, and these two key demands would have been won. But Lindeman yielded on the most emotional issue of all. It had not been wage minimums or arbitration committees that had driven frightened men and women onto Pine Street the morning of August 13. The one issue was recognition of the Guild, and when Lindeman agreed to it, no orator, no matter how persuasive, could stop the tired Guildsmen from embracing their victory. When the agreement was read and Everhardt Armstrong heard the words, "as a result of negotiations between me and a committee of the Seattle Newspaper Guild," he broke into a broad smile and nothing else in the document registered at all. Hull said he felt "uncomfortably like a failure" because he had not convinced the others they should try for more, but he knew that they "are going back to work full of self-confidence and pride."[72]

Recognition of the Guild was implied by the signature of Richard Seller, Guild chairman, on the settlement document. (In Milwaukee, only a few weeks earlier, the settlement had been negotiated and the strike settled by a committee of the Labor Council without the Guild being signatory.) The Seattle agreement was not a contract, "but it is the policy in operation on the paper which will be continued for one year from date and as long thereafter as economic conditions justify."

All striking employees were to return to work without discrimination or prejudice and without reduction of salaries. The cases of Lynch and Armstrong would continue in the National Labor Relations Board.

A forty-hour week in six days until March 1, 1937, and a forty-hour week in five days thereafter were established. Sick leaves with full pay, two-week vacations for employees of more than one year, and a severance plan with one week's pay for each year, after one year and up to five-week maximum, were assured. These terms were essentially the same as those granted in the Milwaukee settlement.[73]

Wage scales agreed on also followed the Milwaukee standard. Editorial department employees with more than three years' experience were guaranteed $40 a week; those with less than three years' time, $25 a week. Library clerks, home economics, and society writers were to be paid a minimum of $25 and $20, and copy boys, office clerks, and messengers were to receive $18 and $15 minimums.[74]

The management promised no discrimination because of Guild membership and agreed to meet with employees to discuss grievances. The settlement was to go into effect when the newspaper was removed from the Labor Council unfair list.[75] Seller promptly notified Charles W. Doyle, secretary of the council, that "all differences" had been "amicably settled," and asked emergency action to remove the paper from the list.

In Tampa, the AFL convention continued, and on the morning of November 25, Jonathan Eddy rose to speak to the delegates: "I am sure that President Green, the Executive Council of the American Federation of Labor, and every delegate in this room will rejoice with me. . . ."[76] The strike was over, but the Guild was moving rapidly away from the AFL toward the new Committee for Industrial Organization.

Six resolutions had been introduced at the convention, calling "for condemnation of William Randolph Hearst, and a boycott of his publications; the reasons offered being the editorial and news policy of his publications and his alleged anti-labor policy." The Executive Council had agreed with Kelly before the convention to prevent any censure of Hearst. The American Newspaper Guild, realizing that the AFL now posed a threat and that its battle with

Hearst was only begun, refused to go along with the Executive Council. When a resolution to condemn and boycott Hearst came on the floor, Eddy supported it." [77] Tobin, the Teamster official, moved that the resolutions be "nonconcurred in," and Beck jumped to his support. [78] The resolutions were disposed of swiftly with Green pronouncing the benediction: ". . . (W)ould we, the defenders of the cardinal principles upon which our government rests, come into a convention and stand before the world as praising freedom of the press with our lips but denying it with our votes?" [79]

The convention also passed a constitutional amendment preventing unfair listing by central labor councils until all affected companies and labor unions had had time to intercede. [80] Eddy considered it a direct attack on the Guild, in view of the role the Seattle Central Labor Council had taken in the *Post-Intelligencer* strike. The Guild officials found solace in the thought that "in the recent past many central labor bodies have been forced to assert their independence in the face of autocratic exercise of dictatorial powers by the Executive Council of the American Federation of Labor." [81]

On Sunday afternoon, November 29, 1936, the *Seattle Post-Intelligencer* presses rolled again. Bundles of the afternoon edition, pre-dated for Monday, were rushed to the street corners, where they rapidly sold out. The next morning, the newspaper exulted at the happy acceptance of its return to Seattle. The newspaper's recovery, endorsed by organized labor, was remarkably rapid and complete. Hearst greeted the readers with a front page message and a startling announcement:

The Seattle Post-Intelligencer resumes publication this morning after its first period of silence in 69 years.

The controversy which rendered it mute was not of our choosing and let us say of it only that we have sought faithfully during all these past three months to bring peace.

An honorable peace is now ours. The Post-Intelligencer looks not to the past, but to the future, and in that spirit we now rededicate the Post-Intelligencer to a fuller service to the whole people of the Seattle region.

The authority to guide the paper during the coming years has been given by me into the hands of the new publisher, John Boettiger. Mr. Boettiger will have absolute freedom in directing the editorial and business policies of the Post-Intelligencer, his only direction being to make it the best newspaper in Seattle.

He brings to his task a long experience as an active newspaperman, and is thus well-fitted to carry out this important assignment.

William Randolph Hearst [82]

The Chief not only had conceded the popularity of the New Deal, but he had turned his paper over to the son-in-law and daughter of the President. Boettiger was a product of the *Chicago Tribune*, but he had married Anna Roosevelt, which was, in effect, marrying into the New Deal's royal family. Boettiger was to show repeatedly his *Chicago Tribune* orientation, but his wife was forthrightly liberal. Whatever would be their later success in publishing the newspaper, their appointment was Hearst's grand and successful maneuver to win popular support for the *Post-Intelligencer*, and perhaps to ease the impact of inevitable scrapes with federal regulatory agencies. [83] Boettiger arrived triumphantly in Seattle and was warmly greeted by Mayor Dore, who once had suggested the paper ought to quit publishing. Toasts to the *Post-Intelligencer* were capped by Dave Beck, who told Boettiger, "I speak for the entire organized labor movement when I say without reservation, mental or otherwise, we welcome the *Post-Intelligencer* back to the field. [84] Boettiger would have reason to recall that toast many times in the coming months. His father-in-law, the President, would be prompted to remind the new Hearst employee "that so far as labor relations go, Seattle is without doubt one of the two or three most difficult places in the United States." [85]

The Guild had won the war for recognition without knowing the outcome of its battle for the reinstatement of Lynch and Armstrong. Hearst had decided to make the battle a legal one — in 1936, with the constitutionality of the National Labor Relations Act still pending before the Supreme Court, the decision was predictable. Of course, he could have agreed as part of the strike settlement to let the two men return to work — a liberal gesture unlike Hearst and certainly in conflict with the attitude of American business generally toward the new labor legislation. So the case had to wend its slow way among the courts, confronting every possible legal test.

The legal battle over Lynch and Armstrong began on the first morning of the strike, when the National Labor Relations Board director in Seattle issued a complaint against the *Post-Intelligencer*. In answer to the Guild's charge of discrimination in the two discharges, the newspaper challenged the constitutionality of the Wagner Act and the jurisdiction of the regional labor relations board. The newspaper operated chiefly within one state, said the answer, and was out of the reach of the interstate jurisdiction of the board. The stage was thus set for the extended hearings of the Labor Board in the case. [86]

The hearings must be viewed against the national legal crisis involving the Wagner Act. Since its passage, business had kept the legislation under steady and severe attack. At the time of the hearing, the American Newspaper Publishers' Association took the position that publishers "should flatly refuse to have anything to do with the National Labor Relations Board, other than to notify it it is without power under the Constitution to interfere with their business." [87] The Supreme Court held the key to enforcement of the Act, and the Board knew that it must offer the court clear-cut, strong cases. The famed Schecter decision that had invalidated the National Recovery Act and its labor provision had been a poor case, regardless of the evident Supreme Court antagonism to the New Deal. Thus, in May, 1936, regional staffs were told to concentrate on cases involving interstate transportation and communication. [88]

The *Post-Intelligencer* case would have been an excellent test of the board's jurisdiction, but it was preceded by nine months by a similarly far-ranging case involving the dismissal of a national Guild officer by the Associated Press. In that case, the board had found AP guilty of an unfair labor practice and had been sustained in July, 1936, by the Circuit Court of Appeals. The AP decision was to be announced in April, 1937, in the court's historic decisions upholding the Wagner Act. Meanwhile, the board had to build substantial evidence that newspapers, as well as wire services, were engaged in interstate commerce. That was the basic strategy in the *Post-Intelligencer* hearings.

The decision of the board was issued on January 13, 1937. The order listed nine counts of interference, restraint, or coercion by the employer against the union. The discharges were discriminatory against union members, the board ruled, and the reinstatement of Lynch and Armstrong was ordered with full back pay.

> The Board is convinced that (Lynch's) ultimate discharge was due to the respondents' displeasure at his refusal to abandon his Guild activities. . . . the Board cannot believe that the respondents would have regarded Armstrong's attitude seriously enough to discharge him if they had not been dominated by antagonism towards the Guild. [89]

The order, as expected, was appealed by the Hearst organization.

As part of the strike settlement, "businessmen" in the community had given Lynch $1,300 and Armstrong $1,820 — the equivalent of six-months' pay. [90] The newspaper had continued to insist that their cases be decided by the labor board, while the Guild had urged arbitration. While he waited, Lynch accepted a job as a deputy sheriff — a kindness by the sheriff that won Lynch's lifelong gratitude. [91] Armstrong rebelled against taking interim employment. The Guild began to plan a testimonial banquet for the two men as another means of applying pressure on the newspaper.

Then, on March 18, 1937, Armstrong died. "The circumstances . . . were not the best," Seller later wrote to Hull. The *Post-Intelligencer*, to Seller's surprise, decided not to print the details. The funeral offered an opportunity to publicly embarrass the newspaper for refusing to reinstate the dead martyr and Lynch. The mayor and other speakers urged the newspaper to hire Lynch as a tribute to Armstrong. The city's major labor leaders spoke or served as pallbearers at the funeral. Seller described the event to Hull:

> There were no ministerial trappings, and it was an impressive rite, with — oddly — a congregation which in itself was a tribute to Armstrong. There were ragged

men from WPA, alongside women in lavish furs. There was the manager of the town's largest department store — Frederick and Nelson — alongside a longshoreman. A seaman stood beside Cecilia Schultz, whose impresario efforts bring Seattle its concerts and dancers.

A peaked-faced man with the soles missing from his shoes stood for a moment before the casket and clicked his heels together and clapped his hand to his forehead in military salute.

It was a demonstration which I will never forget.[92]

It was not the Armstrong funeral, however, that finally prompted the Hearst newspaper to respond on the two dismissals. Even a resolution by the Central Labor Council in February urging reinstatement had not moved management to act, although it was evidently alarmed by labor's reaction to the case. In a letter, Seller reported a conversation with Boettiger that indicated the source of management resistance: Woods, Hearst's attorney, had told Hearst that the two men were fired for cause, and that the labor board decision would be overturned in court.[93] The Chief evidently listened to his counsel.

Guild leaders responded negatively to Boettiger's offer to arrange permanent jobs for the two men — away from the *Post-Intelligencer*. "Boettiger frankly wants to pay the Guild to quit fighting for a just cause," said Hull.[94]

Then, on April 12, the Supreme Court upheld the Wagner Act. The next day, Boettiger refused to reinstate Lynch, pleading that the case was not in his hands.[95] Had Boettiger not yet heard from Hearst? Exactly a week later, Boettiger invited Lynch to return to work, with the matter of back pay to be worked out.

Lynch did not accept the idea graciously.

I wasn't going to talk to (Boettiger) on the P-I. I'd talk to him anywhere else he'd name. . . . So he agreed to meet me over in the Mayflower Hotel, and I remember that he bitched like hell when I showed up there because I think the room cost him two and a half. "I can't go on rentin' rooms all the time. It's costing the paper money."

* * *

And I said, I don't think I want to come back. He says, what do you mean by that. And I says, well, you've lost this decision, you're going to have to take me back eventually, you're not going to go any place just appealing on the constitutionality of this, and in the meantime I'm getting paid for everything. [96]

Boettiger's threat to publicize Lynch's refusal to accept the offer and Seller's pleading to accept the victory persuaded Lynch to return to work.

The final legal step took place on March 23, 1939, when the Ninth Circuit Court of Appeals upheld the NLRB order, ordering back pay to Lynch and to personal representatives of Armstrong. [97]

FOOTNOTES CHAPTER VIII

VICTORY THROUGH DIVISION

1. Daniel J. Leab, *A Union of Individuals* (New York: Columbia University Press, 1970), pp. 243-244.
2. See Irving Bernstein, *The New Deal Collective Bargaining Policy* (Berkeley and Los Angeles: University of California Press, 1950).
3. Richard C. Cortner, *The Wagner Act Cases* (Knoxville: The University of Tennessee Press, 1964), pp. 88-97. See also Edwin Emery, *History of the American Newspaper Publishers' Association* (Minneapolis: The University of Minnesota Press, 1950), pp. 234-235.
4. The Wagner Act was upheld in five decisions read April 12, 1937, by the Supreme Court. Among the decisions recognizing the power of the federal government to protect union organization under the commerce clause of the Constitution was Associated Press v. NLRB, 301 U.S. 103 (1937).
5. Telephone interview with Richard Seller, May, 1959.
6. Seller interview, June, 1961.
7. *Guild Daily*, August 19, 1936.
8. The *Seattle Times*, August 19, 1936.
9. The *New York Times*, August 26, 1936.
10. *Editor & Publisher*, September 5, 1936; Leab, p. 258.
11. Morgan Hull to Jonathan Eddy, September 20, 1936, Newspaper Guild Collection, Archives of Labor History and Urban Affairs, Wayne State University, Detroit. Hereafter referred to as Newspaper Guild Collection.
12. *Ibid.*
13. "Employment Policy in News and Feature Departments," undated, Newspaper Guild Collection.
14. Hull to Eddy, September 20, 1936, Newspaper Guild Collection.
15. "Employment Policy in Editorial Departments," undated, Newspaper Guild Collection.
16. Hull to Eddy, September 20, 1936, Newspaper Guild Collection.
17. Richard Seller to Eddy, September 21, 1936, Newspaper Guild Collection.
18. Walter Galenson, *The CIO Challenge to the AFL* (Cam-

bridge: Harvard University Press, 1960), p. 552.

19. *Guild Daily*, September 14, 1936.

20. Washington State Federation of Labor, *Proceedings of the Thirty-sixth Annual Convention*, Bellingham, Washington, July 12-15, 1937 (Seattle: The Trade Printery, 1937), p. 88.

21. The *Seattle Times*, September 5, 1936.

22. *Ibid.*

23. *Guild Daily*, September 5, 1936.

24. *Current History*, October, 1936, p. 15.

25. C. S. Patterson interview, April, 1959.

26. Cliffe Erickson to Eddy, October 14, 1936, Newspaper Guild Collection.

27. Hull to Eddy, October 2, 1936, Newspaper Guild Collection.

28. *Ibid.*

29. Hull to Eddy, November 1, 1936, Newspaper Guild Collection.

30. Hull to Eddy, October 22, 1936, Newspaper Guild Collection.

31. W. A. Swanberg, *Citizen Hearst* (New York: Charles Scribner's Sons, 1961), pp. 474, 477.

32. National Labor Relations Board, "Transcript of Hearings in Case C-136" (Seattle Hearings), p. 554; testimony of Raymond Holmes, *Post-Intelligencer* librarian.

33. Erickson to Eddy, October 26, 1936, Newspaper Guild Collection.

34. National Labor Relations Board, "Transcript of Hearings in Case C-136" (Washington, D.C. hearings), pp. 231-232.

35. William Green and AFL Executive Council to Claude O'Reilly, October 24, 1936, Newspaper Guild Collection.

36. "A Proposal," attached to letter, Green to O'Reilly, October 24, 1936, Newspaper Guild Collection.

37. Erickson to Eddy, October 26, 1936, Newspaper Guild Collection.

38. Hull to Eddy, October 22, 1936, Newspaper Guild Collection.

39. *Ibid.*

40. Erickson to Eddy, October 29, 1936, Newspaper Guild Collection.

41. *Guild Daily*, October 29, 1936.

42. *Ibid.*, October 30, 1936.

43. Hull to Clyde Beals, November 3, 1936, Newspaper Guild Collection.
44. Heywood Broun, "Shoot the Works," *New Republic*, Hearst was worried in 1936, and which resulted in re-
45. Hull to Eddy, October 24, 1936, Newspaper Guild Collection.
46. *Guild Daily*, October 30, 1936.
47. Eddy to the International Executive Board, December 9, 1936, Newspaper Guild Collection.
48. Swanberg documents the financial crisis about which Hearst was worried in 1936, and which resulted in reorganization in 1937 and 1938. See also Bruce Bliven, "Dear William Randolph," *New Republic*, December 2, 1936, pp. 141-142.
49. *Guild Daily*, November 5, 1936.
50. William Randolph Hearst to H. Richard Seller, November 5, 1936, Newspaper Guild Collection.
51. Eddy to International Executive Board, December 9, 1936, Newspaper Guild Collection.
52. *Ibid.*
53. Neylan to Hearst, March 8, 1944, John F. Neylan Papers (MSS in Bancroft Library, University of California, Berkeley). Hereafter referred to as Neylan Papers.
54. T. J. White to W. R. Hearst, August 30, 1936. Neylan Papers.
55. Swanberg, pp. 483-485.
56. H. Richard Seller to C. B. Lindeman, November 6, 1936, Newspaper Guild Collection.
57. Hull to Beals, November 7, 1936, Newspaper Guild Collection.
58. Hull to Milton Kaufman and Victor Pasche, November 9, 1936, Newspaper Guild Collection.
59. Erickson to Pasche, November 11, 1936, Newspaper Guild Collection.
60. Hull to Eddy, *et al.*, November 12, 1936, Seattle folder, Newspaper Guild Collection.
61. Pasche to Hull, November 14, 1936; Erickson to Eddy, November 12, 1936, Newspaper Guild Collection.
62. *Guild Daily*, November 16, 1936.
63. Harvey J. Kelly interview, April, 1959
64. Dave Beck interview, April, 1959.
65. Kelly interview, April, 1959.

66. Eddy to Clyde, Milt, Vic., etc., undated, Newspaper Guild Collection.
67. Kelly interview, April, 1959.
68. Eddy to International Executive Board, December 9, 1936, Newspaper Guild Collection.
69. Hull to Eddy, November 28, 1936, Newspaper Guild Collection.
70. *Ibid.*
71. C. B. Lindeman interview, April, 1959.
72. Hull to Eddy, November 28, 1936, Newspaper Guild Collection.
73. Untitled copy of agreement between Lindeman and Seller, November 25, 1936, Newspaper Guild Collection.
74. *Ibid.*
75. *Ibid.*
76. American Federation of Labor, *Report of the Proceedings of the Fifty-sixth Annual Convention,* Tampa, Florida, November 16-27, 1936 (Washington: Judd & Detweiler, 1936), p. 665.
77. *Ibid.*
78. *Ibid.,* pp. 665-667.
79. *Ibid.,* p. 668.
80. *Ibid.,* pp. 732, 751.
81. Eddy to International Executive Board, December 9, 1936, Newspaper Guild Collection.
82. *Post-Intelligencer,* November 30, 1936.
83. Swanberg, p. 479.
84. *Post-Intelligencer,* December 4, 1936.
85. Elliott Roosevelt, ed., *F.D.R., His Personal Letters* (New York: Duell, Sloan & Pearce, 1947-1950), Vol. 3, p. 687.
86. National Labor Relations Board, "Transcript of Hearings in Case C-136" (Seattle hearings).
87. Cortner, p. 97.
88. *Ibid.,* p. 103.
89. National Labor Relations Board, *Decisions and Orders of the National Labor Relations Board,* Vol. 2, July 1, 1936-July 1, 1937 (Washington: U.S. Government Printing Office, 1937), p. 530.
90. Hull to Eddy, November 28, 1936, Newspaper Guild Collection.
91. Frank Lynch interview, May, 1959.
92. Seller to Hull, May 1, 1937, Newspaper Guild Collection.

93. Seller to Eddy, February 18, 1937, Newspaper Guild Collection.
94. Hull to Seattle Newspaper Guild, March 15, 1937, Newspaper Guild Collection.
95. Seller to International Executive Board, April 13, 1937, Newspaper Guild Collection. The same day Randolph Hearst wired his father: "After Wagner decision have joined Guild. Hallelujah." Hearst replied: "Ataboy! You better get into politics or some other form of crime. That is the only thing which will pay under the Wagner decision." E. D. Coblentz Papers (MSS in Bancroft Library, University of California, Berkeley).
96. Lynch interview, May, 1959.
97. 102 F2d 658 (1939).

CHAPTER IX

AFTERMATH

The peace which supposedly follows a conflict seldom is realized. So it was for members of the Guild involved in the *Post-Intelligencer* strike. Presumably the Guild won a victory. Through a series of fortuitous circumstances, the nation's most famous publisher was forced to recognize the American Newspaper Guild as a bargaining agent. This was the breakthrough which the union needed nationally, and within a short time Hearst also recognized units in San Francisco and New York. New unit charters were issued across the country as reporters heartened by the victory of the Seattle group sought to gain union benefits. It was the first real triumph the Guild had won through a strike, and this was important to such a fledgling organization.

The members of the Seattle unit were proud of the fight which they had waged and won. They were proud that their efforts had helped strengthen the organization nationally. But, somehow, they never quite felt that those who joined the Guild after it was well established fully appreciated the significance of the strike. Years later Slim Lynch had mellowed considerably from his "bull in a china closet" mood of the 1936 strike days. He maintained his membership in the Guild but played no active part in the organization. The young members then were not even aware of the martyrdom which Lynch had shared with Armstrong during the strike. He was just another photographer who could tell fascinating stories, and eventually this skill earned him a position as a *Post-Intelligencer* columnist. But he remembered the days of the strike, the role which he played, and the courage he showed. He was sure that somewhere in the Guild offices, then located in New York, were people who knew the name of Slim Lynch and what it stood for in the annals of Guild history.

In the late 1930s he made a pilgrimage east and stopped at the Guild headquarters. The people there didn't know who he was any more than the young reporters on the *Post-Intelligencer* knew of his role in the Guild. The name Slim Lynch meant nothing, and the *Post-Intelligencer* strike was only a vague recollection. Lynch was philosophical: "Hell, that's just the way things were." He did stop at the headquarters long enough to propose that a statue be erected to the man he thought was most responsible for the Guild victory in Seattle. He nominated Bart Guild, the Hearst efficiency expert who had created such undesirable working conditions on the *Post-Intelligencer* that the men and women were willing to join the Guild even if it meant becoming martyrs to the union's cause. [1]

Despite the three-and-a-half month strike, the *Post-Intelligencer's* recovery was quick and in many ways amazing. Primarily it was due to William Randolph Hearst, who realized that changes were needed if the paper were to regain any position of financial strength in Seattle.

Hearst's seemingly brilliant strategem was to court public and labor support for the newspaper by replacing its good, gray top executives with an attractive and charming couple who were members of the President's family. John Boettiger and Anna Roosevelt Boettiger came to Seattle immediately after the strike. Boettiger's appointment was a wise move by Hearst. Although the move neither brought internal peace to the newspaper nor improved its quality very much, it did appeal to the citizens of Seattle and helped to counteract the "I Don't Read Hearst" atmosphere which had been so prevalent during the strike.

Boettiger's modest $30,000 annual salary showed he was not a power in the corporation, and other executives said as much. An internal corporate report in 1937 commented: "He may be all right, but the considerations actually involved in his employment would make the possibility that he is a competent newspaper executive a coincident (*sic*)." One of those considerations obviously was that organized labor's help was needed for the newspaper to reopen successfully. Dan Tobin, the international Teamster president and friend of FDR, and Dave Beck agreed completely; the appointment of Boettiger was a fine move. The fanfare for the Boettigers didn't fool Beck, however. He understood that they had been appointed in defiance of corporate tradition solely because the publication was in distress. Beck could be a great help to the *P-I*, but there was the small matter of the libel suits that he wanted to discuss with the new publisher. With Beck's help and the Boettigers' appeal, Hearst was able to re-establish the *Post-Intelligencer* almost immediately. Within a few weeks circulation reached its former level, and advertising lineage rose steadily. [2]

The strikers themselves had no such easy adjustment back to their positions on the paper. The central issue which had precipitated the strike still remained unsettled; the cases of Lynch and Armstrong were still in the hands of the National Labor Relations Board, and the two martyrs were not a part of the group returning to the *Post-Intelligencer* following the general settlement. All future employees would enjoy the better working conditions, better wages, and better hours which the strike had won. But few felt any necessity to express gratitude to the Guild for the conditions of their hiring. And, in addition to the new employees, those who had remained loyal to Hearst during the strike felt more antagonistic than ever toward the Guild and its members. These included Robert Bermann, Fred Niendorff, Douglass Welch, Berne Jacobsen, Paul Stoefel, Marion Stixrood, and many others — nearly half of the editorial department of the paper. The feelings between these people and the strikers were deep and bitter. The returning strikers could sense the resentment, the suspicion, the contempt which many loyal employees felt. There was always the question: "How could you have done that to a paper which had paid your salary for years?" 3

Those suspicious of the political leanings of the Guild seemed to regard its members as dangerous fanatics who waited only for the proper time to betray all that was good and American into the hands of some radical, foreign ideology. Slim Lynch, after his return to the paper, never got over the feeling that some regarded him as sort of a Eugene Debs. 4

Such an atmosphere made the return to work a demoralizing experience rather than a triumph. If the Guild were to be an effective bargaining agent for the editorial employees, it needed the support of most editorial employees. Such was not the case. Those who remained loyal to Hearst were contemptuous of the Guild and went out of their way to show their disdain. They had their own informal organization which was held together by the agreement that none of its members would join the Guild and let the Guild negotiate for them. This was called the "fink unit" by loyal Guild members. 5 For the most part these were the men who had the better salaries and working conditions on the paper and could have gained little from the newspaper union. When notices went up on the bulletin board of Guild meetings, almost immediately a notice went up from the loyalists also calling a meeting. [6] Only one person joined the Guild chapter in the three months following the strike's end. [7] Such conflict bred further bitterness and made it impossible to forget the strike. Considerable consternation arose within the Seattle Chapter at the idea of admitting the so-called "fink" members for fear that new members would control the Seattle Guild. [8]

In addition to such petty actions, some outside the Guild still were opposed to the idea of a newspaper writers' union, and daily these men grew more suspicious as the Guild moved closer and closer to the leftist CIO. There was a strong suspicion that the communist influence within the Guild was growing.

Nationally, the strong and influential New York local Guild provided the radical leftist leadership which was ascending within the organization. Organizers which the Guild was hiring and sending out to help run the strikes were strongly suspected of being sympathetic to, if not members of, the Communist Party. Morgan Hull, who had been sent to represent the national during the *Post-Intelligencer* strike, was suspected by many of being a member of the Communist Party. Those who knew him best certainly realized he leaned toward this solution to the world's problems if he did not actually belong to the party which advocated communism as an absolute answer.[9] The rumor circulated that there was no chance of becoming an organizer for the national Guild unless you were a member of the party, and as the national Guild inched closer to the CIO, the suspicions grew stronger.[10]

Organizers for the Communist Party in Seattle were active during the period of the *Post-Intelligencer* strike. Maurice Rappaport, executive secretary of the Communist Party in the Pacific Northwest, had brought the small party of a few members in 1932 to a membership of nearly 6,000 by 1936. These were spread over the Pacific Northwest, but Seattle provided an important center for the party.[11] Rappaport, always more interested in the blue-collar worker than the so-called intellectual, was not particularly aware nor concerned about the recruiting being done in the newly-organized Guild.

During, and in the few months following the *Post-Intelligencer* strike, several members of the Seattle Guild became members of the party and as a result more sympathetic to the direction in which the national Guild was heading. Several Guild members were approached to join the party. Some saw Marx as providing answers to the discouraging situation facing the United States in the mid 1930s, but only a few. Several Guildsmen were accused of being members of the Communist Party during the state's un-American activities hearings in 1948. [12]

Such commitment provided the Seattle Guild with a strong leftist nucleus from which to work, and from 1936 until after 1940 the battle between the left and right wings of the Seattle Guild was probably the unit's most prominent feature. The eventual wresting of the power from the leftists robbed the Seattle unit of much of the militant spirit which characterized its early days and undoubtedly deprived it of some of its effectiveness in carrying on labor's fight. [13]

The Guild's move from the AFL to the insurgent CIO was responsible for the Seattle unit finding itself in its second major strike within a year, when a picket line was thrown around the *Seattle Star* on July 3, 1937. The resentment growing out of the AFL executive committee's attempt to force settlement of the *Post-Intelligencer* strike had caused bitterness toward AFL unions on the part of the Guild, and the following June, Heywood Broun led his union into the more radical CIO. There were other sound reasons for the move, for now the Guild was placed on an industrial rather than the crafts basis which had characterized the AFL.

As members of the CIO, the Guild's members found themselves more isolated than ever in Seattle. They had to face not only the anti-union men, but also the united force of all labor which stayed within the AFL. The Longshoremen provided the one important source of strength for the Guild, but arrayed against them was the impressive strength commanded by their former ally, Dave Beck and his Teamsters. Within days after the 1937 Guild convention had voted to join the CIO and broaden the base of its membership, Beck moved to counter the new potential strength of the Guild and to block out new recruiting areas for himself.

The *Star* strike was a messy situation for the Guild, for as a national Guild representative termed it, ". . . this strike has just about every bad feature it is possible to imagine.

Except the fact that no strike was ever more justified." [14]

The two strikes presented startling studies in contrasts. Where the dominant factor about the closing of the *Post-Intelligencer* was the unity of the labor front, the very essence of the strike against the *Star* was the division which had taken place in labor. These two factions much more than labor and management brought the picket line around the *Seattle Star*. Whereas Beck and his Teamsters had been important components of the line around the *Post-Intelligencer*, now they were the reason for the picket line.

The act which triggered the strike took place on July 2 when *Star* management called a meeting of nineteen district circulation managers and introduced a Teamster spokesman, Lew Shaw. Shaw generally was regarded as one of Dave Beck's boys and was suspected by many of being responsible for the harrassment of some of the rank and file of the newsboys' unions which attempted to operate in Seattle during the spring of 1937. As the meeting opened, Shaw told the managers present that they would have to join the Teamsters union. All were members of the Newspaper Guild. These circulation managers did no delivery work themselves, but they did have employees working under them who used delivery vehicles. Shaw cited a 1911 executive council order of the AFL which granted the Teamsters jurisdiction over circulation employees. The *Star* circulation managers refused to change their labor affiliation. The *Star* management faced the problem of getting their newspapers delivered. As a result of the circulation managers' vote, the Teamsters employed in delivery walked off the job, and the nineteen Guild circulation workers were asked if they could guarantee delivery. Knowing what the reaction of the Teamsters would be to any such invasion of the truck drivers' responsibilities, the Guildsmen replied they could not. The Teamsters then were asked the same question and, of course, replied that they could guarantee delivery. Forthwith the Guildsmen were fired and replaced by members of the Teamsters union, and the second major Guild strike in Seattle was under way. [15]

This strike, which lasted from July 3, 1937, until February 5, 1938, was the longest Guild strike to that time and brought none of the fruits of victory which had accompanied the *Post-Intelligencer* strike. A strong picket line which closed the *Star* was broken completely a few days later when Mayor John Dore ordered the police to break the picket line, guaranteed safe passage to the *Star* employees, and the newspaper was published without a missed edition. [16]

Although many Guild participants in the *Star* strike were the veterans who a year before had fought with such enthusiasm against Hearst, now these Guildsmen seemed to have lost something. During the important opening days of the *Post-Intelligencer* strike, this desperate group of men and women was convinced they had sealed their doom as far as ever being employed on a newspaper again was concerned. They had had little to lose by the strike, and their main aim was not necessarily to help the American Newspaper Guild but to hurt Hearst. This they had succeeded in doing. They had won the strike, and the effort had won national acclaim as a great boost to the American Newspaper Guild.

But, in a way, it was a hollow victory. It had taken months to have Lynch reinstated on the newspaper, and Armstrong had died before the reinstatement. At times, the Guild was powerless to help its martyrs, and some wondered what the strike had been all about. Certainly it had not won any great position for the Guild as far as the *Post-Intelligencer* was concerned. In addition to those who were discouraged, more were just simply tired. Cliffe Erickson, Dick Seller, Fritzi Swanstrom, Lynch, and others continued to devote much of their extra time to the Guild. The debris from the strike was plentiful, and the financial situation was particularly vexing. The nearly $3,000 in back debts which remained from the *Post-Intelligencer* strike was a great detriment to those who attempted to mount the Guild effort against the *Star*. There were stories by Forrest Williams, Erickson, and others that the creditors of the *Post-Intelligencer* strike planned to sue the individuals involved. [17] Despite this, the Guild members were dedicated and probably in no city in the United States did the organization receive a greater payment of loyalty than in Seattle during the years 1936 and 1937. But the enthusiasm which characterized the strike in 1936 was quite different a year later. Naive enthusiasm can be given to a cause only once. The Guild members had learned.

The leader of the strike again was Dick Seller, and for seven months he led the battle as the National Labor Relations Board and the courts determined jurisdiction over the circulation managers. The Guild battled to cut into the circulation and the advertising of the *Star;* and in a very real sense this action eventually killed the newspaper, for it never was fully able to recover from the advertising and circulation losses which the strike caused. The strike ended practically where it had begun, with both the Teamsters and the Guild represented in the circulation department. The Guild took satisfaction in proving that it could stop Dave Beck from infringing on its organizing province. [18]

There was something admirable, however, about the Newspaper Guild which within eighteen months had, with various degrees of success, conducted two major strikes against newspapers in Seattle. One it had won with the united strength of the city's labor unions, and one it had carried on against much of the strength of the city's labor — and particularly Dave Beck.

Dave Beck — as much if not more than the Guild — gained from the strikes, particularly against the *Post-Intelligencer.* He had taken on the Seattle newspapers in the *Post-Intelligencer* strike, and he, on his own terms, had defeated them. This had nothing to do with the final settlement of the strike, but rather with his own law suits which were filed against both the *Post-Intelligencer* and the *Times.* Both had tried to arouse the community against this pugnacious labor leader and his drive for power. Both had sought to show that Beck's drive for power could lead only to the dominance of the city itself by the former laundry truck driver. And the papers had paid for their efforts. They had paid Beck $25,000 in cash, but they also had learned that it did not pay to oppose Beck. Beck had taught the papers the value of cooperating with the labor union. The consequence of the lesson was the silencing of any voices of opposition to Beck.

Beck had taken offense when General Clarance Blethen of the *Times* had accused him of being a bandit with a gun trained on the entire city of Seattle. "How do you like the look of Dave Beck's gun?" he had asked. "The shame of it."

Beck reacted by filing libel suits against the *Times,* the *Post-Intelligencer,* and at least two of the radio stations that broadcast *P-I* attacks during the strike. The publishers had, during the strike, begun the awkward task of assembling evidence of Beck's organizing tactics, evidence that would essentially prove the truth of the broad-stroke accusations made in print and on the air.

Times lawyers, in their answer to Beck's suit, retreated to literal statements suited to the testimony likely from witnesses the newspapers might recruit. Beck, the *Times* said in answer to his suit, "customarily employed pickets and strong-arm men who conduct unlawful picketing and picketing in an unlawful manner, accompanied by coercion, intimidation, threats, assaults, force and physical violence."[19] The Teamster, however, would have had good reason to expect to win the suits. The words, after all, were libelous on their face — the references to Beck's "gun" and his dictatorship. It also was likely the trial would occur before a jury and judge friendly to labor, if not to Beck, compounding the newspapers' task of making a few provable instances of Teamster violence add up to the defamation they had tagged on Beck.

Thus, when the strike ended, and John Boettiger took the helm of a paper that had to recover ground quickly, Beck was in a solid bargaining position. The Teamsters could do a great deal to help the newspaper reopen, but there still was that troublesome set of libel suits.

Beck's suits against the *Post-Intelligencer* and the *Seattle Times* were settled out of court for $25,000, a sum which Beck later contended was his original stake in real estate which eventually made him a wealthy man.[20]

Time magazine, referring to the 1936 *Post-Intelligencer* strike, commented; "It was the last time a Seattle paper ever spoke a harsh word about him (Beck). Today (1948) they publish editorials praising his statesmanship; critical references by Westbrook Pegler or Drew Pearson are carefully deleted."[21] Less than a year later, Pegler, one of the *Post-Intelligencer's* own columnists, wrote: "Most of the press of the Northwest surrendered to fear of Beck and professed to admire his 'practical' methods of abating friction, business losses, and disorder. With few exceptions, he is flattered and praised. Rarely is he opposed, and derogatory comment is suppressed as morbid pessimism."[22] This Pegler column did not appear in the *Post-Intelligencer*.

How true were the charges against the two large newspapers in Seattle? Had *Time* magazine and Pegler both been unfair in charging that the "newspapers were afraid of Beck and that they treated him cordially or didn't treat him at all?"

Between 1936 and 1944, the *Seattle Times* largely ignored Beck as far as any editorial comment. He was covered as a source of news, but no comment was given. During the war years, Beck began to emerge as more than a leader of brawny crews of laborers. He gained national recognition for bringing peace to the Seattle labor scene.

There were a few complimentary editorials. The *Times* played only a minor role in bringing respectability to Dave Beck. The *Times* did run some editorials from other papers, particularly when Beck was named to the University of Washington's Board of Regents. Criticism was published from the *Portland* (Oregon) *Oregonian;* favorable comment was published from the *Aberdeen* (Washington) *World* and the *Tacoma News Tribune.* 23

In 1957, three editorials appeared in the *Times* concerning Beck's appearance before a Senate committee which cast doubts on many of the tactics which Beck used as national president of the Teamsters. 24 The *Seattle Times's* editorials condemned Beck but were in no way unfair to him in light of the evidence presented before the committee.

As far as columns were concerned, there was evidence that criticisms of Beck were kept from the *Times's* editorial pages. A 1948 column by Victor Riesel, syndicated *New York Post* labor writer, which lambasted International Teamster Vice-President Beck, was strangely missing from the *Seattle Times.* The *Aero Mechanic* newspaper did not fail to note the deletion and charged there was a suppression of pro-union news in the Seattle area. 25 Also omitted from the Seattle newspapers was an anti-Beck column by Robert S. Allen, who called Beck a "strike buster." Again it was the *Aero Mechanic* which brought the story to Seattle, reprinted from the *Minneapolis Star.* 26

The *Times's* relationship to Beck changed considerably following the 1936 strike. Before and during the strike Beck and his labor union methods were strongly criticized. Following the strike and the libel suit, no locally written criticism, either editorial or letters to the editor, was run between 1937 and 1957. There was editorial praise of Beck's handling of labor problems.

The *Post-Intelligencer* during 1937 did run Pegler columns and a guest editorial attacking Beck. Various other

Pegler columns which criticized the Teamsters and Teamster President Dan Tobin were run through the years. [27]

On the *Post-Intelligencer* editorial page, numerous bold-face boxes appeared saying that Pegler had failed to provide copy for that day and that his column would be resumed upon receipt. Not all these omitted columns were critical of Beck after 1937, but none of the critical columns was run.

During the 1940s the *Post-Intelligencer* began to warm to Beck a bit editorially and to praise "Dave Beck's Sound Advice" when he urged cooperation between labor and business to keep Seattle stores open Monday evening during the Christmas shopping period. During a taxicab strike in November, 1944, the *Post-Intelligencer* called the attention of its readers to the fact that "Dave Beck is deserving of support in his vigorous efforts to see that the pledge of the Teamsters' Union against wartime strikes is carried out. . . ." [28]

When Beck was appointed to the University Board of Regents by Governor Mon Wallgren, the *Post-Intelligencer* commented: "Dave Beck should prove a valuable addition . . . as a representative of both organized labor and the general public. He is not an alumnus, but he has as deep a personal interest in the institution as if he were, having a son who just returned there from the Army." [29]

Beck's election in 1952 to head the Teamsters International brought more editorial comment from the *Post-Intelligencer:*

Seattle takes pride in the election of Dave Beck as general president of the International Teamsters Brotherhood. Congratulations should be extended to the union, one of the largest in the nation, on the wisdom it displayed in its choice of a leader. By the firm stand he has taken against communism and his consistent championing of the free enterprise system, Mr. Beck has given ample proof of his qualifications for the enlarged responsibilities of his new post. [30]

In November, 1955, the *Post-Intelligencer* ran another locally-written editorial praising Beck. The occasion was the dedication of the Teamsters' headquarters in Washington, D.C.

Seattle has a peculiar interest in the dedication of the building today since one of our citizens has a leading role in the ceremonies as head of perhaps the largest labor union in the world. Dave Beck not only made his way from humble beginnings here to a position of national leadership, but was so attached to his home city he accepted the presidency of the Teamsters only on the condition that he continue to maintain his home in Seattle. Mr. Beck's own career is a case history in the turbulent but always healthy and dynamic process in which the American way of life has been forged. [31]

The *Post-Intelligencer* ran its last complimentary editorial on January 3, 1956, when the Teamsters Union announced it would invest six million dollars in housing developments. The paper commented on Beck's statement, "The investment will be of direct benefit to the union but it also provides an opportunity for us to help the entire economy of the city."

That Beck is in a position to say this tells a great deal about the labor movement in our country. We think it tells a lot, too, about Dave Beck — a home town boy who made good — and made us like it, for our own good. [32]

This was written just a little more than a year before Beck appeared before the McClellan committee and the nation was shocked by the charges which the committee leveled against the Seattle labor leader. [33]

No doubt the *Post-Intelligencer* strike marked the beginning of the rapid ascendancy of Beck to what was probably the most powerful national figure in labor. Prominent politicians and leaders in the city were well aware after the *Post-Intelligencer* strike of the effort to change the attitude toward Beck. Former Mayor William F. Devin saw the rise of Beck and expressed the view that the press itself did not push Beck to his power position. "However, he couldn't have made the climb if the newspapers had openly opposed him." [34]

A former governor of Washington State echoed a similar belief. Arthur Langlie wrote: "I feel quite sure, looking back on it, that had there been a militant crusading spirit to effectively and intelligently fight this growing Beck domination, the serious consequences of his growing strength would have been halted." [35]

There is little doubt but that the attitude of the newspapers helped David Beck gain respectability in the years following the *Post-Intelligencer* strike. There was truth in the charges made against the Seattle newspapers that criticism vanished, that there was praise, that Beck was rarely challenged. Somehow, the press, which claims to be the watchdog and spokesman for the people, had been strangely quiet.

In a way, it was Beck who had gained the most from the *Post-Intelligencer* and the *Star* strikes. He had demonstrated to Hearst that he had the force to close a newspaper. This lesson was not lost on the *Star* management a year later. The Guild never gained the strength to be a serious challenge to Beck, while in ways it helped Beck demonstrate a strength which for years enabled him to dominate a city.

FOOTNOTES CHAPTER IX

AFTERMATH

1. Frank Lynch interview, May, 1959.
2. Beck interview, March, 1978; F. E. Hagelberg to C. J. Shearn, September 9, 1937, John F. Neylan Papers (MSS in Bancroft Library, University of California, Berkeley). Boettiger resigned as *P-I publisher in 1945* (after two years of military service). *Seattle Post-Intelligencer*, June 15, 1945, p. 1.
3. Lynch interview, May, 1959. See also letters from Dick Seller, Cliffe Erickson, and Forrest Williams to National Guild officials during winter of 1937, Newspaper Guild Collection, Archives of Labor History and Urban Affairs, Wayne State University, Detroit. Hereafter referred to as Newspaper Guild Collection.
4. Lynch interview, May, 1959.
5. See Erickson to Victor Pasche, January 19 and January 23, 1937, Newspaper Guild Collection.
6. Lester Hunt interview, April, 1960.
7. Forrest Williams to Jonathan Eddy, February 21, 1937, Newspaper Guild Collection.
8. See telegrams dated February 1 and 2, by Erickson, Seller, Eddy, Hull, and Pasche regarding the stituation. See also Hull to Eddy and Erickson to Eddy, both dated February 9, 1937, Newspaper Guild collection.
9. See Hull to Charles Daggett, February 10, 1937, Newspaper Guild Collection.
10. Terry Pettus interview, October, 1958.
11. Maurice Rappaport interview, April, 1964.
12. See Joint Legislative Fact-Finding Committee on Un-American Activities, *First and Second Reports on Un-American Activities in Washington State*, 1948. See also Vern Countryman, *Un-American Activities in the State of Washington* (Ithaca: Cornell University Press, 1951).
13. See David L. Evans, "The History and Significance of the Portland Newspaper Strike" (unpublished Master's thesis in Communications, University of Washington, 1966), pp. 287-288.
14. Tad Irvine to Pasche, July 13, 1937, Newspaper Guild Collection.
15. Ellen McGrath and J. P. Dallas, "The Guild Scores

Again," *New Masses*, February 22, 1938, p. 19. See also Irvine to American Newspaper Guild headquarters, July 13, 1937, Newspaper Guild Collection.

16. *Seattle Times*, July 8, 1937.
17. See Erickson to Pasche, January 19, 1936, Newspaper Guild Collection.
18. See McGrath and Dallas, "The Guild Scores Again," *New Masses*, February 22, 1938, p. 19.
19. Dave Beck and Dorothy Beck v. The Times Printing Co., King County (Washington) Superior Court, No. 292311, filed August 25, 1936; answer filed September 14, 1936. Dave Beck and Dorothy Beck v. Hearst Publications, Inc., and Seattle Broadcasting Co., King County (Washington) Superior Court, No. 296157, filed January 27, 1937. Despite the delay in formal filing of the case, the Becks' complaints evidently were served on defendants during the strike. *Seattle Post-Intelligencer*, January 28, 1937, p. 4.
20. Donald Garnel, "Teamsters and Highway Truckers in the West" (unpublished Ph.D. dissertation in Economics, University of California, Berkeley, 1966), I, 165.
21. *Time*, November 29, 1948.
22. *Spokane Spokesman Review*, February 7, 1949.
23. *Ibid.*, May 1, May 4, 1946.
24. See *Seattle Times* for March 22, 28, and May 21, 1957.
25. *Aero Mechanic*, August 19, 1948.
26. *Ibid.*, August 26, 1948.
27. *Post-Intelligencer*, November 25, 1937, for example.
28. *Ibid.*, December 27, 1943 and November 24, 1944.
29. *Ibid.*, April 24, 1946.
30. *Ibid.*, October 20, 1952.
31. *Ibid.*, November 4, 1955.
32. *Ibid.*, January 3, 1956.
33. Beck was convicted of grand larceny and was eventually pardoned by Washington Governor Albert Rosellini. He also was convicted on two counts of charges dealing with the tax returns of a union-related organization for which he was responsible, and served two and one-half years at McNeil Island federal penitentiary. He later was pardoned by President Gerald Ford.
34. Interview with William Devin, June, 1958.
35. Arthur Langlie to Dierdre Randall, May, 1958, quoted in Victor H. Bagnall, Richard Enger and Deirdre Randall,

"Dave Beck and the *Seattle Post-Intelligencer*" (unpublished research paper in Communications, University of Washington, 1958).

BIBLIOGRAPHY

A. BOOKS AND PAMPHLETS

Bernstein, Irving, *The New Deal Collective Bargaining Policy* (Berkeley and Los Angeles: University of California Press, 1950).

——————, *Turbulent Years* (Boston: Houghton Mifflin Co., 1970).

Blanchard, John, and Dorothy Terrill, *Strikes in the Pacific Northwest, 1927-1940* (Portland: Northwest Regional Council, 1942).

Carlson, Oliver, and Ernest Sutherland Bates, *Hearst: Lord of San Simeon* (New York: Viking Press, 1936).

Citizens Committee, *The Truth About the Post-Intelligencer Strike* (Seattle: The Citizens Committee, 1936).

Cortner, Richard C., *The Wagner Act Cases* (Knoxville: The University of Tennessee Press, 1964).

Countryman, Vern, *Un-American Activities in the State of Washington* (Ithaca: Cornell University Press, 1951).

Dulles, Foster Rhea, *Labor in America*, second edition (New York: Thomas Y. Crowell Co., 1955).

Emery, Edwin, *History of the American Newspaper Publishers' Association* (Minneapolis: University of Minnesota Press, 1950).

Emery, Edwin, and Henry Ladd Smith, *The Press and America* (Englewood Cliffs, N.J.: Prentice-Hall, Inc., 1954).

Freidheim, Robert L., *The Seattle General Strike* (Seattle: University of Washington Press, 1964).

Galenson, Walter, *The CIO Challenge to the AFL* (Cambridge: Harvard University Press, 1960).

Garnel, Donald, *The Rise of Teamster Power in the West* (Berkeley: University of California Press, 1972).

Gillingham, J. B., *The Teamsters Union on the West Coast* (Berkeley: Institute of Industrial Relations, University of California, 1956).

Glock, Margaret S., *Collective Bargaining in the Pacific Northwest Lumber Industry* (Berkeley: Institute of Industrial Relations, University of California, 1955).

Hass, Erick, *Dave Beck, Labor Merchant* (New York: New York Labor News Co., 1957).

Kramer, Dale, *Heywood Broun: A Biographical Portrait* (New York: A. A. Wyn, Current Books, 1949).

Leab, Daniel J., *A Union of Individuals* (New York: Columbia University Press, 1970).

Minton, Bruce, and John Stuart, *Men Who Lead Labor* (New York: Modern Age Books, Inc., 1937).

Morgan, Murray, *Skid Road, An Informal Portrait of Seattle*, revised edition (New York: Viking Press, 1960).

Neuberger, Richard L., *Our Promised Land* (New York: The Macmillan Co., 1939).

O'Connor, Harvey, *Revolution in Seattle* (New York: Monthly Review Press, 1964).

O'Connor, Richard, *Heywood Broun* (New York: Putnam, 1975).

Ross, Malcolm, *Death of a Yale Man* (New York: Farrar & Rinehart, Inc., 1939).

Schlesinger, Arthur M., Jr., *The Age of Roosevelt: The Politics of Upheaval* (Boston: Houghton Mifflin Co., 1960), volume III.

Schneider, Betty V. H., and Abraham Siegel, *Industrial Relations in the Pacific Coast Longshore Industry* (Berkeley: Institute of Industrial Relations, University of California, 1956).

Steuben, John, *Strike Strategy* (New York: Gaer Associates, Inc., 1950).

Swanberg, W. A., *Citizen Hearst* (New York: Charles Scribner's Sons, 1961).

Swindler, William F., *Problems of Law in Journalism* (New York: The Macmillan Co., 1955).

Tebbel, John, *The Life and Good Times of William Randolph Hearst* (New York: E. P. Dutton & Co., 1952).

B. GOVERNMENT PUBLICATIONS

National Labor Relations Board, *Decisions of the National Labor Relations Board,* volume II (Washington: U.S. Government Printing Office, 1935).

_____, *Collective Bargaining in the Newspaper Industry* (Washington: Division of Economic Research, 1938).

_____, *Decisions and Orders of the National Labor Relations Board,* volume II, July 1, 1936 — July 1, 1937 (Washington: U.S. Government Printing Office, 1937).

Federal Reporter, second series, volume CII (St. Paul: West Publishing Co., 1939).

Washington State Legislature, Joint Fact-Finding Committee on Un-American Activities, *First Report. Un-American Activities in Washington State* (Olympia: State of Washington, 1948).

Washington State Legislature, Joint Fact-Finding Committee on Un-American Activities, *Second Report. Un-American Activities in Washington State* (Olympia: State of Washington, 1948).

C. LABOR UNION AND MANAGEMENT PUBLICATIONS

American Federation of Labor, *Report of Proceedings of the Fifty-sixth Annual Convention of the American Federation of Labor,* Tampa, Florida, November 16-27, 1936 (Washington: Judd & Detweiler, 1936).

American Newspaper Guild, *Constitution.* Adopted by 1936 Convention.

National Association of Manufacturers, *Labor Relations Bulletin,* July 30, 1936.

Washington State Federation of Labor, *Proceedings of the Thirty-fifth Annual Convention,* Vancouver, Washington, July 13-16, 1936 (Seattle: The Trade Printery, 1936).

_____, *Proceedings of the Thirty-sixth Annual Convention*, Bellingham, Washington, July 12-15, 1937 (Seattle: The Trade Printery, 1937).

D. NEWSPAPERS

Aero Mechanic (Seattle), January-December, 1948.

Bellingham Herald, August 26, 1936 — December, 1936.

Business Chronicle (Seattle), October 2, 1937.

The Daily Worker (New York), August 15-30, 1936.

Guild Daily (Seattle), August 15, 1936 — November 27, 1936.

Guild Reporter (Washington), December, 1933 — January, 1937.

Guild Striker (Seattle), August 14, 1936.

New York Times, August 14, 1936 — September 20, 1936.

New York World-Telegram, August 7, 1933.

Portland Oregonian, 1936—1956.

Seattle Daily Times, 1936—1956.

Seattle Municipal News, August-November, 1936.

Seattle Post-Intelligencer, 1936-1956.

Seattle Star, August 13, 1936 — November 30, 1936.

Spokane Spokesman Review, 1936—1956.

E. PERIODICALS

"A Question of Affiliation," *The Nation,* CXL (April 24, 1935), 484-485.

Bliven, Bruce, "Dear William Randolph," *New Republic,* LXXXIX (December 2, 1936), 141-142.

Broun, Heywood, "An Army with Banners," *The Nation,* CXL (February 13, 1935), 184-185.

_____, "Because the Judge Says So," *The Nation,* CXL (March 20, 1935), 336-337.

_____, "Broun's page," *The Nation,* CXLII (March 11, 1936), 320.

_____, "Broun's page," *The Nation,* CXLIII (August 8, 1936), 158.

_____, "Broun's page," *The Nation,* CXLIII (August 24, 1936), 243.

_____, "The Industry," *The Nation,* CXL (February 20, 1935), 223.

_____, "Professional or Trade Unionist?", *Literary Digest,* CXXII (November 28, 1936), 33-34.

Editor & Publisher, XIX-LXX (August, 1936 — January, 1937).

"Embattled Guild," *Literary Digest,* CXXI (June 13, 1936), 30.

Emery, Edwin, "William Randolph Hearst: A Tentative Appraisal," *Journalism Quarterly,* XXVIII (Summer, 1949), 429-440.

"Furious Strike of Guild in Far West; Hearst-owned *Seattle P-I* Suspends in Battle," *Literary Digest,* CXXII (August 29, 1936), 25.

"Gift on a Platter," *Business Week,* August 3, 1935.

"Hearst," *Fortune,* XII (October, 1935), 42 ff.

"The Herdsman," *Time,* LII (November 29, 1948), 24-27.

Johnston, Alva, "Seattle's One-Man Revolution," *The Saturday Evening Post,* January 16, 1937.

Keating, Isabelle, "Reporters Become of Age," *Harper's Monthly,* CLXX (April 1935), 601-612.

Kritzberg, Barry, "An Unfinished Chapter in White Collar Unionism: the Formation Years of the Chicago Newspaper Guild, Local 71, American Newspaper Guild, A.F.L.-C.I.O.", *Labor History,* XIV (Summer, 1973), 397-413.

Levin, Ruben, "The People vs. Hearst," *The New Republic,* XXXVI (March 4, 1936), 106-107.

McGrath, Ellen, and J. P. Dallas, "Boettiger — His Master's Voice," *The Nation*, CXLIV (February 6, 1937), 150-151.

——————————, "The Guild Scores Again," *New Masses*, XXVI (February 22, 1938), 19-20.

Menefee, Selden, "Hearst Loses to Public Opinion," *Christian Century*, LIII (December 9, 1936), 1654-1656.

Meyers, W. Cameron, "The Chicago Newspaper Hoax in the '36 Election Campaign," *Journalism Quarterly*, XXXVII (Summer, 1960), 356-364.

Miller, Joe, "Dave Beck Comes Out of the West," *The Reporter*, IX (December 8, 1953), 20-23.

Neuberger, Richard L., "Labor's Overlords," *American Magazine*, CXXV (March, 1938), 16-17, 166-170.

"Newshawks' Union," *Time*, XXVII (June 8, 1936), 24, 26.

"The Newspaper Guild Attains Man's Stature," *Literary Digest*, XVIII (July 28, 1934).

"Strike: Broun Defies," *Newsweek*, V (March 23, 1935), 23.

OTHER SOURCES

A. INTERVIEWS

Beck, Dave, June, 1958, Seattle, Washington.

——————————, April, 1959, Seattle, Washington.

——————————, March, 1978, Seattle, Washington.

Brier, Howard, October, 1963, Seattle, Washington.

Camozzi, Robert, May, 1959, Seattle, Washington.

Daggett, Emerson, March, 1966, San Francisco, California.

Devin, William, June, 1958, Seattle, Washington.

Dore, John F., April, 1959, Seattle, Washington.

Farquharson, Mrs. Mary, May, 1969, Seattle, Washington.

Fay, Jean, May, 1963, Seattle, Washington.

French, Art, May, 1959, Seattle, Washington.

Gettings, William, April, 1959, Seattle, Washington.

Gies, Ethel, May, 1959, Seattle, Washington

Hillman, Mr. and Mrs. C. Kirk, April, 1959, Seattle, Washington.

Hunt, Lester, April, 1960, Indianapolis, Indiana.

Jacobsen, Berne, April, 1959, Seattle, Washington.

Kelly, Harvey J., April, 1959, Coeur d' Alene, Idaho.

Larkin, Mr. and Mrs. Floyd, May, 1959, Eatonville, Washington.

——————————, Floyd, July, 1960, Eatonville, Washington.

Lindeman, Charles, April, 1959, Seattle, Washington.

Lewis, Al, April, 1959, Seattle, Washington.

Lynch, Frank, May, 1959, Seattle, Washington.

Patterson, C. S., April, 1959, Seattle, Washington.

Pettus, Mr. and Mrs. Terry, October, 1959, Seattle, Washington.

——————————, Terry, December, 1960, Seattle, Washington.

——————————, June, 1961, Seattle, Washington.

Rappaport, Maurice, April, 1963, Petaluma, California.

——————————, April, 1964, Petaluma, California.

Reddington, Bernice, April, 1959, Seattle, Washington.

——————————, May, 1959, Seattle, Washington.

Rohlfs, Mr. and Mrs. Marcus, April, 1959, Seattle, Washington.

Ryerson, Roy, April, 1959, Seattle, Washington.

Seller, Richard, May, 1959, Portland, Oregon.

——————————, June, 1961, Seattle, Washington.

Smith, Mr. and Mrs. Claude, August, 1960, Seattle,

Washington.

Wakefield, Lowell, July, 1966, Seattle, Washington.

Weston, Edward, April, 1959, Seattle, Washington.

Williams, Forrest, April, 1959, Seattle, Washington.

B. DOCUMENTS

Stephen Chadwick Papers (MSS in Manuscript Division, University of Washington Library).

Citizens Committee. Public statement, undated.

_____. Press release, undated.

Eddy, Jonathan. Report to the International Executive Board, December 9, 1936.

Hunt, Lester. Letter to Roger Simpson, May 14, 1960.

_____. Letter to William Ames, December 23, 1959.

Kelly, Harvey. Letter to Roger Simpson, June 13, 1959.

National Labor Relations Board. Transcript of Hearings in Case C-136; William Randolph Hearst, etc., and American Newspaper Guild, Seattle Chapter, 1936. Included Seattle hearings, September 10-29, 1936, pp. 1-2095; Washington hearings, November 9-10, 1936, pp. 1-300, and respondents and board exhibits.

Newspaper Guild Collection, Archives of Labor History and Urban Affairs, Wayne State University, Detroit.

John D. Neylan Papers (MSS in Bancroft Library, University of California, Berkeley).

Terry Pettus Papers (MSS in Manuscript Division, University of Washington Library).

Report of Investigator A. K. #4 to Federal Bureau of Investigation, Folder 227, Peyser Papers (MSS in Manuscript Division, University of Washington Library).

Seattle Central Labor Council. Proceedings, July-December, 1936.

Seattle Chamber of Commerce, Board of Trustees, Minutes, June-December, 1936.

Seattle Chapter, American Newspaper Guild. Audit of financial records, July 22, 1937.

C. UNPUBLISHED MATERIALS

American Newspaper Guild. Historical Report on *Seattle Post-Intelligencer* Strike, prepared in April, 1959.

Anderson, Paul, early thesis draft on the *Voice of Action*, 1966.

Bagnall, Victor H., "An Appraisal of the Editorial Treatment of the Rise and Fall of Dave Beck by the *Seattle Post-Intelligencer* (1950-1958)." Term paper for Professor William Ames, University of Washington, 1958.

——————————, "Etiology of the 1936 Strike Against the *Seattle Post-Intelligencer* by the American Newspaper Guild." Term paper for Professor William Ames, University of Washington, 1959.

——————————, and others, seminar report to Association for Education in Journalism, History Section, 1958.

——————————, Richard Enger, and Deirdre Randall, "Dave Beck and the *Seattle Post-Intelligencer.*" Unpublished research paper in Communications, University of Washington, 1958.

Bowers, Robert Scott, "The International Brotherhood of Teamsters and a Theory of Jurisdiction." Unpublished Ph.D. dissertation, University of Wisconsin, 1951.

Dailey, John, "Labor Omnia Vincit, A Study of Dave Beck on Communism." Term paper for Professor William Ames, University of Washington, 1959.

Evans, David L., "The History and Significance of the Portland Newspaper Strike." Unpublished Master's thesis in Communications, University of Washington, 1966.

Garnel, Donald, "Teamsters and Highway Truckers in the West: The Evaluation of Multiemployer Bargaining in the

Western Highway Trucking Industry." Unpublished Ph.D. dissertation in Economics, University of California (Berkeley), 1966.

Hillman, Arthur, "The Unemployed Citizens League of Seattle." Unpublished Master's thesis in History, University of Washington, 1934.

Hogan, John A., "The Decline of Self-Help and the Growth of Radicalism Among Seattle's Organized Unemployed." Unpublished Master's thesis in History, University of Washington, 1934.

Kling, Alice J., "A Political Press; policies of the Washington Commonwealth Federation." Unpublished Master's thesis in Communications, University of Washington, 1966.

Simpson, Roger A., "The American Newspaper Guild and the *Seattle Post-Intelligencer* Strike of 1936." Unpublished Master's thesis in Journalism, University of Wisconsin, 1961.

_____, "The American Newspaper Guild's First Major Victory." Unpublished paper presented at the national convention of the Association for Education in Journalism, Lincoln, Nebraska, 1963.

Wolfard, John Addison, "The History and Significance of the American Newspaper Guild Strike Against the Seattle Post-Intelligencer." Unpublished Master's thesis in History, University of Washington, 1937.

APPENDIX

AGREEMENT

November 25, 1936

As a result of negotiations between me and a committee of the Seattle Newspaper Guild for the purpose of ending the strike against the Post-Intelligencer the following formula was agreed to:

1. — It is understood and agreed that all striking employes shall be returned to work without discrimination or prejudice and without reduction of salaries upon resumption of publication by the Seattle Post-Intelligencer, publication to be resumed within 96 hours after settlement is reached and the Post-Intelligencer is removed from the "unfair" list of the Seattle Central Labor Council.

2. — It is agreed that the Guild will see to it that the Seattle Central Labor Council removes the Post-Intelligencer from its "unfair" list, or any similar list by whatever name known, as its first regular meeting or a special meeting that may be called following ratification of this agreement; that the Central Labor Council will notify affiliates and other Pacific Northwest Central Labor bodies of its action and ask them to do likewise; that the strike be discontinued and that pickets be removed from the Post-Intelligencer plant at Sixth and Pine Street, Seattle, and elsewhere under its jurisdiction.

3. — It is agreed that the provision for reinstatement of all striking employes shall apply to the following persons:

A. C. Shoemaker	H. R. Seller
Walter Rue	John Jarvis
Claude Smith	Forrest Williams
R. McConnell	Hugh Evans
Bruce Helberg	J. Corbett
Richard Sharp	Mike Donohue
Edna Daw	Georgina Swanstrom
J. Rowland	R. D. Holmes
Abe Cohen	Cliffe Erickson
Boyd Smith	Max Sarchett
W. Partymiller	E. A. French
Mary Swanstrom	Carl Venstrom
Ruth Sutherland	Perry Ross
Duke Ledford	

4. — The cases of Frank Lynch and Philip E. Armstrong will continue in the hands of the National Labor Relations Board.

5. — The Post-Intelligencer herewith outlines its office policy in settlement of all disputes concerning hours, wages and conditions of service. This is not a contract but it is the policy in operation on the paper which will be continued for one year from date and as long thereafter as economic conditions justify.

For the purpose of this statement, editorial department employes shall be classified as those actually engaged in editorial work, to-wit: Newspapermen including all directly charged with reporting, writing, preparing or editing news of all kinds, editors of social notes and feature materials, photographers, artists and chief librarians, editors including copy desk slot men, make up men, swing men, telegraph editors, dramatic editors, editorial writers, library clerks, copy clerks, office clerks, messengers and home economics employes.

No editorial department employe shall work more than forty hours per week, the said forty hours to fall within five consecutive days. This provision shall become effective on or before March 1, 1937. In the interim no editorial employes shall work more than forty hours per week, the said forty hours to fall within six consecutive days. This shall not interfere with the completion of assignments by employes nor with the performance of emergency assignments.

Any overtime resulting from the completion of assignments or the performance of emergency assignments shall be allowed to accumulate and shall be compensated for in the discretion of the publisher by an allowance of days off equivalent to hours of overtime performed or by paying for such overtime work at the regular rate of pay of the employe to whom such compensation is due.

All necessary adjustments for overtime work shall be made at not less than quarter-annual intervals.

Sick leave is granted with full pay, provided, however, that the duration and frequency of such benefit payments are to be decided by the management in each individual case.

Two weeks vacation is granted to those who have been employed more than one year; one week to those who have been employed six months but not more than one year.

Employes dismissed after one year of service for causes other than willful misconduct will be given one week's pay at current rates for each year of service up to a maximum of five weeks.

All editorial department employes as defined above, except those specifically covered hereinafter, shall be paid not less than the following scales:

A — Those having less than three years' newspaper experience on any comparable daily newspaper, news feature syndicate or press association, shall be paid not less than $25. per week.

B — Those having more than three years' newspaper experience as defined in paragraph A shall be paid not less than $40. per week.

It is understood that in paragraphs A and B, "experience" refers to previous or present employment in classifications covered by the foregoing minimums.

All library clerks, home economics employes and society department employes who have had less than three years' experience in their particular departments on any comparable daily newspaper shall be paid not less than $20 per week.

All library clerks, home economic employes and society department employes who have more than three years' experience as defined above shall be paid not less than $25, per week.

All copy clerks, office clerks, and messengers with less than three years' experience shall be paid not less than $15 per week.

All copy clerks, office clerks and messengers with more than three years' experience shall be paid not less than $18. per week.

We definitely state that there will be no discrimination against any editorial department employe, nor will any editorial department employe be discharged because of membership in the Guild or any other organization.

The management will be glad any time to meet with employes or a committee representing employes for the purpose of discussing grievances.

H. Richard Seller
Seattle Newspaper Guild

C. B. Lindeman
Seattle Post-Intelligencer

INDEX

172

Time Magazine, 149

Tobin, Daniel, 118, 120, 151

The Truth About The Post-Intelligencer Strike, 95

Union Record, 45, 90

"Unionism or Hearst" stamps, 106

University of Washington, 88-89, 151

Usatalo, William, 61-2

Van Ettisch, Ray, 29

Voice of Action, 16, 90

Volz, Ed J., 51, 117

Wadleigh, Helen, 91

Wakefield, Lowell, 16-17, 44, 45-6, 47, 90

Washington Commonwealth Federation, 81, 90

Washington Federation of Labor, 116

Washington Industrial Council, Inc., 70

Washington Posten, 19

Washington State Federation of Labor, 41

Watson, Rowland, 93, 116, 117

Watts, Robert, 114

Welch, Douglass, 91, 143

Weston, Ed, 34, 84, 90

White, Edith, 39, 92

Williams, Forrest, 17, 19, 22, 25, 28, 35, 36, 41, 43, 46, 54, 55, 63, 67, 92, 147

Wisconsin News °(Milwaukee), xviii, 18, 25, 31, 63, 101, 113

Women of Washington, 87

Woods, Edward, 27, 92, 114, 115, 134

Workers Alliance, 101